C++ Programming PowerPack

C++ Programming PowerPack

Michael Vilot

SAMS
PUBLISHING

A Division of Prentice Hall Computer Publishing
11711 North College, Carmel, Indiana 46032 USA

To C++ programmers everywhere who face a deadline.

Copyright © 1993 by Sams Publishing

First Edition

All rights reserved. No part of this book shall be reproduced, stored in a retrieval system, or transmitted by any means, electronic, mechanical, photocopying, recording, or otherwise, without written permission from the publisher. No patent liability is assumed with respect to the use of the information contained herein. Although every precaution has been taken in the preparation of this book, the publisher and author assume no responsibility for errors or omissions. Neither is any liability assumed for damages resulting from the use of the information contained herein. For information, address Sams Publishing, 11711 N. College Ave., Carmel, IN 46032.

International Standard Book Number: 0-672-30279-9

Library of Congress Catalog Card Number: 92-62681

96 95 94 93   4 3 2 1

Interpretation of the printing code: the rightmost double-digit number is the year of the book's printing; the rightmost single-digit, the number of the book's printing. For example, a printing code of 93-1 shows that the first printing of the book occurred in 1993.

Trademarks

All terms mentioned in this book that are known to be trademarks or service marks have been appropriately capitalized. Sams Publishing cannot attest to the accuracy of this information. Use of a term in this book should not be regarded as affecting the validity of any trademark or service mark.

Composed in AGaramond and MCPdigital
by Prentice Hall Computer Publishing

Printed in the United States of America

Publisher
   Richard K. Swadley

Acquisitions Manager
   Jordan Gold

Acquisitions Editor
   Stacy Hiquet

Development Editor
   Dean Miller

Editors
   Fran Hatton
   Melba Hopper

Editorial Coordinators
   Rebecca S. Freeman
   Bill Whitmer

Editorial Assistants
   Rosemarie Graham

Technical Editor
   Bruce Graves

Cover Designer
   Tim Amrhein

Director of Production and Manufacturing
   Jeff Valler

Production Manager
   Corinne Walls

Imprint Manager
   Matthew Morrill

Book Designer
   Michele Laseau

Production Analyst
   Mary Beth Wakefield

Proofreading/Indexing Coordinator
   Joelynn Gifford

Graphics Image Specialists
   Dennis Sheehan
   Sue VandeWalle

Production
   Terri Edwards
   Carla Hall-Batton
   Tim Montgomery
   Juli Pavey
   Angela Pozdol
   Linda Quigley
   Michelle Self
   Susan Shepard
   Alyssa Yesh

Indexer
   Joy Dean Lee

Overview

	Introduction	xiii
Chapter 1	Using the PowerPack	1
Chapter 2	Structures Class Strategy	45
Chapter 3	Tools Class Category	129
Chapter 4	Support Class Category	169
Appendix	Source Code Listings	211
	Glossary	251
	Bibliography	253
	Index	255

Contents

Introduction xiii

Chapter 1 Using the PowerPack   1

Library Overview 2
    Library Contents 2
Library Organization 6
    Type Parameterization 7
    Inheritance 8
    Containment 11
Design Discussion 11
    Templates 11
    Exceptions 15
    Representation 17
    Storage Management 22
    Process Synchronization 28
    Iteration 34
Example 37
The Rest of the Book 42
    Coding Style 44

Chapter 2 Structures Class Strategy   45

Bag 46
Deque 51
Directed_Graph 56
Undirected_Graph 66
Double_List 76
Single_List 83
Map 89
Queue 94
Ring 98
Set 103
Stack 107
Variable_String 110

Arbitrary_Tree 115
Binary_Tree 122

Chapter 3 Tools Class Category   129

Introduction 129
Input_Filter 131
Output_Filter 133
Process_Filter 135
Pattern_Match 137
Graph_Search 140
List_Search 143
Tree_Search 145
Search 147
Graph_Sort 149
Sort 151
Character_Utilities 154
Float_Utilities 157
Integer_Utilities 160
String_Utilities 162

Chapter 4 Support Class Category   169

Bounded_Simple_List 173
Exception 178
Storage_Manager 181
Bounded_Heap 184
Node 188
Counter, Shared 195
Semaphore, Monitor, Lock 198
Simple_List 202
Simple_Vector 206

Appendix Source Code Listings   211

Example Source Code Listings 211
Components—Structures 217
Components—Support 231
Makefiles 248

Glossary   251

Bibliography   253

Index   255

About the Author

Michael Vilot, MSE, is president of ObjectCraft, Inc. and consults on object-oriented design and the C++ programming language. He is an expert in both topics, having used them extensively in his work since 1986. Among his recent projects was the design and implementation of The C++ Booch Components® library, a commercial software product containing reusable data structure and algorithm classes. He is a columnist for "The C++ Report" on object-oriented design, and he chairs the Library Working Group of the ANSI X3J16 committee working to standardize the C++ language and its library. He can be reached at (603) 883-1268, and electronically at mjv@objects.mv.com or 70461,2142 on CompuServe.

Introduction

Interest in C++ and object-oriented development (OOD) is growing at an amazing rate. Informal estimates place the C++ development community at more than 300,000 people at the close of 1992, with the population doubling every nine months. At that rate, most of the world's existing C programmers (estimates range from 800 thousand to 2 million) will be using C++ in a couple of years.

A language doesn't get to be this popular just because it has some clever features, or because it was invented at AT&T Bell Labs—literally hundreds of programming languages can offer counterexamples. One reason for C++'s popularity is that it can significantly improve your productivity by making it easier to build reusable software components. Indeed, support for libraries was one of the language's design goals, and many developers have found that C++ fulfills this goal remarkably well, as the growing number of commercially available C++ library products demonstrates.

The C++ Booch Components is one of these successful software component libraries. Starting in 1990, I worked with Grady Booch to design, implement, and evolve this library. His original version of the library, written in Ada in 1984, required more than 150,000 lines of code. The most recent release of the C++ version, providing the same functionality, consists of only 15,000 lines of code. This dramatic reduction illustrates the great economy of expression possible through the use of classes, inheritance, and type parameterization.

The library builds on the experience of earlier library products and provides an example of how OOD influences the development of a reusable component library. It also uses some of the most powerful aspects of the C++ programming language, including templates, exceptions, and multiple inheritance.

About This Book

The primary goal of this book is to provide a concise reference for the C++ Booch Components library. It contains substantially the same contents as the Class Catalog and Quick Reference Guide that are included with the full distribution kit for the library. Our hope is that readers of this book will gain an appreciation for the scope and quality of the library and understand the library's value enough to consider purchasing it—a "try before you buy" approach not unlike the shareware products available on many electronic bulletin boards.

Because this book is not a tutorial in C++, OOD, or data structures and algorithms, readers should have some experience with programming in general, and C++ programming in particular. This book is meant to be a detailed and consise reference text, providing a lot of detail. It should be useful to anyone considering purchasing a C++ class library. It should also be useful to C++ developers who are considering designing their own class library—at the very least, it provides a comprehensive example of how to organize and describe such a library.

Structure of the Book

The book is organized around the structure of the library itself. Chapter 1, "Using the PowerPack," provides an overview of this design, introducing the Structures, Tools, and Support class categories. Chapter 2, "Structures Class Strategy," provides a reference manual for the Structures components. Chapter 3, "Tools Class Category," is a reference for the Tools. Chapter 4, "Support Class Category," is a reference for the Support components.

Chapter 1 contains a small C++ application that illustrates how to use a component from the library. Appendix A lists the source code for the example, as well as the sample code for the components used. The disk that accompanies the book also contains this code.

System Requirements

The code in this library is written entirely in standard C++. It can be used directly by compilers that support templates, such as Borland's 3.0 and 3.1 releases or USL's cfront 3.0 release. Although it is possible to use the library with earlier releases, the library's extensive use of templates makes this awkward—a preprocessor that understands template syntax and generates simpler C++ code is required, and the preprocessor supports only the essential subset of template capabilities.

The library is commercially available and tested on a number of platforms, including Borland and Comeau C++ on PCs, Apple MPW on the Macintosh, IBM C++ on the RS/6000, and USL cfront on various platforms. The library's source code is identical on all platforms; only the details of assembling C++ programs (most notably template instantiation mechanisms) differ.

Acknowledgments

I cannot give enough thanks to the many people who have influenced and guided me over the years. However, I would like to call attention to those people whose work relates directly to this book:

- Bjarne Stroustrup, for that engineering compromise called C++. Through many conversations over the years, I've come to appreciate the design ideas embodied in the language.

- Grady Booch, for the opportunity to work on the C++ Booch Components library. He's been very generous with his time and other resources, and I have enjoyed working with him.

- Jon Williams, Brock Peterson, and the other folks at Rational who distribute and support the C++ Booch Components library product.

- Stacey Hiquet and the staff at Sams who helped create this book.

Nashua, New Hampshire
February, 1993

USING THE POWERPACK

This chapter provides a high-level overview of the C++ Booch Components library. The first section explains the contents of the library, and how it is organized. The second section describes some key aspects of the library's, including how C++ language features such as derived classes, templates, and exceptions all work to support the economical expression of the design. The third section presents a small example using one of the components from the library (Appendix A contains the full source code for the example and the component used, and the accompanying disk contains the software). Finally, the fourth section explains the format and style used in the remaining chapters of the book.

Library Overview

Library Contents

The C++ Booch Components are a carefully designed collection of domain-independent data structures and algorithms. This class library was designed with several goals in mind:

Completeness: The library provides classes for many of the basic data structures and algorithms required in production-quality software; additionally, for each kind of structure, the library offers a family of classes, united by a shared interface but each employing a different representation, so that a developer can select the one with the time and space semantics most appropriate to a given application.

Adaptability: The library's environment-specific aspects are clearly identified and are isolated using template arguments, so that local substitutions may be made; in particular, a developer has control over the storage management policy used by each structure, as well as the semantics of process synchronization, for those forms of a class designed for use in the presence of more than one thread of control (such as with the AT&T_ task library).

Efficiency: Our goal was to provide easily assembled components (efficient in compilation resources) that impose minimal runtime and memory overhead (efficient in execution resources) and that are more reliable than hand-built mechanisms (efficient in developer resources).

Safety: Each class is designed to be type-safe so that static assumptions about the behavior of a class may be enforced by the compilation system; additionally, exceptions are used to identify conditions under which a class's dynamic semantics are violated, but without corrupting the state of the object that threw the exception.

Using the PowerPack

Ease of use: A clear and consistent organization makes it easy to identify and select appropriate forms of each structure and tool.

Extensibility: It is possible for developers to independently add new data structures and algorithms, yet at the same time preserve the design integrity of the library.

This library represents an application of Grady Booch's object-oriented design (OOD) method [Booch, 1991], which was used to both design and document its contents. This library is carefully organized and precisely defined; as a result, there is an opportunity to formally specify the behavior of all classes in the library.

The C++ Booch Components are a mature library, having evolved from an Ada version first released in 1984, and now in use in over 300 different organizations in the U.S., Europe, and the Pacific Rim. The C++ version is more than a simple port of the Ada version; rather, it was designed to take advantage of C++'s unique features, including classes, multiple inheritance, polymorphism, templates, and exceptions. The C++ Booch Components have undergone over a year of internal use since their first public exposure at the 1990 OOPSLA/ECOOP conference [Booch, 1990], and in so doing have evolved to take advantage of experiences gained in using the OOD method on several large commercial C++ projects.

The C++ Booch Components are contained in four class categories, as the class diagram in Figure 1.1 illustrates.

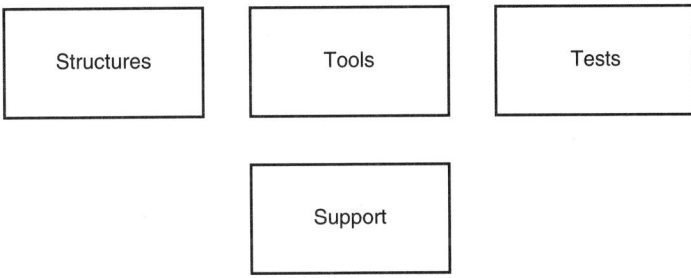

Figure 1.1. Library Organization.

All the data structures are placed in the category labeled Structures, and all the algorithms are placed in the category labeled Tools. As this figure indicates, all the data structures and algorithms in the library are constructed from more primitive classes, found in the category named Support. Additionally, there exists a Test category, which contains comprehensive tests of all the structures and tools, which are included as part of software distribution.

In general, application developers must concern themselves only with the classes found in Structures and Tools. Library developers and power users, however, may want to make use of the more primitive abstractions found in Support, from which new structures and tools can be constructed, or through which the behavior of existing classes can be modified.

As this figure suggests, the C++ Booch Components are organized as a forest of classes, rather than as a tree; there exists no single base class.

As diagrammed in Figure 1.2, the Structures category is further divided into the following categories:

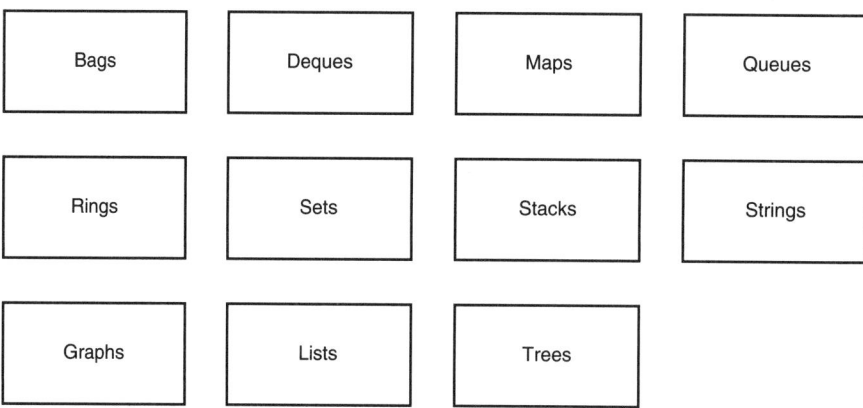

Figure 1.2. Structures.

These eleven categories provide the following abstractions:

Bags	A collection of items from some domain; may contain duplicates.
Deques	A sequence in which items may be added and removed from either end.
Graphs	An unrooted collection of nodes and arcs; may contain cycles and cross-references; structural sharing is permitted.
Lists	A sequence of zero or more items; structural sharing is permitted.
Maps	A collection forming a dictionary of domain/range pairs.
Queues	A sequence in which items may be added from one end and removed from the opposite end.

Rings   A sequence in which items may be added and removed from the top of a circular structure.

Sets   A collection of items from some domain; may not contain duplicates.

Stacks   A sequence in which items may be added and removed from the same end.

Strings   A sequence of zero or more items.

Trees   A rooted collection of nodes and arcs; may not contain cycles or cross-references; structural sharing is permitted.

Each of these categories stands alone: there are no dependencies among categories at this level.

The Deques, Queues, Graphs, Lists, and Trees categories are all further divided, with each subcategory representing a family of classes that specializes the more general abstraction (such as in Priority_Queues and Directed_Graphs).

The top eight categories in Figure 1.2 represent each of the *monolithic* structures. A monolithic structure is one that is always treated as a single unit: there are no identifiable, distinct components, and thus referential integrity is guaranteed. Alternatively, a *polylithic* structure is one in which structural sharing is permitted; for example, we can have objects that denote a sublist of a longer list, a branch of a larger tree, or individual vertices and arcs of a graph. The fundamental distinction between monolithic and polylithic structures is that in monolithic structures, the semantics of copying, assignment, and equality are deep, whereas in polylithic structures, copying, assignment, and equality are all shallow (meaning that aliases may share a reference to a part of a larger structure).

As Figure 1.3 diagrams, the Tools category is further divided into five categories:

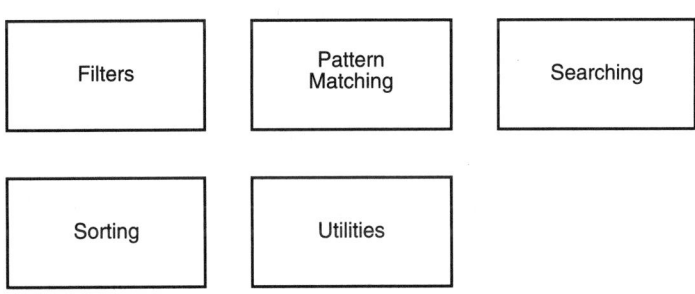

Figure 1.3. Tools.

These five categories provide the following abstractions:

`Filters`	Input, output, and process transformations.
`Pattern matching`	Vector multi-item searching operations.
`Searching`	Graph, list, tree, and vector single-item searching operations.
`Sorting`	Graph and vector ordering operations.
`Utilities`	Primitive class operations.

Each of these categories also stands alone: there are no dependencies among categories at this level, although many of these tools operate upon objects that are instances of certain structural classes.

The `Support` category is not further divided, although it does provide several distinct groups of abstractions, namely:

`Bound`	Elementary stack-based lists.
`Except`	Definitions of exceptional conditions.
`Free`	Facilities for free list management.
`Heap`	Facilities for stack-based heap management.
`Node`	Elementary containers.
`Shared`	Primitive counting abstractions.
`Synch`	Facilities for process management.
`Unbound`	Elementary free list-based lists.
`Vector`	Elementary stack-based vectors.

The semantics of each of the classes found in the `Structures`, `Tools`, and `Support` categories are provided in Chapter 2, "Structures Class Strategy," Chapter 3, "Tools Class Category," and Chapter 4, "Support Class Category."

LIBRARY ORGANIZATION

The design of any genuinely useful class library demands the delicate balance of competing and often conflicting technical and social requirements. In a general sense, the C++ Booch Components are simply one solution in the design space of constructing a set of domain-independent foundation classes. The design of this particular library was guided by the principles described in *Object-Oriented Design with Applications*, together with a set of pragmatic design rules that we have evolved through our participation in the development of several large C++

applications. In this section, we describe these principles and heuristics, because they contribute to the clear and consistent organization of the C++ Booch Components and thus are of immediate relevance to any user of this library. Additionally, the style employed in the construction of this library has general applicability to other software domains and may be of value to developers in other application domains.

In this section and the next, we will use the Queue class to illustrate our style; its semantics are described in complete detail in Chapter 2.

Object-oriented programming offers three facilities for organizing a rich collection of classes: inheritance, type parameterization, and containment. Inheritance is certainly the most visible (and popular) aspect of object-oriented design; however, it is not the only structuring principle. Indeed, in this library, type parameterization combined with multiple inheritance is central to the design of the structures and tools.

Type Parameterization

Except for a few cases, the classes provided in this library are actually templates for classes, using the type parameterization facility described in [Ellis, 1990], and now an official part of the C++ language. This kind of type parameterization is a fundamental mechanism for combining building blocks and creating the individual classes needed for the application at hand, yet at the same time preserving a measure of type safety. In this library, templates are used to parameterize each structure with the kind of item it contains. Thus, for example, we can devise a Queue class whose instances behave the same way, whether these objects hold primitive items such as integers and pointers or user-defined items such as windows and inventory records. For the abstract base class Queue, we may indicate that it is parameterized according to the kind of the Item held in each queue object, as follows:

```
template<class Item>
class Queue...
```

To denote a queue of integers, therefore, we can write Queue<int>, or for a queue of windows, Queue<Window>.

Templates can also be used to provide certain implementation information to a class. Using a slightly different mechanism, a client can additionally import certain Item operations in a type-safe manner.

Inheritance

A second principle central to the design of this library is the concept of building families of classes related by lines of inheritance. For each kind of structure, the library provides several different classes united by a shared interface (such as the abstract base class `Queue`), but with several concrete subclasses. Each of these subclasses has a slightly different representation, and thus each has different time and space semantics. In this manner, a developer can select the one concrete class whose time and space semantics best fit the needs of a given application, yet still be confident that no matter which concrete class is selected, it will behave functionally the same as any other concrete class in the family. Because of this intentional and clear separation of concerns between an abstract class and its concrete classes, a developer initially can select one concrete class and later, as the application is being tuned, replace it with a sibling concrete class with minimal effort (the only real cost is the recompilation of all uses of the new class). The developer can be confident that the application will still work, because all sibling concrete classes share the same interface and the same basic behavior. Another implication of this organization is that it is possible to copy, assign, or test for equality among objects of the same family of classes, even if each object has a radically different representation.

In a sense, an abstract base class serves to capture all the relevant public design decisions about the abstraction. Another use of abstract base classes in this library is the cache state that might otherwise be expensive to compute. This can convert an `O(n)` computation to an `O(1)` retrieval. The cost of this style is the required cooperation between the abstract base class and its derived classes, to keep the cached result up to date.

We call these time/space variations the *forms* of an abstraction. In our experience, there are two fundamental forms of an abstraction, which any developer must consider when building a serious application. The first of these is the form of representation, which establishes the concrete implementation of an abstract base class. Ultimately, there are only two meaningful choices for in-memory structures: the structure is stored on the free list (the heap), or it is stored on the stack. We call these variations the *unbounded* and *bounded* forms of an abstraction, respectively:

Unbounded The structure is stored on the free list and thus can grow to the limits of available memory.

Bounded The structure is stored on the stack and thus has a static size; clients must specify the structure's size at the time of template instantiation.

Because the unbounded and bounded forms of an abstraction share a common interface (as well as some common state), we choose to make them direct subclasses of the abstract base class for each structure.

The second important variation concerns process synchronization. Many useful applications involve only a single process: we call them *sequential* systems, because they involve only a single thread of control. Certain applications, especially those involving real-time control, may require the synchronization of several simultaneous threads of control within the same system: we call such systems *concurrent*.

The synchronization of multiple threads of control is important because of the issues of mutual exclusion. Simply stated, it is improper to allow two or more threads of control to directly act upon the same object at the same time, because they may interfere with the state of the object and ultimately corrupt its state. Consider two active agents that both try to add an item to the same Queue object. (An active agent is one that embodies its own threat of control, and thus may operate autonomously.) The first agent might start to add the new item, be preempted, and so leave the object in an inconsistent state for the second agent.

Basically, there are three design alternatives possible, requiring different degrees of cooperation among the agents that interact with a shared object:

Sequential The semantics of the structure are guaranteed only in the presence of a single thread of control.

Guarded The semantics of the structure are guaranteed in the presence of multiple threads of control; client processes must cooperate in the use of a shared semaphore; a client must specify the guard class at the time of template instantiation.

Synchronized The semantics of the structure are guaranteed in the presence of multiple threads of control; each operation is considered atomic, and no explicit collaboration among client processes is required; a client must specify the monitor class at the time of template instantiation.

The simplest of these three variations is the sequential form, which is equivalent to the behavior of the unbounded and bounded forms described earlier. Because the guarded and synchronized forms of an abstraction share a common interface (as well as some common state) with each corresponding concrete representation class, we choose to make the guarded and synchronized forms direct subclasses of the unbounded and bounded concrete classes.

Bringing these concepts together, the interactions among the abstract base class, the representation forms, and the synchronization forms yield the following family of classes (Figure 1.4) for every structure in the library:

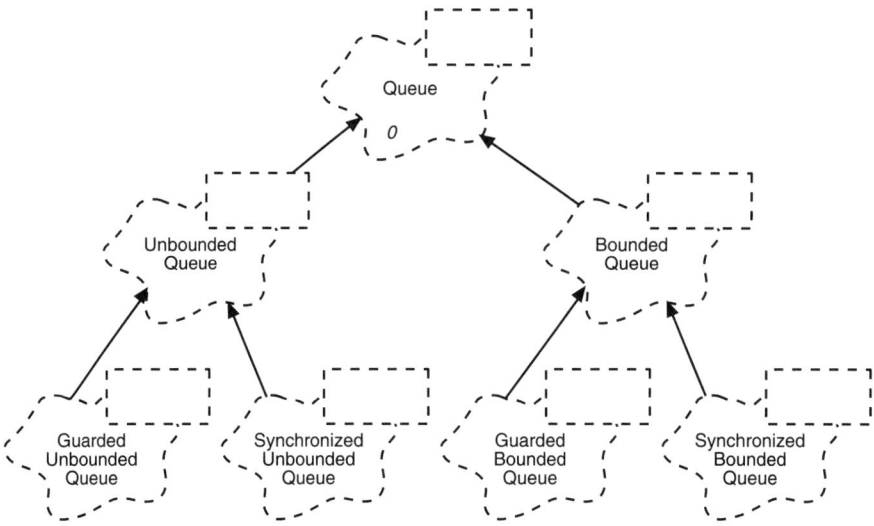

Figure 1.4. Fundamental Forms.

As this figure illustrates, the cardinality of the class Queue is zero, indicating it is an abstract class and so may have no direct instances. The cardinality of all other classes is unspecified, indicating (once instantiated) these classes may have any number of instances.

The most important implication of this style is that the C++ Booch Components represent a forest of classes, not a strict tree of classes. We deliberately chose this topology for four reasons:

- It accurately reflects the regular structure of the component forms.
- It involves less complexity and overhead when selecting one component from the library.
- It avoids the endless ontological debates engendered by a pure object-oriented approach.
- It simplifies integrating this library with other libraries.

As described further in Chapter 2, we also apply inheritance to construct layered abstractions: for example, a `Priority_Queue` is a kind of `Queue`.

Containment

Containment is the third structuring principle used in this library. For example, all guarded forms of a structure use a `Semaphore`, but are not themselves a kind of `Semaphore`.

Because most of the data structure abstractions in the library are container classes, containment plays a fairly central role in their design. This affects storage management considerably, as explored later in the next section.

Design Discussion

In this section, the key design issues that influence both the library's organization and the use of C++ language features are described. These five topics are covered: the use of templates for type (and other) parameterization; the use of exceptions as a consistent error reporting mechanism; support for Bounded and Unbounded representation; support for process/thread synchronization; and iterator design.

Templates

A template class specifies how individual classes can be constructed, much as a class declaration specifies how individual objects can be constructed [Stroustrup, 1991]. A template class does not stand alone, but must first be instantiated, before any objects are declared. Instantiation involves the participation of at least two classes: the template class itself, and the class denoting the kind of item to be stored in the structure. Figure 1.5 shows the declaration of the object `window_directory`, as an instance of class `Bounded_Queue`.

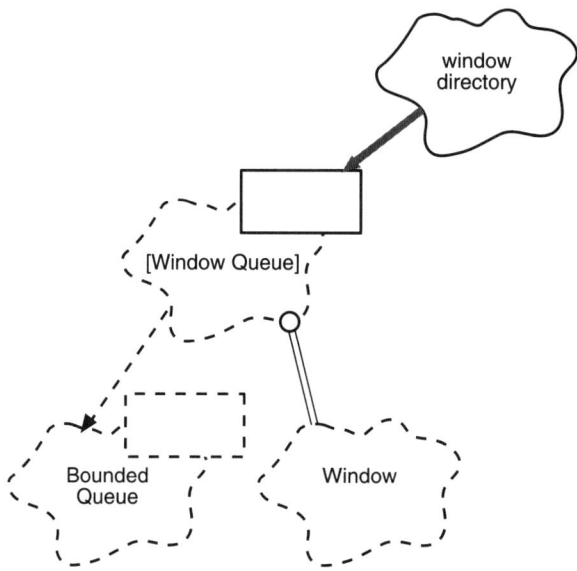

Figure 1.5. Instantiating a Template.

Following is the equivalent declaration, in C++. Given the following incomplete declarations:

```
template<class Item, unsigned int Size>
class Bounded_Queue...

class Window {
public:

  unsigned order() const; // the stacking order of the window
};
```

declare a bounded queue object as follows:

```
Bounded_Queue<Window, 36> window_directory;
```

Because the actual instantiated class is anonymous (that is, it has no simple name), a name for it is provided in brackets (see Figure 1.5).

C++ templates are deliberately underspecified, which leaves a degree of flexibility (and responsibility) in the hands of developers who instantiate templates. It also creates opportunities for optimization, such as sharing definitions of member functions, and not instantiating unnecessary member functions, which otherwise would lead to large amounts of code being generated.

In this library, the primary use of templates is to parameterize each structure with the kind of item it contains; this is why such structures are often called *container classes*. As the previous example illustrates, templates may also be used to provide certain implementation information to a class. In fact, all bounded classes (such as `Bounded_Queue` in the previous example) require that an instantiator provide an unsigned integer representing the static size of its objects. This same approach is also used to import the kind of container used by each unbounded structure, and to import agents responsible for process synchronization.

A more complicated situation involves tools that use structures in their implementation. For example, the tool `Graph_Search`, which provides a facility for depth-first and breadth-first graph traversal, uses an iterator, set, stack, and queue in its implementation. Its partial declaration appears as follows:

```
template<class Vertex, class Arc, class Graph,
        class Imp_Vertex_Iter, class Imp_Set,
        class Imp_Stack, class Imp_Queue>
class Graph_Search...
```

The convention is to name template arguments with the prefix `Imp` to indicate that they are needed only for the purposes of implementing the tool. An alternative implementation would have been to simply choose an appropriate iterator, set, stack, and queue class, but this approach would have required us to select a specific form of each in these classes. Only the instantiator has sufficient information to know what time/space semantics are needed in the context of the tool's use, and so we must leave this decision up to the instantiator. This style does require more work on the part of the instantiator, but it does offer much greater flexibility in the use of the tool.

As an example, following is an instantiation of the tool `Graph_Search`, constructed to operate on graphs whose nodes and arcs contain characters, and which uses all unbounded abstractions in its implementation. First we provide a number of `typedef`s, to make the declaration more readable:

```
typedef
  Unbounded_Directed_Vertex<char, Shared_Graph_Char_Node>
    Char_Vertex_U;
typedef
  Unbounded_Directed_Arc<char, Shared_Graph
_Char_Node>
    Char_Arc_U;
typedef
  Unbounded_Directed_Graph<char, Shared_Graph_Char_Node>
    Char_Graph_U;
```

```
typedef Directed_Vertex_Active_Iterator<char> Vertex_Iter;
typedef Unbounded_Set<Char_Vertex_U, Vertex_Node> V_Set_U;
typedef Unbounded_Stack<Char_Vertex_U, Vertex_Node> V_Stack_U;
typedef Unbounded_Queue<Char_Vertex_U, Vertex_Node> V_Queue_U;
```

Next, we provide an instantiation of `Graph_Search` itself:

```
Graph_Search<Char_Vertex_U, Char_Arc_U, Char_Graph_U,
         Vertex_Iter, V_Set_U, V_Stack_U, V_Queue_U>
  graph_search;
```

Importing classes and values as template arguments means that every object of the instantiated class shares the same arguments. In some circumstances, it is better if each individual object can have slightly different arguments. For example, consider a `Priority_Queue`, which is a kind of `Queue`, except that its items are stored in some order, according to its priority. Under these circumstances, we may want different objects of the same instantiation to use different priority functions (for example, one queue might hold items in ascending priority, another in descending priority). Rather than import this priority function as a template argument, we have more degrees of freedom if we import it via a member function.

The partial declaration of the class `Priority_Queue` is as follows:

```
template<class Item>
class Priority_Queue : public Queue<Item> {
public:

  Priority_Queue();
  Priority_Queue(int (*priority)(Item&));
  Priority_Queue(const Priority_Queue<Item>&);
  virtual ~Priority_Queue();

  virtual Queue<Item>& set_priority_function(int (*priority)(Item&));

};
```

Our style is to provide a constructor and a modifier, whereby a client can supply a pointer to a priority function. The semantics of this particular structure are such that a client may set a priority function exactly once for each object. Thus, a client might declare an object using a default constructor, and then call `set_priority_function`, or just use the special constructor function directly. In any case, if an object already has been given a priority function and the client tries to set a new one, an exception will be thrown, as described in the following section. We must enforce this protocol, because otherwise it would be possible to corrupt the state of the queue by having items inserted according to different priorities.

The other advantage of importing a priority function in this manner is that it correctly addresses the problem of instantiations that involve pointers to objects. For example, given the following partial declaration:

```
typedef Window* Window_Ptr;
```

we may declare a bounded queue object as follows:

```
Bounded_Queue<Window_Ptr, 100U> directory;
```

However, we want the priority function to operate upon the windows themselves, not the pointers. Therefore, we might write a function such as the following:

```
unsigned window_priority(window_ptr p)
{
   return p->order();
}
```

Now, we can set the priority function:

```
directory.set_priority_function(&window_priority);
```

We use this style in all of the priority forms of the classes Deque and Queue, for importing hash functions in the class Map, and for importing various kinds of operations, such as ordering operations, in many tools.

EXCEPTIONS

Whereas we may use the C++ language itself to enforce most static assumptions about an abstraction, we must have some means of reporting any dynamic violations, such as trying to add an item to an already full queue, or removing an item from an empty queue. In this library, we apply the exception facility as described in *The Annotated C++ Reference Manual*, and now an official part of C++. Our design uses a generalized notion of exceptions, and separates them from the mechanisms involved in reporting them. As described further in Chapter 4, we provide a base Exception class and derived classes to describe exceptional conditions. We also provide a mechanism for creating instances of exceptions and reporting them to library users.

A partial declaration of the base class Exception appears as follows:

```
class Exception {
public:

   Exception(const char* name, const char* who, const char* what);
   virtual ~Exception();
```

```
    virtual void display(ostream&) const;

    const char* name() const;
    const char* who() const;
    const char* what() const;

};
```

For every exception, we may attach its name, who threw it, and why it was thrown. Additionally, we provide a means for displaying an exception on an output stream.

Member functions in library classes only throw exceptions; they neither try nor catch exceptions. For example, consider the implementation of the member function pop in the abstract base class Queue:

```
template<class Item>
Queue<Item>& Queue<Item>::pop()
{
  if (rep_length == 0)
    throw(Underflow("Queue<Item>::pop()", _EMPTY));
  --rep_length;
  return *this;
}
```

Underflow is a subclass of the base class Exception. In the above function, if the queue object is already empty, we throw the exception. Our convention is to provide the name of the member function that threw the exception, together with some meaningful phrase explaining the reason.

We do not implement an exception handling mechanism in the library. Instead, we simulate the throw_expression with calls to a _catch function, passing it a reference to an Exception object. Therefore, in the absence of a translator that fully supports exceptions, we must use the preproessor to redefine throw to be a call to _catch.

The library provides a simple definition of _catch, which reports the exception on the standard error stream, and then exits the program:

```
void _catch(const Exception& e)
{
  cerr << "EXCEPTION: " << e << '\n';
  terminate();
}
```

Our approach achieves the goal of error notification, but does not pretend to provide robust error handling (specifically, it does not unwind the stack and invoke all the appropriate destructors automatically). However, our design is compatible with the current definition of C++, and ensures simple evolution to future language implementation. In particular, no code changes need be made to any class in the library, when used with a translator that fully implements the C++ exception facility.

Using `Exception` as a base class, clients can derive new kinds of exceptions; the library already provides several such useful subclasses. Library clients can also control the basic error handling mechanism. In particular, developers can replace the default `_catch` implementation above with functions to call, for example, `longjmp` (assuming that such clients also have solutions to the stack unwinding/destructor invocation issues involved).

One very important aspect of our use of exceptions is that they are guaranteed not to corrupt the state of any object that throws an exception, except in the case of out-of-memory conditions. Member functions always throw an exception before any changes to the state of the object are made. For example, in the implementation of the member function `pop` above, we first check that all preconditions to the function are satisfied, and only then do we alter the state of the object. This is a style that has been carefully followed, and should be preserved by any subclasses derived from this library.

REPRESENTATION

Each abstract base class in this library primarily describes behavior. As we described earlier, to provide the variety of time/space performance offered in this library, every abstract base class has two immediate subclasses, each using a different representation:

Unbounded   The structure is stored on the free list, and thus may grow to the limits of available memory.

Bounded   The structure is stored on the stack, and thus has a static size; clients must specify the structure's size at the time of template instantiation.

Unbounded forms are applicable in those cases where the ultimate size of the structure cannot be predicted, and where allocating and deallocating storage from the heap is neither too costly nor unsafe (as it may be in certain time-critical applications). Alternatively, bounded forms are better suited to smaller structures, whose average and maximum sizes are predictable, and where heap usage is deemed insecure. Because both concrete representations of a structure share the same interface and behavior, a developer can choose one representation or the other, with minimal impact to the semantics of the application. Additionally, because of the manner in which copying, assignment, and equality are implemented, it is possible to perform these operations among objects that share the same abstract base class, yet are of different representational subclasses.

One fundamental design decision in this library was the concept of separating policy from implementation. In a sense, any of the structures in this library are merely abstractions that enforce a certain protocol or policy upon a list or a vector. For example, the policy of a Stack object permits adding and removing items only from the top; the policy of a Queue object permits adding from one end and removing from the other. More complicated classes, such as the class Ring, are no different: the policy of a Ring permits adding and removing from one point in a list that wraps back around on itself.

A domain analysis of all the structures in this library reveals that by separating policy from implementation, we can extract a significant amount of redundancy among the classes, ultimately resulting in a smaller, more versatile library. This discovery led us to create three low-level classes, upon which all structures are layered. In general, the typical developer using this library need never be concerned with these low-level abstractions, although knowledge of them will help in understanding the time/space trade-offs they represent.

These three lower-level classes include:

Simple_List	A singly linked list, whose nodes are stored on the heap.
Simple_Bounded_List	A singly linked list, whose nodes are stored on the stack.
Simple_Vector	A simple sequence, whose nodes are stored on the stack.

Lists and vectors represent fundamentally different abstractions. As described further in Chapter 4, a list offers an abstraction that permits the efficient and arbitrary manipulation of linked nodes. Vectors, on the other hand, provide the abstraction of a well ordered sequence, whose items may be indexed by some ordinal number. Both kinds of classes have a representation optimized to these abstractions: in lists, manipulating nodes is very fast, but finding a particular item is slow (on the order of O(n)), and in vectors, manipulating items is slow (the worst case is only O(n/2), however), whereas finding an item is very fast (on the order of O(1)).

We apply a mix-in style of multiple inheritance to construct both the unbounded and bounded concrete classes, as Figure 1.6 illustrates.

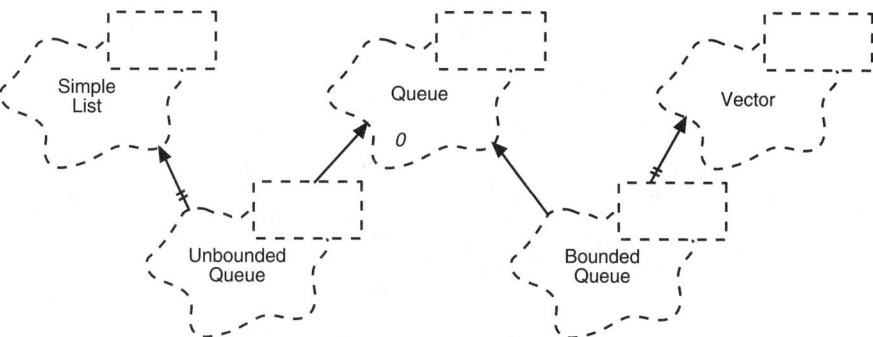

Figure 1.6. Layering Abstractions.

As this figure shows, our style involves using public inheritance to share interfaces, and private inheritance to share implementation. Private derivation ensures that the implicit conversion rules (that is, using a derived object as a base object) do not apply. Notice that we use the class `Simple_Vector` rather than `Simple_Bounded_List` in the bounded forms. We do so because the `Simple_Vector` class is much more space-efficient (as a bounded form should be): the `Simple_Bounded_List` requires storage for an additional unsigned integer for every item. However, this added complexity of the `Simple_Bounded_List` is required for the class `Map` and all of the polylithic structures.

The major implication of separating policy from implementation in this manner is that each concrete representation form becomes almost trivial. For example, the implementation of the member function `pop` for the `Unbounded_Queue` is as follows:

```
template<class Item, class Container>
Queue<Item>& Unbounded_Queue<Item, Container>::pop()
{
  Queue<Item>::pop();
  Simple_List<Item>::remove();
  return *this;
}
```

Because the protocols of the list and vector low-level classes are somewhat the same, the implementation of the bounded forms of structures parallels the unbounded forms fairly closely.

Unbounded forms raise the issues of storage management: one must choose a policy whereby nodes are allocated and deallocated from the heap. We will elaborate upon these issues later, but, briefly, our design is to place this policy decision in the hands of the developer, not the library, thus offering many more degrees of freedom in tuning the library for serious applications. We achieve this design by constructing the `Simple_List` so that it manipulates containers of the class Node or its subclasses. Therefore, the template signature of every unbounded form is roughly the same because each must provide an argument for the instantiator to supply a particular kind of container. The `Unbounded_Queue` is a typical example of this style:

```
template<class Item, class Container>
class Unbounded_Queue : private Simple_List<Item>,
                       public Queue<Item>...
```

Notice our use of public and private inheritance. To instantiate this class, an instantiator must provide an item and a container for that item, as follows:

```
typedef Node<char> Char_Node;
Unbounded_Queue<char, Char_Node> char_queue_1;
```

Here, we again introduce a `typedef` only for the purpose of readability.

Bounded forms are different, in that items are stored directly on the stack, and so do not require any containers for storage management. However, an instantiator is responsible for specifying the size of a structure at the point of instantiation, and so the template signature of every bounded form appears similar to the following example:

```
template<class Item, unsigned int Size>
class Bounded_Queue : private Simple_Vector<Item, Size>,
                     public Queue<Item>...
```

Notice again our use of public and private inheritance. To instantiate this class, an instantiator must provide an item and a size, as follows:

```
Bounded_Queue<char, 100U> char_queue_2;
```

All bounded forms provide the member function available, which allows a client to query how much space is available in the structure.

The design of both the unbounded and bounded concrete representation mix-in classes raises some subtle issues concerning the use of references. We explore these issues here, not only because they impact the interface of every template class in the library, but also because they are fundamental issues that must be faced by the designer of any nontrivial class library.

References in C++ provide an aliasing mechanism that can improve performance. However, references must be used carefully to avoid creating unsafe situations at runtime. In this library, we use references to improve the performance of passing arguments to member functions. However, all structures store values, not references, in their respective concrete forms (nodes for the unbounded forms, and arrays for the bounded forms). This style prevents creating references to transient objects on the runtime stack. For the same reason, we rejected an alternative design involving storing pointers to items, because this approach exhibits very undesirable behavior when instantiating a template with built-in types.

These issues are significant when designing the interface to template classes, because clients can instantiate the templates with arbitrary types. There are three cases to consider, and we must design the library so that it strikes a balance among all three.

First, built-in types can be passed by reference and copied into concrete representations with no difficulty. Declaring the argument types as constant references avoids warnings due to temporaries involved in type conversion (see [Ellis, 1990, page 155]).

Second, user-defined types can be passed by reference and copied, even if they provide copy constructors and the assignment operator. Although the references permit polymorphic operations (passing an object of a derived class instead of the declared class supplied in the instantiation), the copying will not be polymorphic. Assigning the object of the representation will "slice" the object to an instance of the base class (see [Ellis, 1990, page 297]).

Third, polymorphic uses of the library will have to instantiate the templates with pointers to the base class(es) involved. Although passing the pointers by reference does not improve performance, copying pointers into the representation preserves the polymorphism of the derived objects involved.

Library clients are ultimately not greatly impacted by this design. For example, given the class `Bounded_Queue`, we can declare the following:

```
typedef Window* Window_Ptr;

Bounded_Queue<int, 10U> int_queue;
Bounded_Queue<Window, 50U> wq_1;
Bounded_Queue<Window_Ptr, 100U> wq_2;
```

Clients of the third queue object above are most likely handling windows polymorphically in their code: storing and retrieving pointers is therefore the most appropriate arrangement.

There are two implications of storing values instead of references or pointers to items, regarding the construction and destruction of items in a structure. First, the item classes used to instantiate a structure must provide at least a copy constructor and an assignment operator. Second, items may not be destroyed immediately upon removal from a structure. In bounded forms, for example, destructors for items (which are ultimately stored in arrays) are not called until the structure itself is destroyed. Similarly, for unbounded forms, destructors may not be called until the node surrounding the item is itself destroyed, which may not happen until the application terminates, in the case of certain managed and controlled nodes (as discussed in the next section).

Because of the presence of structural sharing, most polylithic structures do not use the Simple_List or Simple_Vector classes for constructing their concrete representational classes. Instead, most unbounded polylithic forms directly manipulate items of the class Node, and most bounded polylithic forms use the class Simple_Bounded_List.

Earlier, we indicated that this library is designed such that a client may copy, assign, and test for equality among objects of the same abstract base class, yet each with different representation. We achieve this capability through an elegant use of iterators and helper functions. This style allows us, in the abstract base class, to traverse any structure in a representation-independent manner. For example, in the class Queue we find:

```
template<class Item>
Queue<Item>& Queue<Item>::operator=(Queue<Item>& q)
{
  if (this == &q)
    return *this;
  q.lock_argument();
  purge();
  Queue_Active_Iterator<Item> iter(q);
  while (!iter.is_done()) {
    append(*iter.item());
    iter.next();
  }
  q.unlock_argument();
  return *this;
}
```

Assignment proceeds by traversing the structure of the argument q, using a queue iterator. We apply the protected helper function append to add new items to the structure.

STORAGE MANAGEMENT

Storage management is an issue for all unbounded forms, because the library designer must consider their policies for allocating and deallocating nodes from the heap. A naive approach will simply use the global new and delete functions defined for each item, but this strategy can have very poor runtime performance. With a little more work, a library can be constructed with a much more robust facility, as we shall see.

Recall that the low-level class `Simple_List` is defined to work upon containers of the class `Node` and its subclasses. A basic node is the most primitive of all containers, and consists of an item value and a pointer to the next node. This structure is sufficient for many structures, but not expressive enough for structures such as the classes `Bag`, `Map`, and `Ring`.

A domain analysis reveals that exactly six kinds of nodes are sufficient for all the monolithic structures in this library:

`Node`	The most primitive container, consisting of an item value and a pointer to the next node.
`Double_Node`	A kind of `Node`, with the addition of a pointer to the previous node.
`Tree_Node`	A kind of `Double_Node`, with the addition of a pointer to a parent node.
`Graph_Node`	A kind of `Tree_Node`, with the addition of a pointer to a connected node.
`Counting_Node`	A kind of `Node`, with the addition of a counter.
`Association_Node`	A kind of `Node`, with the addition of a second value.

Polylithic structures offer a greater challenge. Because C++ does not directly provide any mechanisms for automatic garbage collection, clients must be very particular about storage management in objects that allow structural sharing, otherwise large amounts of garbage will be generated, and the application will quickly run out of usable heap space. Our style in this library was to design all such components so that storage leaks were eliminated, except in the case of intentional abuses by the client, which no library can defend against. For example, when manipulating a list, we would like all relevant nodes to be reclaimed, once that list or any parts of that list could no longer be reached. We achieve this behavior through the interaction of two techniques. First, the interfaces of all polylithic classes are carefully designed to export only those operations that are guaranteed not to produce any memory leaks, unless grossly misused. Specifically, most polylithic operations generally do not create new objects, but rather, alias existing ones. Second, we use simple reference counting on nodes, which we get in-expensively by mixing in the class `Shared` (a reference counting class) to each of the six basic node classes above.

The mix-in class `Shared`, as described in Chapter 4, is quite simple: it provides a counter, which a polylithic structure uses to keep track of how many references there are to the node. When a modifier function causes this count to drop to zero, then the structure can safely reclaim the node.

It is reasonable to ask how the low-level class `Simple_List` works properly with any of these twelve or other kinds of nodes. Basically, a client of `Simple_List` (such as any unbounded structure) is responsible for allocating the kind of node appropriate to that structure and placing it in the list in its proper place. We have designed every unbounded structure, so that allocation is isolated in exactly one member function, thus simplifying the task of any developer who wishes to specialize an existing concrete unbounded class. `Simple_List` then relies upon the polymorphic behavior of nodes, especially with regard to their constructors, destructors, and copying operations, so that the behavior of the given node subclass is correctly performed.

Stopping our design at this point yields the naive solution to storage management described above. This is not necessarily a terrible solution: it may be sufficient for simple applications. However, this solution can have some distressing run time characteristics. Specifically, when nodes are allocated and deallocated at arbitrary times, interleaved with the allocation and deallocation of other items on the heap, the heap can become very fragmented, ultimately leading to the application running out of usable heap space. Additionally, for certain time-critical applications where microseconds count, the cost of allocating nodes at critical moments may actually be prohibitive.

In light of these circumstances, there are at least three meaningful storage management policies we may employ. This library provides predefined mechanisms for all of them, plus the facilities that allow library developers to create their own policies.

Unmanaged

We call the first storage management policy unmanaged, because it involves doing nothing. Under this policy, allocation and deallocation rely upon the behavior of the global functions `new` and `delete`, respectively.

Managed

The second policy is called managed. Under this policy, nodes are allocated and deallocated from a free list, managed by an instance of the class `Storage_Manager`, described further in Chapter 4. Unused nodes of any kind are reclaimed to this free list, and allocation takes nodes from the free list unless it is empty, in which case new nodes of an appropriate size are allocated from the heap. This policy has the advantages that it minimizes new allocation from the heap and localizes references to often used nodes, but has the disadvantage that, when structures grow very large and then shrink to a small size in the steady state, the free list becomes filled with storage that is unusable outside all clients of the storage manager. To mitigate this problem, we do make it possible for a client to purge the free list.

The library achieves the managed policy through the collaboration of the concrete class `Storage_Manager`, the mix-in class `Managed`, and the various node classes.

The responsibility of the class `Storage_Manager` is to provide a single free list that may be shared by all objects of a managed instantiation. The head of this free list is a static declaration in the `Storage_Manager`, and so may be shared by all of its instances. A key feature of this design uses the fact that the semantics of constructors and destructors in C++ guarantee that the correct size of an object is passed to the new and delete operators. This makes it possible for the `Storage_Manager` to maintain free lists of the proper size, even when derived classes are larger than base classes.

The responsibility of the mix-in class `Managed` is to provide a redefinition of the new and delete member functions, using this storage manager. By mixing in the class `Managed` with each of the previously discussed kinds of nodes, we produce a new family of nodes that uses the free list. In this manner, the interaction between all unbounded forms and managed storage management is indirect: the essential link is through the specialized behavior of all the managed kinds of nodes. Because each kind of managed node object knows how to copy itself and respond to the operators new and delete (inherited from the `Managed` mix-in), no other member functions have to be redefined. This style not only reduces the overall size of the library, but also contributes to its reliability and maintainability.

Controlled

The third policy is called controlled and is required in certain circumstances because of the semantics of process synchronization. For all sequential applications, the simpler unmanaged and managed policies are generally sufficient. For some multi-threaded applications, these policies may indeed still apply. As we will discuss in the next section, we make the assumption that for every object of a guarded or synchronized form, there may be more than one active agent that manipulates it. By implementing these forms so that their member functions are treated as atomic actions, we can guarantee that there is mutual exclusion over any actions that manipulate the free list, and so are safe in the presence of multiple threads of control. However, there is one hybrid situation that must be considered. Suppose we can guarantee that exactly one active agent will manipulate an object at one time. Under these circumstances, we do not need the complexity of the guarded or concurrent forms, because there are no problems of mutual exclusion within an object. Specifically, no one object may have its state manipulated by more than one thread of control at a time. However, there are problems of mutual exclusion within the class. Although individual objects are not shared by active agents, any free list is common to all such objects, and so must be given mutual exclusion. This leads us to to create the mix-in class Controlled. Controlled is exactly like the class Managed, except that allocation and deallocation are guaranteed to be atomic actions. In this manner, we achieve mutual exclusion over the free list, without having to use the more complex guarded or synchronized forms.

To make this library more adaptable, we give the instantiator control over which storage management policy is used, on a class-by-class basis. This places some small additional demands upon the instantiator, but yields the much greater benefit of giving us a library that can be tuned for serious applications.

Our strategy requires instantiators to provide a suitable kind of node, at the point of instantiation. It is for this reason, as we described earlier, that the template signature of all unbounded forms includes a Container argument, as the following example illustrates:

```
template<class Item, class Container>
class Unbounded_Queue : private Simple_List<Item>,
                       public Queue<Item>...
```

To apply the unmanaged policy, we provide a suitable primitive container, as follows:

```
typedef Node<char> Char_Node;

Unbounded_Queue<char, Char_Node> unmanaged_queue;
```

Similarly, to apply the managed policy, we provide a slightly different container, as follows:

```
typedef Managed_Node<char> Managed_Char_Node;

Unbounded_Queue<char, Managed_Char_Node> managed_queue;
```

In both cases, we introduce typedefs to improve readability.

Because our library exposes all of these primitive facilities as support classes, it is trivial for a library developer to introduce new storage management policies. For example, consider a policy that preallocates space in the free list, producing what amounts to a contiguous heap segment that virtually eliminates fragmentation problems. A developer need only produce a new mix-in class, similar to Managed, but whose constructor preallocates this storage exactly one time. The library developer then produces a new family of node classes (derived from Node or its subclasses), and then makes them available to the application developer, who applies them in the same style shown above.

Bounded

Our design thus far addresses the needs of all the unbounded monolithic and polylithic structures. Bounded monolithic structures need no storage managers, because every object has complete control over its storage. However, bounded polylithic structures pose a different problem, because here, all the objects of a given class share the same pool of storage.

These circumstances are what led us to introduce the class Simple_Bounded_List. Its semantics parallel the free list-based class, Simple_List. Whereas a Simple_List draws its nodes from the heap, a Simple_Bounded_List draws its nodes from a pool of nodes kept on the stack. We call this pool a bounded heap, and provide a support class that implements this abstraction.

Chapter 4 describes the semantics of the class Bounded_Heap in more detail, but briefly, a Bounded_Heap provides the semantics of allocation and deallocation just like the predefined new and delete operators, except that these operations draw from the stack. Whereas the heap associated with a Simple_List is globally visible, we must explicitly associate a Bounded_Heap with a Simple_Bounded_List, so that list knows where to draw its storage.

Just as for unbounded structures, we produce a family of bounded nodes, as well as its shared variations, yielding twelve low-level classes. Similarly, we provide subclasses of the Bounded_Heap for each of these classes. The semantics of the Simple_Bounded_List are guaranteed, no matter what kind of bounded heap is used, because, like the Simple_List, the Simple_Bounded_List relies upon the polymorphic behavior of its nodes.

A bounded heap ultimately stores its bounded nodes in an array of values, not references or pointers. For this reason, we must have a different kind of bounded heap for every kind of bounded node; to do otherwise would introduce slicing. As Chapter 4 explains, however, we can build a hierarchy of bounded heaps, thus extracting all common state and behavior, and elevating it to a base class.

All bounded polylithic structures use bounded heaps, which are kept as static members, so that all instances of such a class can share the same pool of storage (as for regular heaps). It is the responsibility of the instantiator, therefore, to also provide a declaration of this static member.

The class `Bounded_Map` also uses bounded heaps. Its use of an open hash table requires all buckets to share the same pool of storage. This heap is not a static member, but rather is uniquely a part of the state of every such map object.

Process Synchronization

An important feature of this library is its support for concurrent uses of the structures. A purely sequential version of the library could be made to work in a concurrent environment (for example, with client applications that manually guarded every call to any library operation). However, besides being tedious and error-prone, such an approach can be inefficient. Certain operations (especially in complex components) can be made more effective when implemented at the finer granularity available to the library's implementor.

The design of this library makes the following assumption: those developers that care about concurrency will have ported or implemented at least a `Semaphore` class for synchronizing light-weight processes, such as found in the AT&T task library. Other clients won't care, and won't miss not having the guarded or synchronized forms of structures (and will appreciate not having to pay the overhead). The guarded and synchronized forms are an independent, layered part of the library, and rely upon local implementations of concurrency mechanisms. The library's only dependencies upon the local implementation are intentionally isolated in the implementation of the class `Semaphore`.

As we described in an earlier section, the guarded and synchronized forms of monolithic structures provide varying degrees of explicit and implicit process synchronization. Just as we did for storage management, we desire to separate the policies of process synchronization from its implementation. For this reason, the template signature of every guarded form imports a guard, which is responsible for providing a binding to the local implementation of a semaphore or its equivalent. Similarly, the template signature of every synchronized form imports a monitor, which is similar to a semaphore but, as we will discuss, permits a higher degree of concurrency.

Guarded

A guarded class is a direct subclass of its concrete representation class; a guarded class contains a guard as a member object. All guarded classes introduce the member functions seize and release, which allow an active agent to gain exclusive access to the object.

For example, consider the class `Guarded_Unbounded_Queue`, which is a kind of `Unbounded_Queue`:

```
template<class Item, class Container, class Guard>
class Guarded_Unbounded_Queue : public Unbounded_Queue<Item,
                                        Container> {
public:

  Guarded_Unbounded_Queue();
  Guarded_Unbounded_Queue
    (const Guarded_Unbounded_Queue<Item, Container, Guard>&);
  virtual ~Guarded_Unbounded_Queue();

  Guarded_Unbounded_Queue<Item, Container, Guard>&
    operator=(Guarded_Unbounded_Queue<Item, Container, Guard>&);

  virtual Queue<Item>& seize();
  virtual Queue<Item>& release();

protected:

  Guard rep_guard;

};
```

Notice our introduction of the type-safe copy constructor and assignment operator, which we provide for every subclass of a structure's abstract base class.

This library provides the interface of one predefined guard: the class `Semaphore`, described further in Chapter 4. Users of this library must complete the implementation of this class, according to the needs of the local definition of light-weight processes.

Given this predefined guard, an instantiator may declare the following:

```
typedef Node<char> Char_Node;
```

```
Guarded_Unbounded_Queue<char, Char_Node, Semaphore> guarded_queue;
```

Clients who use guarded objects must follow the simple protocol of first seizing the object, operating upon it, and then releasing it (especially in the face of any exceptions thrown). To do otherwise is considered socially inappropriate, because aberrant behavior on the part of one agent denies the fair use by other agents. Seizing a guarded object and then failing to release it blocks the object indefinitely; releasing an object which was never first seized by the agent is subversive. Lastly, ignoring the seize/release protocol is simply irresponsible.

The primary benefit offered by the guarded form is its simplicity, although it does require the fair collective action of all agents that manipulate the same object. Another key feature of the guarded form is that it permits agents to form critical regions, in which several operations performed upon the same object are guaranteed to be treated as an atomic transaction.

Similar to the mechanism of storage management, the template signature of guarded forms imports the guard rather than making it an immutable feature. This makes it possible for library developers to introduce new process synchronization policies. Using the predefined class Semaphore as a guard, the library's default policy is to give every object of the class its own semaphore. This policy is acceptable only up to the point where the total number of processes reaches some practical limit set by the local implementation.

An alternate policy involves having several guarded objects share the same semaphore. A developer need only produce a new guard class that provides the same protocol as Semaphore (but is not necessarily a subclass of Semaphore). This new guard might then contain a Semaphore as a static member object, meaning that the semaphore is shared by all its instances. By instantiating a guarded form with this new guard, the library developer introduces a different policy whereby all objects of that instantiated class share the same guard, rather than there being one guard per object. The power of this policy comes about when the new guard class is used to instantiate other structures: all such objects ultimately share the same guard. The policy shift is subtle, but very powerful: not only does it reduce the number of processes in the application, but it also permits a client to globally lock a group of otherwise unrelated objects. Seizing one such object blocks all other objects that share this new guard, even if those objects are entirely different types.

Synchronized

A synchronized class is also a direct subclass of its concrete representation class; a synchronized class contains a monitor as a member object. Synchronized classes do not introduce any new member functions, but rather, redefine every virtual member function inherited from their base class. The semantics added by a synchronized class cause every member function to be treated as an atomic transaction. Whereas clients of guarded forms must explicitly seize and release an object to achieve exclusive access, synchronized forms provide this exclusivity, without requiring any special action on the part of their clients. For example, consider the class Synchronized_Unbounded_Queue, which is a kind of Unbounded_Queue:

Using the PowerPack

```
template<class Item, class Container, class Monitor>
class Synchronized_Unbounded_Queue :
  public Unbounded_Queue<Item, Container> {
public:

  Synchronized_Unbounded_Queue();
  Synchronized_Unbounded_Queue
    (const Synchronized_Unbounded_Queue<Item, Container, Monitor>&);
  virtual ~Synchronized_Unbounded_Queue();

  Synchronized_Unbounded_Queue<Item, Container, Monitor>&
    operator=(Synchronized_Unbounded_Queue<Item, Container,
              Monitor>&);
  virtual int operator==(Queue<Item>&) const;

  virtual Queue<Item>& clear();
  virtual Queue<Item>& add(Item&);
  virtual Queue<Item>& pop();

  virtual unsigned length() const;
  virtual int is_empty() const;
  virtual Item& front() const;

protected:

  Monitor rep_monitor;

  virtual void lock_argument();
  virtual void unlock_argument();

};
```

Notice again our introduction of the type-safe copy constructor and assignment operator, plus the specialization of the two helper member functions.

This library provides two predefined process synchronization policies:

- `Single`   Guarantees the semantics of a structure in the presence of multiple threads of control, with a single reader or writer.

- `Multiple`   Guarantees the semantics of a structure in the presence of multiple threads of control, with multiple simultaneous readers or a single writer.

A writer is an agent that alters the state of an object; writers are those agents that invoke modifier member functions. A reader is an agent that operates upon an object, yet preserves its state; readers are those objects that only invoke selector functions. The multiple form therefore provides the greatest amount of parallelism possible.

These two policies are implemented via the predefined monitors `Single_Read_Write_Monitor` and `Multiple_Read_Write_Monitor`, respectively. These classes are both subclasses of the base class `Read_Write_Monitor` and are layered on top of the class `Semaphore`.

Monitors collaborate with the predefined classes `Read_Lock` and `Write_Lock` to achieve exclusive invocation of each individual member function. As described further in Chapter 4, a lock contains a semaphore or a monitor as the agent responsible for process synchronization, and the lock is responsible for seizing this agent upon construction and releasing it upon destruction. The class `Write_Lock` has a very simple declaration, as follows:

```
class Write_Lock {
public:

  Write_Lock (const Read_Write_Monitor&);
  Write_Lock ();

private:

  Read_Write_Monitor& rep_monitor;

};
```

By separating the abstractions of the lock and its monitor, our design permits a client to attach a different policy to the mechanism of locking.

The definition of the class `Read_Lock` is equally simple. When used with the class `Multiple_Read_Write_Monitor`, a read lock object permits multiple simultaneous readers, but when used with the class `Single_Read_Write_Monitor`, a read lock object treats readers and writers the same.

The definition of each member function in a synchronized form uses locks to wrap around the corresponding operation inherited from its superclass:

```
template<class Item, class Container, class Monitor>
Queue<Item>&
  Synchronized_Unbounded_Queue<Item, Container, Monitor>::pop()
{
  Write_Lock _x(rep_monitor);
  return Unbounded_Queue<Item, Container>::pop();
}
```

Here, we employ a write lock, because we are guarding a modifier. The simple elegance of this design is that it guarantees that every member function represents an atomic action, even in the face of exceptions and without any explicit action on the part of a reader or writer.

In a similar fashion, we employ a read lock object to guard selectors:

```
template<class Item, class Container, class Monitor>
unsigned
  Synchronized_Unbounded_Queue<Item, Container, Monitor>::length() const
{
  Read_Lock _x(rep_monitor);
  return Queue<Item>::length();
}
```

Given the predefined monitors, an instantiator may declare the following:

```
typedef Node<char> Char_Node;
Synchronized_Unbounded_Queue
  <char, Char_Node, Multiple_Read_Write_Monitor> concurrent_queue;
```

Clients who use synchronized objects need not follow any special protocol, because the mechanism of process synchronization is handled implicitly, and so is less prone to the deadlocks and livelocks that may result from incorrect usage of guarded forms. A developer should choose a guarded form instead of a synchronized form, however, if it is necessary to invoke several member functions together as one atomic transaction. The synchronized form only guarantees that individual member functions are atomic.

Our design renders synchronized forms relatively free of circumstances that might lead to a deadly embrace. For example, assigning an object to itself or testing an object for equality with itself is potentially dangerous because in concept it requires locking the left and right elements of such expressions, which in these cases is the same object. Because once constucted an object cannot change its identity, these tests for self-identify are performed first, before either object is locked.

Even then, member functions that have instances of the class itself as arguments must be carefully designed to ensure that such arguments are properly locked. Our solution relies upon the polymorphic behavior of two helper functions, `lock_argument` and `unlock_argument`, defined in every abstract base class. Each abstract base class provides a default implementation of these two functions that does nothing; synchronized forms provide an implementation that seizes and releases the argument. As shown in an earlier example, member functions such as `operator=` use this technique:

```
template<class Item>
Queue<Item>& Queue<Item>::operator=(Queue<Item>& q)
{
  if (this == &q)
    return *this;
```

```
    q.lock_argument();
    purge();
    Queue_Active_Iterator<Item> iter(q);
    while (!iter.is_done()) {
      append(*iter.item());
      iter.next();
    }
    q.unlock_argument();
    return *this;
}
```

Notice the initial test for self-identity. Our solution for locking arguments works no matter what process synchronization policy is used by the argument, even if it differs from the policy of the instantiation.

Just as for the guarded forms, a library developer may introduce new policies of process synchronization by defining new kinds of monitors.

In all monolithic structures, we lock the class arguments of every member function, including operator=, operator==, and operator!=, plus operations such as append and insert for the class Variable_String (which have overloaded versions that use arguments of the same class). The one exception to this rule involves copy constructors, which do not guarantee such locking and so must be applied cautiously (or avoided altogether) when copying synchronized objects.

The family of classes provided with each polylithic structure does not include the guarded or the synchronized forms, because the presence of structural sharing renders any localized solutions to mutual exclusion dangerous (because they may inadvertently lead to a deadly embrace) and insufficient (there are no means of locating all the objects that share a structure). A similar problem arises with iterators, which we discuss in the next section, because iterators introduce a form of structural sharing. In either case, using polylithic structures or iterators in the presence of multiple threads of control is intrinsically difficult, so the instantiator must proceed with extreme caution.

Iteration

Every structure provides an iteration mechanism, whereby clients may visit all items in the structure in some meaningful order. For example, a client might wish to iterate through all the items in a queue to see if a certain item has already been added.

For each structure, we provide two forms of iteration. Iterators thus serve as agents that traverse a structure. An active iterator requires that clients explicitly advance the iterator; in one logical expression, a passive iterator applies a client-supplied function, and so requires less collaboration on the part of the client. We define different iterators for each kind of structure, for reasons of type safety. Additionally, the protocol of certain iterators, such as for the class Graph, are subtly different and so do not lend themselves to a common iterator class.

The following incomplete declaration illustrates a typical active iterator:

```
template <class Item>
class Queue_Active_Iterator {
public:

  Queue_Active_Iterator(const Queue<Item>&);
  virtual ~Queue_Active_Iterator();

  virtual void reset();
  virtual int next();

  virtual int is_done();
  virtual Item* item();

};
```

At the time of its construction, every iterator is bound to a particular object. Iteration begins at the "top" of a structure, whatever that might mean for the given abstraction.

For an active iterator, a client obtains a pointer to the current item through the member function item; the pointer is null if iteration is complete or if the structure is empty. A client advances the iterator to the next successive item through the member function next. The selector is_done allows the client to query the progress of iteration, and returns 0 if the iteration is complete or if the structure is empty. The reset member function allows multiple traversals over the same object.

As an example, given the following declarations:

```
typedef Node<char> Char_Node;

Unbounded_Queue<char, Char_Node> unbounded_queue;

typedef Queue_Active_Iterator<char> Active_Iterator;
```

we might use an active iterator to print the contents of the queue:

```
int process(char* item)
{
  cout << *item;
  return 1;
}
```

```
void display_active (Queue<char>& q)
{
  Active_Iterator iter(q);
  while (!iter.is_done()) {
    process(iter.item());
    iter.next();;
  }
  cout << "\n";
}
```

The implementation of the function `display_active` uses an idiom employed by most clients of active iterators.

A passive iterator is an applicator, meaning that it applies some function to every item in the structure. The following incomplete declaration illustrates a typical passive iterator:

```
template <class Item>
class Queue_Passive_Iterator {
public:

  Queue_Passive_Iterator(const Queue<Item>&);
  virtual ~Queue_Passive_Iterator();

  virtual int apply(int (*)(Item*));

};
```

Passive iterators operate on all items in a structure in a (logically) single operation. The `apply` function visits each item in the structure and invokes the supplied function on each. It continues until reaching the last item, or when the supplied function returns a result of 0. The `apply` member function allows multiple traversals over the same object.

As an example, given the following declarations:

```
typedef Queue_Passive_Iterator<char> Passive_Iterator;
```

we might use a passive iterator to print the contents of the queue:

```
extern int process(char*);

void display_passive (Queue<char>& q)
{
  Passive_Iterator iter(q);
  iter.apply(process);
  cout << "\n";
}
```

Both kinds of iterators are defined as friends of the abstract base class, and rely upon the polymorphic behavior of the base class's helper functions. Iterators may therefore be applied to objects of any subclass of a structure. This behavior is what makes it possible for structures to copy, assign, and test for equality among objects of the same structure, but with different representations.

During iteration, it is always safe to invoke a selector upon the current item. However, care must be taken when changing the number and order of elements within a structure. Doing so safely requires an intimate understanding of the representation of the object being traversed. The implementation of the member function `intersection` for the class `Set` provides an idiom for deletion of an item during iteration.

EXAMPLE

In this section, we examine a small program that illustrates how to set up and use a component. The example program is straightforward: it takes a list of filenames for C or C++ source code, and searches through them to find any `#include` directives. The program uses a `Bag` component to store any included filenames it finds. (See Chapter 2 for a description of a Bag abstraction.) At the end, it iterates over the `Bag`, displaying the names found and how many times they are included.

Although the example is simple, some of the details are not. Given the great diversity of C++ implementation environments and the fact that templates are a relatively novel feature, writing portable template code can be a challenge. Check the details of template instantiation for each implementation.

Appendix A lists the complete source text of all the files on the accompanying PowerPack disk, including the C++ Booch Components files used. In this section, we walk through the example translation unit (found in the file example.C on UNIX, example.cpp on DOS, and example.cp on the Macintosh).

The first part of the file contains the preprocessor `#include` directives necessary to make certain declarations available:

```
#include <stdlib.h>       // for EXIT_SUCCESS, EXIT_FAILURE
#include <fstream.h>      // for ifstream
#include <iomanip.h>      // for setw
#include "str.h"          // for simple String class
#include "bag_b.h"        // for Bounded_Bag template
```

The file stdlib.h is from the standard C library, which will also be part of the standard C++ library. The files fstream.h and iomanip.h are from the standard C++ iostreams library. The file str.h defines a simple String class, which encapsulates the details of storage management and character handling so that we can concentrate on the matter at hand. The file bag_b.h is from the C++ Booch Components library.

Next, we declare some typedefs to cause template expansion. These are not needed in C++ implementations supporting Automatic Template Instantiation (ATI), such as UNIX-based cfront environments. They are used by Borland's implementation and for pre-3.0 implementations, a separate preprocessor (tpl) included in the C++ Booch Components distribution.

The typedef for Collect gives us a shorthand for the Bounded_Bag we use to store the included filenames. The Iterator typedef is a similar shorthand for an active iterator we use to get each name after we have handled all the files.

```
// typedefs cause template instantiation for Borland, tpl:
typedef Bag<String>                       bag;
typedef Simple_Vector<String, 100U>       _vec;
typedef Unsigned_Vector<100U>             _uvec;
typedef Bounded_Bag<String, 100U>         Collect;
typedef Bag_Active_Iterator<String>       Iterator;
```

Next, we provide forward declarations of some support defined later in this translation unit. The error() function reports we had trouble, and exits. The class Include is a special kind of String that knows about the format of #include directives. As we see later, constructing the string is sufficient to parse the directive and find the included file's name. The includes() function hides the details of how we go through the lines in the file looking for the directives.

```
// Local definitions:

static void error(const char* const);

class Include : public String {
public:
  Include(const char* const);         // parse an #include directive
};

static Include includes(ifstream&);      // find Includes in file
                                 // returns "" String at eof()
```

The main() function is straightforward, because we've pushed so many of the messy details into supporting abstractions and functions. The function iterates over the command line arguments and attempts to open the named file. If the file exists and opens correctly, we then look for all the included filenames and store them away in the bag.

When we are done with all the files named on the command line, we iterate over the bag and list its contents. A Bag is like a Set, except we can add the same item more than once—where a Set throws a Duplicate exception, a Bag increments a counter associated with the item. We, therefore, can also see how many times a given file was included.

```
int main(int argc, char* argv[])    // list #included files
{
  Collect bag;        // collect up the #included file names

  cout << "Files and their includes:" << endl;
  for (int i=1; i<argc; ++i) {
    const String file = argv[i];
    cout << file << ':' << endl;
    ifstream f = argv[i];    if (!f) error(argv[i]);

    Include s = includes(f);
    while ( s ) {
      cout << '\t' << s << endl;
      bag.add(s);
      s = includes(f);
    }
  }

  cout << "\nSummary:" << endl;
  for (Iterator iter(bag); !iter.is_done(); iter.next() ) {
    cout << setw(15) << *iter.item() << " included "
         << setw(2)  <<  iter.size() << " times" << endl;
  }
  return EXIT_SUCCESS;
}
```

Most of the details have been encapsulated in supporting abstractions: the iostreams handle the details of files and their input/output buffering; the Bags handle the details of in-memory data structures for adding and counting the files of interest; and the Strings handle the details of character storage and comparison.

We also have some local support functions, tailored to the problem at hand. The error() function is just a quick way to print an error string and exit the program:

```
// Auxiliary support:

static void error(const char* const s)
```

```
{
  cerr << "Error: " << s << endl;
  exit(EXIT_FAILURE);
}
```

The constructor for the derived Include class hides the details of parsing an #include directive. It looks through a NUL-terminated character sequence and finds the subsequence that identifies the included file. As in standard C, C++ supports two styles of identifying such files: the <> form for "library" files, and the "" form for local files.

```
#include <string.h> // for strchr
#include <stddef.h> // for ptrdiff_t

Include::Include(const char* const s)
// parses the string s to find the text between <> or ""
// examples:   #include <iostream>  ==> iostream
//             #include "mine.h"    ==> mine.h
{
  if (s) {
    const char* start = s;
    const char* end = start;
    register const char* p = strchr(s,'<');
    if (p) {
      start = p+1;
      p = strchr(start, '>');
      if (!p) error("Include");
      end = p-1;
    } else {
      p = strchr(s, '"');
      if (!p) error("Include");
      start = p+1;
      p = strchr(start, '"');
      if (!p) error("Include");
      end = p-1;
    }
    ptrdiff_t len = (end>=start) ? end-start+1 : start-end+1;
    if (len) assign(start, len);   // inherited
  }
}
```

Finally, the function includes() encapsulates the details of getting each line from a file and looking for #include directives. It returns an empty Include string when it reaches the end of the file, indicating to the caller that it's time to move on to the next file.

This is a simplistic version, looking only for the literal sequence "#include". A more sophisticated version would check for any white space between the '#' and the "include". Also, the fixed-size character buffer is a limiting factor:

it's bound to be too small for a file. A more sophisticated version might use a dynamic-mode `strstream` to accept lines of any length.

```
static Include includes(ifstream& f)
// iterate over the file a line at a time, looking for lines
// of the form "#include ..." => return the include filename
{
  static char buf[120];         // wimpy, but effective
  static const String include = "#include";

  while (f.good() && f.getline(buf, sizeof buf)) {
    if (include.matches(buf)) {
      Include line = buf;       // do the parsing
      return line;              // return the file name
    }
  }
  return 0;                     // return null string @ eof
```

When we compile, link, and run this program on its own files, we get the following result:

```
> example example.cp str.cp

Files and their includes:
example.cp:
    stdlib.h
    fstream.h
    iomanip.h
    str.h
    bag_b.h
    string.h
    stddef.h
str.cp:
    str.h
    string.h
    iostream.h

Summary:
    iostream.h included  1 times
     stddef.h included   1 times
     string.h included   2 times
      bag_b.h included   1 times
        str.h included   2 times
     iomanip.h included  1 times
     fstream.h included  1 times
      stdlib.h included  1 times
```

See Appendix A for details regarding the contents of the supporting abstractions.

The Rest of the Book

This chapter has presented a quick overview of the design of the C++ Booch Components library. It has described the overall content and organization of the library, discussed some of the key design issues, and presented a small example.

The remaining chapters of the book contain the detailed reference material for all of the library's contents. It is organized to be concise and striaghtforward to read. All the entries follow the same documentation style.

The definition of every abstract base class and concrete class in the library follows a consistent style, as follows:

```
template<...>
class Name {
public:

    // constructors
    // virtual destructor

    // operators

    // modifiers

    // selectors

protected:

    // member objects

    // helper functions

private:

    // friends
```

For example, the definition of the abstract base class Queue begins as follows:

```
template<class Item>
class Queue {
```

Next, we provide the usual set of constructors and destructors:

```
Queue();
Queue(const Queue<Item>&);
virtual ~Queue();
```

Notice that the destructor is virtual, because we want polymorphic behavior when an object of this class is destroyed. Next, we have the declaration of all operators:

```
Queue<Item>& operator=(Queue<Item>&);
virtual int operator==(Queue<Item>&) const;
virtual int operator!=(Queue<Item>&) const;
```

In this case, the `operator=` is not declared virtual, for reasons of type safety. It is the responsibility of subclasses to provide a similar member function, but using a function signature of their own class.

We next provide all modifiers, which are operations that may alter the state of the object. Each of these functions returns a reference to the object they operate upon. This is consistent with the inserter and extractor functions of the C++ iostreams library, and the approach illustrated in [Lippman, 1989]. This style provides a very convenient way to invoke multiple modifying operations on the same object within the same expression.

```
virtual Queue<Item>& clear();
virtual Queue<Item>& add(Item&);
virtual Queue<Item>& pop();
```

We use the const qualifier to indicate (and let the language enforce) the use of selector functions that observe, but do not modify, the state of an object.

```
virtual unsigned length() const;
virtual int is_empty() const;
virtual Item& front() const = 0;
```

We have declared the member function `front` as pure, thus letting the language enforce our design decision that this is an abstract base class.

We declare such member functions as virtual, although in some classes, certain members functions are not virtual, as an indication of our design decision that they should never be specialized. In some support classes (such as the class `Node`), we also make various constructors and operators private, thus intentionally restricting how instances of that class may be initialized.

The protected part of every class begins with any member objects that form the representation of the abstraction. For all abstract base classes, this generally includes some cached information about the size of the structure. For example, in the class `Queue` we have:

```
unsigned rep_length;
```

We make such declarations protected rather than private, so that all subclasses may have direct visibility to the state of a class's objects.

We follow these member objects with any helper functions, which are used by all concrete subclasses to implement the abstract base class. The class Queue provides a typical set of these member functions:

```
virtual void purge();
virtual void append(Item&);

virtual void lock_argument();
virtual void unlock_argument();

virtual void* iter_first() const = 0;
virtual void* iter_next(void*) const = 0;
virtual int iter_is_done(void*) const = 0;
virtual Item* iter_item(void*) const = 0;
```

It is important to remember that all of these members are insignificant to clients that manipulate instances of the class; protected members are relevant only to clients that specialize the abstract base class, or to friends of the class.

Lastly, we provide a private part, which typically contains only friend declarations:

```
friend class Queue_Active_Iterator<Item>;
friend class Queue_Passive_Iterator<Item>;
```

We describe the meaning and use of iterators in more detail in Chapter 3.

Coding Style

In general, code formatting and indentation follow the AT&T style [Stroustrup, 1991].

We follow some additional conventions not directly covered by the AT&T style:

- Class names have a leading upperclass letter, such as Queue; adjective modifiers (representing the forms of an abstraction) precede the name, and are separated by an underscore, as in Unbounded_Queue.
- Member functions are written in lowercase: modifiers are active verbs such as add, and selectors are generally predicates such as is_empty or nouns representing an attribute of the object such as length and front.
- Member objects, forming the representation of a class, are given the prefix rep, as in rep_length.

Structures Class Strategy

In the context of this library, a structure represents a single, cohesive abstraction. The C++ Booch Components provide classes for many domain-independent data structures:

- Bag
- Deque

    Balking_Deque

    Priority_Deque

    Balking_Priority_Deque

- Directed_Graph
- Undirected_Graph
- Double_List

- `Single_List`
- `Map`
- `Queue`

    `Balking_Queue`

    `Priority_Queue`

    `Balking_Priority_Queue`

- `Ring`
- `Set`
- `Stack`
- `Variable_String`
- `Arbitrary_Tree`
- `Binary_Tree`

This section documents each of these structural classes, in the form of UNIX man pages.

BAG

NAME

`Bag`—A collection of items from some domain may contain duplicates.

SYNOPSIS

```
template<class Item>
class Bag {
public:

  Bag();
  Bag(const Bag<Item>&);
  virtual ~Bag();

  Bag<Item>& operator=(Bag<Item>&);
  virtual int operator==(Bag<Item>&) const;
  virtual int operator!=(Bag<Item>&) const;
```

```
    virtual Bag<Item>& clear();
    virtual Bag<Item>& add(Item&);
    virtual Bag<Item>& remove(Item&);
    virtual Bag<Item>& bag_union(Bag<Item>&);
    virtual Bag<Item>& intersection(Bag<Item>&);
    virtual Bag<Item>& difference(Bag<Item>&);

    virtual unsigned extent() const;
    virtual unsigned size() const;
    virtual unsigned number(Item&) const;
    virtual int is_empty() const;
    virtual int is_member(Item&) const;
    virtual int is_subset(Bag<Item>&) const;
    virtual int is_proper_subset(Bag<Item>&) const;

};
```

DESCRIPTION

A bag denotes a collection of items drawn from some well-defined universe. Unlike a set, a bag may contain duplicate items. A bag actually owns only one copy of each unique item: duplicates are counted, but not stored with the bag.

`template<class Item>`

The template item denotes the universe from which the bag draws its items. The class `Item` may be either a primitive type or a user-defined class. If the latter, the class must provide a default constructor, copy constructor, assignment operator, and equality operator.

The template signature of the unbounded form requires a class `Container`, which must be a kind of `Counting_Node`. The template signature of the bounded form requires an unsigned integer `Size`, representing the static size of all instances of the class. Additionally, the template signature of the guarded form requires a class `Guard` (such as the class `Semaphore`), and the template signature of the synchronized form requires a class `Monitor` (such as a kind of `Read_Write_Monitor`).

`Bag();`

Construct an empty bag.

`Bag(const Bag<Item>&);`

Copy the given bag; items in the copied bag are themselves copied.

`virtual ~Bag();`

Destroy the bag. For unbounded forms, individual items may or may not be destroyed, according to the semantics of the bag's container. For bounded forms, individual items are destroyed.

```
Bag<Item>& operator=(Bag<Item>&);
```

Replace the state of the bag with the items in the given bag; the bag is initially cleared, and items (if any) in the given bag are themselves copied.

```
virtual int operator==(Bag<Item>&) const;
```

Return 1 if and only if both bags have the same number of distinct items, the same number of total items, and the same items themselves; return 0 otherwise. Equality of distinct items uses the default test for equality provided by the class Item.

```
virtual int operator!=(Bag<Item>&) const;
```

Return the logical negation of operator==.

```
virtual Bag<Item>& clear();
```

Empty the bag of all items. For unbounded forms, individual items may or may not be destroyed, according to the semantics of the bag's container. For bounded forms, individual items are not destroyed.

```
virtual Bag<Item>& add(Item&);
```

Add the item to the bag. If the item is not already a distinct member of the bag, copy the item and add it to the bag. If the item already exists, increment the number of that item. The test for membership of an item uses the default test for equality provided by the class Item.

```
virtual Bag<Item>& remove(Item&);
```

If the bag is empty, throw the exception Underflow. If the item is not a member of the bag, throw the exception Not_Found. Otherwise, if there is originally more than one item in the bag, simply decrement its number; if there is exactly one item in the bag, remove the item from the bag. For unbounded forms, the removed item may or may not be destroyed according to the semantics of the bag's container. For bounded forms, the removed item is not destroyed. The test for membership of an item uses the default test for equality provided by the class Item.

```
virtual Bag<Item>& bag_union(Bag<Item>&);
```

Perform a logical bag union. At the completion of this operation, the bag contains the distinct items and number of items found in its original state combined with the given bag. For each item in the given bag, if the item is not already a distinct member of the bag, copy the item (and its number) and add it to the bag. If the item already is a member, increment its number by the number of that item in the given bag. The test for membership of an item uses the default test for equality provided by the class `Item`.

```
virtual Bag<Item>& intersection(Bag<Item>&);
```

Perform a logical bag intersection. At the completion of this operation, the bag contains the distinct items and number of items found both in its original state and in the given bag. For each item in the given bag, if the item is not already a distinct member of the bag, do nothing. If the item already is a member and if there are more items than in the given bag, simply decrement its number by the number of that item in the given bag; otherwise, do nothing. Items in the original bag but not in the given bag are also entirely removed. For unbounded forms, the removed item may or may not be destroyed according to the semantics of the bag's container. For bounded forms, the removed item is not destroyed. The test for membership of an item uses the default test for equality provided by the class `Item`.

```
virtual Bag<Item>& difference(Bag<Item>&);
```

Perform a logical bag difference. At the completion of this operation, the bag contains the distinct items and number of items found in its original state, less those found in the given bag. For each item in the given bag, if the item is not already a distinct member of the bag, do nothing. If the item already is a member and if there are more items than in the given bag, simply decrement its number by the number of that item in the given bag; otherwise, remove the item from the bag. For unbounded forms, the removed item may or may not be destroyed according to the semantics of the bag's container. For bounded forms, the removed item is not destroyed. The test for membership of an item uses the default test for equality provided by the class `Item`.

```
virtual unsigned extent() const;
```

Return the number of distinct items in the bag.

```
virtual unsigned size() const;
```

Return the total number of items in the bag.

```
virtual unsigned number(Item&) const;
```

If the item is not a member of the bag, throw the exception `Not_Found`. Otherwise, return the number of the given item.

```
virtual int is_empty() const;
```

Return 1 if and only if there are no items in the bag.

```
virtual int is_member(Item&) const;
```

Return 1 if and only if the item exists in the bag. The test for membership of an item uses the default test for equality provided by the class `Item`.

```
virtual int is_subset(Bag<Item>&) const;
```

Return 1 if and only if the bag has the same or fewer distinct items than in the given bag and equal or fewer numbers of each such item than in the given bag.

```
virtual int is_proper_subset(Bag<Item>&) const;
```

Return 1 if and only if the bag has fewer distinct items than in the given bag and fewer numbers of each item than in the given bag.

EXCEPTIONS

`Not_Found` —thrown by `remove` and `number` if the item is not a member of the bag.

`Overflow` —thrown by any bounded form member function, when the static limits of the object are exceeded.

`Storage_Error` —thrown by any unbounded form member function, when no more storage can be allocated.

`Underflow` —thrown by `remove` if the bag is empty.

OPTIONS

Bags form a typical family of classes, supporting all the usual representation and process synchronization forms:

- `Bag`
- `Unbounded_Bag`
- `Guarded_Unbounded_Bag`
- `Synchronized_Unbounded_Bag`
- `Bounded_Bag`
- `Guarded_Bounded_Bag`
- `Synchronized_Bounded_Bag`

Bags provide the usual active and passive iterators, with some simple variations. The bag active iterator includes the member function `size`, which returns the number of the current item, and zero if the iterator is done. Similarly, the signature of the apply function in the passive iterator requires an unsigned argument for the number of the current item.

FILES

In the bags class category:

```
bag      Bag
         Bag_Active_Iterator
         Bag_Passive_Iterator
bag_u    Unbounded_Bag
bag_ug   Guarded_Unbounded_Bag
bag_us   Synchronized_Unbounded_Bag
bag_b    Bounded_Bag
bag_bg   Guarded_Bounded_Bag
bag_bs   Synchronized_Bounded_Bag
```

SEE ALSO

Node (especially Counting_Node)

Synch

DEQUE

NAME

Deque—A sequence in which items may be added and removed from either end.

SYNOPSIS

```
enum Location {FRONT, BACK};

template<class Item>
class Deque {
public:

  Deque();
  Deque(const Deque<Item>&);
  virtual ~Deque();

  Deque<Item>& operator=(Deque<Item>&);
  virtual int operator==(Deque<Item>&) const;
  virtual int operator!=(Deque<Item>&) const;

  virtual Deque<Item>& clear();
  virtual Deque<Item>& add(Item&, Location location = BACK);
  virtual Deque<Item>& pop(Location location = FRONT);
```

```
virtual unsigned length() const;
virtual int is_empty() const;
virtual Item& front() const;
virtual Item& back() const;
```

};

DESCRIPTION

A deque denotes a sequence of items, in which items may be added and removed from either end of the sequence.

```
enum Location {FRONT, BACK};
```

Location is used by certain member functions to denote the specific end of the deque upon which to operate.

```
template<class Item>
```

The template item denotes the universe from which the deque draws its items. The class Item may be either a primitive type or a user-defined class. If the latter, the class must provide a default constructor, copy constructor, assignment operator, and equality operator.

The template signature of the unbounded form requires a class Container, which must be a kind of Node. The template signature of the bounded form requires an unsigned integer Size, representing the static size of all instances of the class. Additionally, the template signature of the guarded form requires a class Guard (such as the class Semaphore), and the template signature of the synchronized form requires a class Monitor (such as a kind of Read_Write_Monitor).

```
Deque();
```

Construct an empty deque.

```
Deque(const Deque<Item>&);
```

Copy the items in the given deque, preserving their order; items in the copied deque are themselves copied.

```
virtual ~Deque();
```

Destroy the deque. For unbounded forms, individual items may or may not be destroyed, according to the semantics of the deque's container. For bounded forms, individual items are destroyed.

```
Deque<Item>& operator=(Deque<Item>&);
```

Replace the state of the deque with the items in the given deque, preserving their order; the deque is initially cleared, and items (if any) in the given deque are themselves copied.

```
virtual int operator==(Deque<Item>&) const;
```

Return 1 if and only if both deques have the same length and the same items in the same order; return 0 otherwise. Equality of items uses the default test for equality provided by the class Item.

```
virtual int operator!=(Deque<Item>&) const;
```

Return the logical negation of operator==.

```
virtual Deque<Item>& clear();
```

Empty the deque of all items. For unbounded forms, individual items may or may not be destroyed, according to the semantics of the deque's container. For bounded forms, individual items are not destroyed.

```
virtual Deque<Item>& add(Item&, Location location = BACK);
```

Add the item to the deque at the given location; the item itself is copied.

```
virtual Deque<Item>& pop(Location location = FRONT);
```

If the deque is empty, throw the exception Underflow. Otherwise, remove the item from the deque at the given location. For unbounded forms, the removed item may or may not be destroyed according to the semantics of the deque's container. For bounded forms, the removed item is not destroyed.

```
virtual unsigned length() const;
```

Return the number of items in the deque.

```
virtual int is_empty() const;
```

Return 1 if and only if there are no items in the deque.

```
virtual Item& front() const;
```

If the deque is empty, throw the exception Underflow. Otherwise, return a reference to the item at the front of the deque.

```
virtual Item& back() const;
```

If the deque is empty, throw the exception Underflow. Otherwise, return a reference to the item at the back of the deque.

EXCEPTIONS

Overflow —thrown by any bounded form member function, when the static limits of the object are exceeded.

Storage_Error —thrown by any unbounded form member function, when no more storage can be allocated.

Underflow —thrown by `pop`, `front`, and `back` if the deque is empty.

OPTIONS

Deques form a typical family of classes, supporting all the usual representation and process synchronization forms:

- Deque
- Unbounded_Deque
- Guarded_Unbounded_Deque
- Synchronized_Unbounded_Deque
- Bounded_Deque
- Guarded_Bounded_Deque
- Synchronized_Bounded_Deque

Deques provide the usual active and passive iterators.

In addition to the core family of deque classes, there are three subclasses that provide variations on the theme:

- Balking_Deque
- Priority_Deque
- Balking_Priority_Deque

Each of these three abstractions provides the usual family of classes.

With the `Balking_Deque`, items may be removed from arbitrary positions in the deque. Items are numbered starting at the front of the deque, from 1 to the deque's length. `Balking_Deque` is a direct subclass of `Deque`, and adds the following operations:

```
virtual Deque<Item>& remove(unsigned position);
```

If the given position is zero or greater than the length of the deque, throw the exception `Range_Error`. Otherwise, remove the item at the given ordinal position.

For unbounded forms, the removed item may or may not be destroyed according to the semantics of the deque's container. For bounded forms, the removed item is not destroyed.

```
virtual unsigned position(Item&) const;
```

Return the ordinal position of the item in the deque. If the item does not exist in the deque, return 0. The test for existence of an item uses the default test for equality provided by the class `Item`.

With the priority form, items are ordered in the deque according to their priority, from highest to lowest priority. Priority is an integer, and the higher the number, the higher the priority; negative values are permitted. The class `Item` must provide a function that returns the priority of the item, which may be set exactly once for each deque, either at the time of the deque's construction, or via the member function `set_priority_function`. `Priority_Deque` is a direct subclass of `Deque`, and redefines one operation and adds one operation:

```
virtual Deque<Item>& add(Item&, Location location = BACK);
```

Add the item to the deque in order of its priority; the item itself is copied. When adding from the front, the item is added ahead of existing items with equal priority. When adding from the back, the item is added behind existing items with equal priority.

```
virtual Deque<Item>& set_priority_function(int (*priority)(Item&));
```

If the priority function is already set, throw the exception `Duplicate`. Otherwise, set the priority function to the given function.

`Balking_Priority_Deque` is a direct subclass of `Deque`, and adds the behavior of both the `Balking_Deque` and the `Priority_Deque`.

FILES

In the deques class category:

```
deque    Deque
         Deque_Active_Iterator
         Deque_Passive_Iterator
deq_u    Unbounded_Deque
deq_ug   Guarded_Unbounded_Deque
deq_us   Synchronized_Unbounded_Deque
deq_b    Bounded_Deque
deq_bg   Guarded_Bounded_Deque
deq_bs   Synchronized_Bounded_Deque
```

In the `balking_deques` class category:

```
bdeq       Balking_Deque
bdeq_u     Unbounded_Balking_Deque
bdeq_ug    Guarded_Unbounded_Balking_Deque
bdeq_us    Synchronized_Unbounded_Balking_Deque
bdeq_b     Bounded_Balking_Deque
bdeq_bg    Guarded_Bounded_Balking_Deque
bdeq_bs    Synchronized_Bounded_Balking_Deque
```

In the `priority_deques` class category:

```
pdeq       Priority_Deque
pdeq_u     Unbounded_Priority_Deque
pdeq_ug    Guarded_Unbounded_Priority_Deque
pdeq_us    Synchronized_Unbounded_Priority_Deque
pdeq_b     Bounded_Priority_Deque
pdeq_bg    Guarded_Bounded_Priority_Deque
pdeq_bs    Synchronized_Bounded_Priority_Deque
```

In the `balking_priority_deques` class category:

```
bpdeq      Balking_Priority_Deque
bpdeq_u    Unbounded_Balking_Priority_Deque
bpdeq_ug   Guarded_Unbounded_Balking_Priority_Deque
bpdeq_us   Synchronized_Unbounded_Balking_Priority_Deque
bpdeq_b    Bounded_Balking_Priority_Deque
bpdeq_bg   Guarded_Bounded_Balking_Priority_Deque
bpdeq_bs   Synchronized_Bounded_Balking_Priority_Deque
```

SEE ALSO

```
Node
```

```
Synch
```

DIRECTED_GRAPH

NAME

`Directed_Graph`—An unrooted collection of nodes and unidirectional arcs; may contain cycles and cross-references; structural sharing is permitted.

SYNOPSIS

```
enum Arc_Direction {OUTGOING, INCOMING};

template<class Item>
class Directed_Vertex {
public:

  Directed_Vertex();
  Directed_Vertex(Directed_Vertex<Item>&);
  virtual ~Directed_Vertex();

  virtual Directed_Vertex<Item>& operator=(Directed_Vertex<Item>&);
  virtual int operator==(Directed_Vertex<Item>&) const;
  virtual int operator!=(Directed_Vertex<Item>&) const;

  virtual Directed_Vertex<Item>& clear();
  virtual Directed_Vertex<Item>& set_item(Item&);

  virtual int is_null() const;
  virtual int is_shared() const;
  virtual Item& item() const;
  virtual unsigned arity(Arc_Direction direction = OUTGOING) const;
  virtual unsigned number_of_outgoing_arcs() const;
  virtual unsigned number_of_incoming_arcs() const;

};

template<class Item>
class Directed_Arc {
public:

  Directed_Arc();
  Directed_Arc(Directed_Arc<Item>&);
  virtual ~Directed_Arc();

  virtual Directed_Arc<Item>& operator=(Directed_Arc<Item>&);
  virtual int operator==(Directed_Arc<Item>&) const;
  virtual int operator!=(Directed_Arc<Item>&) const;

  virtual Directed_Arc<Item>& clear();
  virtual Directed_Arc<Item>& set_item(Item&);
  virtual Directed_Arc<Item>&
    set_source_vertex(Directed_Vertex<Item>&);
  virtual Directed_Arc<Item>&
    set_destination_vertex(Directed_Vertex<Item>&);

  virtual int is_null() const;
  virtual int is_shared() const;
  virtual Item& item() const;
```

```cpp
    virtual void get_source_vertex(Directed_Vertex<Item>&) const;
    virtual void get_destination_vertex(Directed_Vertex<Item>&) const;

};

template<class Item>
class Directed_Graph {
public:

  Directed_Graph();
  virtual ~Directed_Graph();

  virtual Directed_Graph<Item>& clear();
  virtual Directed_Graph<Item>&
    create_vertex(Directed_Vertex<Item>&, Item&);
  virtual Directed_Graph<Item>&
    create_arc(Directed_Arc<Item>&, Item&,
               Directed_Vertex<Item>& source,
               Directed_Vertex<Item>& destination);
  virtual Directed_Graph<Item>&
    destroy_vertex(Directed_Vertex<Item>&);
  virtual Directed_Graph<Item>& destroy_arc(Directed_Arc<Item>&);

  virtual int is_empty() const;
  virtual int is_member(Directed_Vertex<Item>&) const;
  virtual int is_member(Directed_Arc<Item>&) const;
  virtual unsigned number_of_vertices() const;
  virtual unsigned number_of_arcs() const;

};
```

DESCRIPTION

A directed graph denotes an unrooted collection of nodes and unidirectional arcs. A graph may contain cycles and cross-references. Graphs are polylithic structures; hence, the semantics of copying, assignment, and equality involve structural sharing. Care must be taken in manipulating the same vertex or arc named by more than one alias.

This graph abstraction involves the collaborative behavior of three classes: Directed_Vertex, Directed_Arc, and Directed_Graph. These classes are all siblings, and are defined independently of the undirected graph. Instances of the classes Directed_Vertex and Directed_Arc are aliases of concrete vertices and arcs, respectively, but are themselves not the concrete vertices and arcs. For this reason, the semantics of Directed_Vertex and Directed_Arc involve structural sharing. Copying, assigning, and testing for equality among graphs as a whole are marginally useful operations and are computationally expensive (on the order of O(n2)); therefore, the Directed_Graph explicitly disallows these operations.

This abstraction has been carefully constructed to eliminate all storage leaks, except in the case of intentional abuses. Concrete vertices and arcs may only be created and destroyed in the context of a graph. Vertices and arcs are always reachable, meaning there is no circumstance whereby a concrete vertex or arc can ever be "lost." Furthermore, this design protects against dangling references: a concrete vertex or an arc cannot be destroyed if aliases to it exist.

Each concrete vertex and arc is a member of exactly one instance of Directed_Graph. Furthermore, an arc and its source and destination vertices are guaranteed to be members of the same graph. This guarantee is provided by an implementation strategy, whereby every graph is given a unique identification upon construction. Similarly, the creation of a concrete vertex or arc, always in the context of some graph, uses the graph's identification to denote the vertex or arc's enclosing graph. A vertex or arc is known to be a member of a given graph if its enclosing graph matches the graph's identification.

```
enum Arc_Direction {OUTGOING, INCOMING};
```

Direction is used by the vertex member function arity to denote the arcs for which the given vertex is either the source (OUTGOING) or the destination (INCOMING).

```
template<class Item>
```

The template item denotes the universe from which the vertices and arcs draw their items. The class Item may be either a primitive type or a user-defined class. If the latter, the class must provide a default constructor, copy constructor, assignment operator, and equality operator.

The template signature of the unbounded form requires a class Container, which must be a kind of Shared_Graph_Node. The template signature of the bounded form requires an unsigned integer Size, representing the static size of all instances of the class. Additionally, the template signature of the guarded form requires a class Guard (such as the class Semaphore), and the template signature of the synchronized form requires a class Monitor (such as a kind of Read_Write_Monitor).

The representation of the bounded form of Directed_Graph includes the static declaration of a bounded heap, from which all the objects of this instantiation draw their storage for vertices and arcs. A client must provide a definition of this bounded heap, which must be a kind of Shared_Bounded_Graph_Node_Heap.

Following are the member functions for the class Directed_Vertex, whose instances represent aliases to concrete vertices in the graph:

```
Directed_Vertex();
```

Construct a null vertex.

```
Directed_Vertex(Directed_Vertex<Item>&);
```

If the given vertex is null, construct a null vertex. Otherwise, construct a vertex so that it structurally shares the concrete vertex denoted by the given vertex.

```
virtual ~Directed_Vertex();
```

Destroy the vertex. The concrete vertex (if not null) is no longer structurally shared by this alias.

```
virtual Directed_Vertex<Item>& operator=(Directed_Vertex<Item>&);
```

Clear the vertex. If the given vertex is not null, set the state of the vertex so that it structurally shares the concrete vertex denoted by the given vertex.

```
virtual int operator==(Directed_Vertex<Item>&) const;
```

Return 1 if and only if both vertices are null or are an alias to the same concrete vertex.

```
virtual int operator!=(Directed_Vertex<Item>&) const;
```

Return the logical negation of operator==.

```
virtual Directed_Vertex<Item>& clear();
```

If the vertex is not null, remove this alias to the concrete vertex and make the vertex null.

```
virtual Directed_Vertex<Item>& set_item(Item&);
```

If the vertex is null, throw the exception Is_Null. Otherwise, set the item of the associated concrete vertex.

```
virtual int is_null() const;
```

Return 1 if and only if the vertex does not denote any concrete vertex.

```
virtual int is_shared() const;
```

Return 1 if and only if the concrete vertex has an alias.

```
virtual Item& item() const;
```

If the vertex is null, throw the exception Is_Null. Otherwise, return a reference to the item of the designated concrete vertex.

```
virtual unsigned arity(Arc_Direction direction = OUTGOING) const;
```

If the vertex is null, throw the exception Is_Null. Otherwise, return a count of the arcs for which the vertex is the source (OUTGOING) or for which the vertex is the destination (INCOMING).

```
virtual unsigned number_of_outgoing_arcs() const;
```

If the vertex is null, throw the exception Is_Null. Otherwise, return a count of the arcs for which the vertex is the source.

```
virtual unsigned number_of_incoming_arcs() const;
```

If the vertex is null, throw the exception Is_Null. Otherwise, return a count of the arcs for which the vertex is the destination.

Following are the member functions for the class Directed_Arc, whose instances represent aliases to concrete arcs in the graph:

```
Directed_Arc();
```

Construct a null arc.

```
Directed_Arc(Directed_Arc<Item>&);
```

If the given arc is null, construct a null arc. Otherwise, construct an arc so that it structurally shares the concrete arc denoted by the given arc.

```
virtual ~Directed_Arc();
```

Destroy the arc. The concrete arc (if not null) is no longer structurally shared by this alias.

```
virtual Directed_Arc<Item>& operator=(Directed_Arc<Item>&);
```

Clear the arc. If the given arc is not null, set the state of the arc so that it structurally shares the concrete arc denoted by the given arc.

```
virtual int operator==(Directed_Arc<Item>&) const;
```

Return 1 if and only if both arcs are null or are an alias to the same concrete arc.

```
virtual int operator!=(Directed_Arc<Item>&) const;
```

Return the logical negation of operator==.

```
virtual Directed_Arc<Item>& clear();
```

If the arc is not null, remove this alias to the concrete arc and make the arc null.

```
virtual Directed_Arc<Item>& set_item(Item&);
```

If the arc is null, throw the exception Is_Null. Otherwise, set the item of the associated concrete arc.

```
virtual Directed_Arc<Item>&
  set_source_vertex(Directed_Vertex<Item>&);
```

If the arc or the vertex is null, throw the exception `Is_Null`. If the arc and the given vertex are not members of the same graph, throw the exception `Container_Error`. Otherwise, change the source vertex of the arc to the given vertex. This change requires that the arc be removed from the list of outgoing arcs in the original source vertex and added to the list of outgoing arcs in the given source vertex. The given source vertex and the arc's destination vertex may denote the same concrete vertex, in which case the arc represents a self-loop.

```
virtual Directed_Arc<Item>&
  set_destination_vertex(Directed_Vertex<Item>&);
```

If the arc or the vertex is null, throw the exception `Is_Null`. If the arc and the given vertex are not members of the same graph, throw the exception `Container_Error`. Otherwise, change the destination vertex of the arc to the given vertex. This change requires that the arc be removed from the list of incoming arcs in the original destination vertex and added to the list of incoming arcs in the given destination vertex. The arc's source vertex and the given destination vertex may denote the same concrete vertex, in which case the arc represents a self-loop.

```
virtual int is_null() const;
```

Return 1 if and only if the arc does not denote any concrete arc.

```
virtual int is_shared() const;
```

Return 1 if and only if the concrete arc has an alias.

```
virtual Item& item() const;
```

If the arc is null, throw the exception `Is_Null`. Otherwise, return a reference to the item of the designated concrete arc.

```
virtual void get_source_vertex(Directed_Vertex<Item>&) const;
```

If the arc is null, throw the exception `Is_Null`. Otherwise, set the given vertex to be an alias of the arc's source vertex.

```
virtual void get_destination_vertex(Directed_Vertex<Item>&) const;
```

If the arc is null, throw the exception `Is_Null`. Otherwise, set the given vertex to be an alias of the arc's destination vertex.

Following are the member functions for the class `Directed_Graph`, whose instances represent collections of concrete vertices and arcs:

```
Directed_Graph();
```

Construct an empty graph.

```
virtual ~Directed_Graph();
```

If any of the graph's concrete vertices and arcs have aliases (which would otherwise introduce dangling references), throw the exception `Storage_Error`. Otherwise, destroy the graph, including all its concrete vertices and arcs. For unbounded forms, individual vertex and arc items may or may not be destroyed, according to the semantics of the graph's container. For bounded forms, individual vertex and arc items are destroyed.

```
virtual Directed_Graph<Item>& clear();
```

If any of the graph's concrete vertices and arcs have aliases (which would otherwise introduce dangling references), throw the exception `Storage_Error`. Otherwise, empty the graph of all its concrete vertices and arcs. For unbounded forms, individual vertex and arc items may or may not be destroyed, according to the semantics of the graph's container. For bounded forms, individual vertex and arc items are not destroyed.

```
virtual Directed_Graph<Item>&
  create_vertex(Directed_Vertex<Item>&, Item&);
```

Create a new concrete vertex and add it to the graph. Set the given vertex to be an alias of the new concrete vertex.

```
virtual Directed_Graph<Item>&
  create_arc(Directed_Arc<Item>&, Item&,
             Directed_Vertex<Item>& source,
             Directed_Vertex<Item>& destination);
```

If either or both vertices are null, throw the exception `Is_Null`. If both vertices are not members of the same graph, throw the exception `Container_Error`. Otherwise, create a new concrete arc with the given source and destination vertices, and add it to the graph. The arc is added to the list of outgoing arcs in the given source vertex, and added to the list of incoming arcs in the given destination vertex. Set the given arc to be an alias of the new concrete arc. The source and destination vertices may denote the same concrete vertex, in which case the arc represents a self-loop.

```
virtual Directed_Graph<Item>& destroy_vertex(Directed_Vertex<Item>&);
```

If the given vertex is null, throw the exception `Is_Null`. If the given vertex is not a member of the graph, throw the exception `Container_Error`. If the given vertex has aliases (which would otherwise introduce dangling references), throw the exception `Storage_Error`. Otherwise, remove the designated concrete vertex from the graph and destroy it; set the given vertex to be null. For unbounded forms, the vertex item may or may not be destroyed, according to the semantics of the graph's container. For bounded forms, the vertex item is not destroyed.

```
virtual Directed_Graph<Item>& destroy_arc(Directed_Arc<Item>&);
```

If the given arc is null, throw the exception `Is_Null`. If the given arc is not a member of the graph, throw the exception `Container_Error`. If the given arc has aliases (which would otherwise introduce dangling references), throw the exception `Storage_Error`. Otherwise, the arc is removed from the list of outgoing arcs in its source vertex, and removed from the list of incoming arcs in its destination vertex. Remove the designated concrete arc from the graph and destroy it; set the given arc to be null. For unbounded forms, the arc item may or may not be destroyed, according to the semantics of the graph's container. For bounded forms, the arc item is not destroyed.

```
virtual int is_empty() const;
```

Return 1 if and only if the graph does not contain any concrete vertices or arcs.

```
virtual int is_member(Directed_Vertex<Item>&) const;
```

Return 1 if and only if the given vertex is non-null and denotes a concrete vertex in the graph.

```
virtual int is_member(Directed_Arc<Item>&) const;
```

Return 1 if and only if the given arc is non-null and denotes a concrete arc in the graph.

```
virtual unsigned number_of_vertices() const;
```

Return the number of concrete vertices in the graph.

```
virtual unsigned number_of_arcs() const;
```

Return the number of concrete arcs in the graph.

EXCEPTIONS

`Container_Error` —thrown by `set_source_vertex` and `set_destination_vertex` if the arc and given vertex are not members of the same graph.

—thrown by `create_arc` if the given vertices are not members of the graph.

—thrown by `destroy_vertex` if the vertex is not a member of the graph.

—thrown by `destroy_arc` if the arc is not a member of the graph.

STRUCTURES CLASS STRATEGY

Is_Null —thrown by `set_item`, `item`, `set_source_vertex`, and `set_destination_vertex` if the vertex or arc is null.

—thrown by `arity`, `number_of_outgoing_arcs`, and `number_of_incoming_arcs` if the vertex is null.

—thrown by `get_source_vertex` and `get_destination_vertex` if the arc is null.

—thrown by `create_arc` if either or both given vertices are null.

—thrown by `destroy_vertex` if the vertex is null.

—thrown by `destroy_arc` if the arc is null.

Overflow —thrown by any bounded form member function when the static limits of the object are exceeded.

Storage_Error —thrown by any unbounded form member function when no more storage can be allocated.

—thrown by clear if the graph's concrete vertices and arcs have aliases.

—thrown by `destroy_vertex` if the vertex has aliases.

—thrown by `destroy_arc` if the arc has aliases.

OPTIONS

Directed graphs are polylithic structures and so must be used cautiously in the presence of multiple threads of control. For this reason, we provide only the representation forms of directed graphs:

- Directed_Vertex

  Directed_Arc

  Directed_Graph

- Unbounded_Directed_Vertex

  Unbounded_Directed_Arc

  Unbounded_Directed_Graph

- Bounded_Directed_Vertex

  Bounded_Directed_Arc

  Bounded_Directed_Graph

We provide two sets of iterators, one for iterating across all the arcs associated with a vertex, and one for iterating across all the vertices in a graph. With these two sets of iterators, it is possible to visit every vertex and every arc in a graph.

The usual active and passive iterators are provided for the class Directed_Vertex, with some simple variations. The vertex active iterator includes the member function get_arc, which sets the given arc to be an alias of the current concrete arc. Similarly, the signature of the apply function in the passive iterator requires an arc argument.

The usual active and passive iterators are provided for the class Directed_Vertex, with some simple variations. The graph active iterator includes the member function get_vertex, which sets the given vertex to be an alias of the current concrete vertex. Similarly, the signature of the apply function in the passive iterator requires a vertex argument.

FILES

In the directed_graphs class category:

```
dgraph     Directed_Vertex
           Directed_Arc
           Directed_Graph
           Directed_Vertex_Active_Iterator
           Directed_Vertex_Passive_Iterator
           Directed_Graph_Active_Iterator
           Directed_Graph_Passive_Iterator
dgraph_u   Unbounded_Directed_Vertex
           Unbounded_Directed_Arc
           Unbounded_Directed_Graph
dgraph_b   Bounded_Directed_Vertex
           Bounded_Directed_Arc
           Bounded_Directed_Graph
```

SEE ALSO

Node (especially Shared_Graph_Node)

Heap (especially Shared_Bounded_Graph_Node_Heap)

Undirected_Graph

NAME

Undirected_Graph—An unrooted collection of nodes and undirected arcs; may contain cycles and cross-references; structural sharing is permitted.

SYNOPSIS

```
template<class Item>
class Undirected_Vertex {
public:

  Undirected_Vertex();
  Undirected_Vertex(Undirected_Vertex<Item>&);
  virtual ~Undirected_Vertex();

  virtual Undirected_Vertex<Item>&
    operator=(Undirected_Vertex<Item>&);
  virtual int operator==(Undirected_Vertex<Item>&) const;
  virtual int operator!=(Undirected_Vertex<Item>&) const;

  virtual Undirected_Vertex<Item>& clear();
  virtual Undirected_Vertex<Item>& set_item(Item&);

  virtual int is_null() const;
  virtual int is_shared() const;
  virtual Item& item() const;
  virtual unsigned arity() const;

};

template<class Item>
class Undirected_Arc {
public:

  Undirected_Arc();
  Undirected_Arc(Undirected_Arc<Item>&);
  virtual ~Undirected_Arc();

  virtual Undirected_Arc<Item>& operator=(Undirected_Arc<Item>&);
  virtual int operator==(Undirected_Arc<Item>&) const;
  virtual int operator!=(Undirected_Arc<Item>&) const;

  virtual Undirected_Arc<Item>& clear();
  virtual Undirected_Arc<Item>& set_item(Item&);
  virtual Undirected_Arc<Item>&
    set_first_vertex(Undirected_Vertex<Item>&);
  virtual Undirected_Arc<Item>&
    set_second_vertex(Undirected_Vertex<Item>&);

  virtual int is_null() const;
  virtual int is_shared() const;
  virtual Item& item() const;
  virtual void get_first_vertex(Undirected_Vertex<Item>&) const;
  virtual void get_second_vertex(Undirected_Vertex<Item>&) const;

};
```

```
template<class Item>
class Undirected_Graph {
public:

  Undirected_Graph();
  virtual ~Undirected_Graph();

  virtual Undirected_Graph<Item>& clear();
  virtual Undirected_Graph<Item>&
    create_vertex(Undirected_Vertex<Item>&, Item&);
  virtual Undirected_Graph<Item>&
    create_arc(Undirected_Arc<Item>&, Item&,
               Undirected_Vertex<Item>& first,
               Undirected_Vertex<Item>& second);
  virtual Undirected_Graph<Item>&
    destroy_vertex(Undirected_Vertex<Item>&);
  virtual Undirected_Graph<Item>& destroy_arc(Undirected_Arc<Item>&);

  virtual int is_empty() const;
  virtual int is_member(Undirected_Vertex<Item>&) const;
  virtual int is_member(Undirected_Arc<Item>&) const;
  virtual unsigned number_of_vertices() const;
  virtual unsigned number_of_arcs() const;

};
```

DESCRIPTION

An undirected graph denotes an unrooted collection of nodes and undirected arcs. A graph may contain cycles and cross-references. Graphs are polylithic structures; hence the semantics of copying, assignment, and equality involve structural sharing. Care must be taken in manipulating the same vertex or arc named by more than one alias.

This abstraction has been carefully constructed to eliminate all storage leaks, except in the case of intentional abuses. Concrete vertices and arcs may only be created and destroyed in the context of a graph. Vertices and arcs are always reachable, meaning that there is no circumstance whereby a concrete vertex or arc can ever be "lost." Furthermore, this design protects against dangling references: a concrete vertex or an arc cannot be destroyed if aliases to it exist.

This graph abstraction involves the collaborative behavior of three classes: Undirected_Vertex, Undirected_Arc, and Undirected_Graph. These classes are all siblings and are defined independently of the directed graph. Instances of the classes Undirected_Vertex and Undirected_Arc are aliases of concrete vertices and arcs, respectively, but are themselves not the concrete vertices and arcs. For this reason, the semantics of Undirected_Vertex and Undirected_Arc involve structural sharing. Copying, assigning. and testing for equality among graphs as a whole are marginally useful operations, and are computationally expensive (on the order of O(n2)); therefore, the `Undirected_Graph` explicitly disallows these operations.

Each concrete vertex and arc is a member of exactly one instance of `Undirected_Graph`. Furthermore, an arc and its vertices are guaranteed to be members of the same graph. This guarantee is provided by an implementation strategy, whereby every graph is given a unique id upon construction. Similarly, the creation of a concrete vertex or arc, always in the context of some graph, uses the graph's id to denote the vertex or arc's enclosing graph. A vertex or arc is known to be a member of a given graph if its enclosing graph matches the graph's id.

```
template<class Item>
```

The template item denotes the universe from which the vertices and arcs draw their items. The class `Item` may be either a primitive type or a user-defined class. If the latter, the class must provide a default constructor, copy constructor, assignment operator, and equality operator.

The template signature of the unbounded form requires a class `Container`, which must be a kind of `Shared_Graph_Node`. The template signature of the bounded form requires an unsigned integer `Size`, representing the static size of all instances of the class. Additionally, the template signature of the guarded form requires a class `Guard` (such as the class `Semaphore`), and the template signature of the synchronized form requires a class `Monitor` (such as a kind of `Read_Write_Monitor`).

The representation of the bounded form of `Undirected_Graph` includes the static declaration of a bounded heap, from which all the objects of this instantiation draw their storage for vertices and arcs. A client must provide a definition of this bounded heap, which must be a kind of `Shared_Bounded_Graph_Node_Heap`.

Following are the member functions for the class `Undirected_Vertex`, whose instances represent aliases to concrete vertices in the graph:

```
Undirected_Vertex();
```

Construct a null vertex.

```
Undirected_Vertex(Undirected_Vertex<Item>&);
```

If the given vertex is null, construct a null vertex. Otherwise, construct a vertex so that it structurally shares the concrete vertex denoted by the given vertex.

```
virtual ~Undirected_Vertex();
```

Destroy the vertex. The concrete vertex (if not null) is no longer structurally shared by this alias.

```
virtual Undirected_Vertex<Item>& operator=(Undirected_Vertex<Item>&);
```

Clear the vertex. If the given vertex is not null, set the state of the vertex so that it structurally shares the concrete vertex denoted by the given vertex.

```
virtual int operator==(Undirected_Vertex<Item>&) const;
```

Return 1 if and only if both vertices are null or are an alias to the same concrete vertex.

```
virtual int operator!=(Undirected_Vertex<Item>&) const;
```

Return the logical negation of operator==.

```
virtual Undirected_Vertex<Item>& clear();
```

If the vertex is not null, remove this alias to the concrete vertex and make the vertex null.

```
virtual Undirected_Vertex<Item>& set_item(Item&);
```

If the vertex is null, throw the exception Is_Null. Otherwise, set the item of the associated concrete vertex.

```
virtual int is_null() const;
```

Return 1 if and only if the vertex does not denote any concrete vertex.

```
virtual int is_shared() const;
```

Return 1 if and only if the concrete vertex has an alias.

```
virtual Item& item() const;
```

If the vertex is null, throw the exception Is_Null. Otherwise, return a reference to the item of the designated concrete vertex.

```
virtual unsigned arity() const;
```

If the vertex is null, throw the exception Is_Null. Otherwise, return a count of the arcs attached to the vertex. Self-loops are counted twice.

Following are the member functions for the class Undirected_Arc, whose instances represent aliases to concrete arcs in the graph:

```
Undirected_Arc();
```

Construct a null arc.

```
Undirected_Arc(Undirected_Arc<Item>&);
```

If the given arc is null, construct a null arc. Otherwise, construct an arc so that it structurally shares the concrete arc denoted by the given arc.

```
virtual ~Undirected_Arc();
```

Destroy the arc. The concrete arc (if not null) is no longer structurally shared by this alias.

```
virtual Undirected_Arc<Item>& operator=(Undirected_Arc<Item>&);
```

Clear the arc. If the given arc is not null, set the state of the arc so that it structurally shares the concrete arc denoted by the given arc.

```
virtual int operator==(Undirected_Arc<Item>&) const;
```

Return 1 if and only if both arcs are null or are an alias to the same concrete arc.

```
virtual int operator!=(Undirected_Arc<Item>&) const;
```

Return the logical negation of operator==.

```
virtual Undirected_Arc<Item>& clear();
```

If the arc is not null, remove this alias to the concrete arc and make the arc null.

```
virtual Undirected_Arc<Item>& set_item(Item&);
```

If the arc is null, throw the exception Is_Null. Otherwise, set the item of the associated concrete arc.

```
virtual Undirected_Arc<Item>&
  set_first_vertex(Undirected_Vertex<Item>&);
```

If the arc or the vertex is null, throw the exception Is_Null. If the arc and the given vertex are not members of the same graph, throw the exception Container_Error. Otherwise, change the first vertex of the arc to the given vertex. This change requires that the arc be removed from the list of arcs in the original first vertex and added to the list of arcs in the given first vertex. The given first vertex and the arc's second vertex may denote the same concrete vertex, in which case the arc represents a self-loop.

```
virtual Undirected_Arc<Item>&
  set_second_vertex(Undirected_Vertex<Item>&);
```

If the arc or the vertex is null, throw the exception Is_Null. If the arc and the given vertex are not members of the same graph, throw the exception Container_Error. Otherwise, change the second vertex of the arc to the given vertex. This change requires that the arc be removed from the list of arcs in the original second vertex and added to the list of arcs in the given second vertex. The arc's first vertex and the given second vertex may denote the same concrete vertex, in which case the arc represents a self-loop.

```
virtual int is_null() const;
```

Return 1 if and only if the arc does not denote any concrete arc.

```
virtual int is_shared() const;
```

Return 1 if and only if the concrete arc has any alias.

```
virtual Item& item() const;
```

If the arc is null, throw the exception Is_Null. Otherwise, return a reference to the item of the designated concrete arc.

```
virtual void get_first_vertex(Undirected_Vertex<Item>&) const;
```

If the arc is null, throw the exception Is_Null. Otherwise, set the given vertex to be an alias of the arc's first vertex.

```
virtual void get_second_vertex(Undirected_Vertex<Item>&) const;
```

If the arc is null, throw the exception Is_Null. Otherwise, set the given vertex to be an alias of the arc's second vertex.

Following are the member functions for the class Undirected_Graph, whose instances represent collections of concrete vertices and arcs:

```
Undirected_Graph();
```

Construct an empty graph.

```
virtual ~Undirected_Graph();
```

If any of the graph's concrete vertices and arcs have aliases (which would otherwise introduce dangling references), throw the exception Storage_Error. Otherwise, destroy the graph, including all its concrete vertices and arcs. For unbounded forms, individual vertex and arc items may or may not be destroyed, according to the semantics of the graph's container. For bounded forms, individual vertex and arc items are destroyed.

```
virtual Undirected_Graph<Item>& clear();
```

If any of the graph's concrete vertices and arcs have aliases (which would otherwise introduce dangling references), throw the exception Storage_Error. Otherwise, empty the graph of all its concrete vertices and arcs. For unbounded forms, individual vertex and arc items may or may not be destroyed, according to the semantics of the graph's container. For bounded forms, individual vertex and arc items are not destroyed.

```
virtual Undirected_Graph<Item>&
  create_vertex(Undirected_Vertex<Item>&, Item&);
```

Create a new concrete vertex and add it to the graph. Set the given vertex to be an alias of the new concrete vertex.

```
virtual Undirected_Graph<Item>&
  create_arc(Undirected_Arc<Item>&, Item&,
             Undirected_Vertex<Item>& first,
             Undirected_Vertex<Item>& second);
```

If either or both vertices are null, throw the exception `Is_Null`. If both vertices are not members of the same graph, throw the exception `Container_Error`. Otherwise, create a new concrete arc with the given first and second vertices, and add it to the graph. The arc is added to the list of arcs in the given first and second vertices. Set the given arc to be an alias of the new concrete arc. The first and second vertices may denote the same concrete vertex, in which case the arc represents a self-loop.

```
virtual Undirected_Graph<Item>&
  destroy_vertex(Undirected_Vertex<Item>&);
```

If the given vertex is null, throw the exception `Is_Null`. If the given vertex is not a member of the graph, throw the exception `Container_Error`. If the given vertex has aliases (which would otherwise introduce dangling references), throw the exception `Storage_Error`. Otherwise, remove the designated concrete vertex from the graph and destroy it; set the given vertex to be null. For unbounded forms, the vertex item may or may not be destroyed, according to the semantics of the graph's container. For bounded forms, the vertex item is not destroyed.

```
virtual Undirected_Graph<Item>& destroy_arc(Undirected_Arc<Item>&);
```

If the given arc is null, throw the exception `Is_Null`. If the given arc is not a member of the graph, throw the exception `Container_Error`. If the given arc has aliases (which would otherwise introduce dangling references), throw the exception `Storage_Error`. Otherwise, the arc is removed from the list of arcs in its first and second vertices. Remove the designated concrete arc from the graph and destroy it; set the given arc to be null. For unbounded forms, the arc item may or may not be destroyed, according to the semantics of the graph's container. For bounded forms, the arc item is not destroyed.

```
virtual int is_empty() const;
```

Return 1 if and only if the graph does not contain any concrete vertices or arcs.

```
virtual int is_member(Undirected_Vertex<Item>&) const;
```

Return 1 if and only if the given vertex is non-null and denotes a concrete vertex in the graph.

```
virtual int is_member(Undirected_Arc<Item>&) const;
```

Return 1 if and only if the given arc is non-null and denotes a concrete arc in the graph.

```
virtual unsigned number_of_vertices() const;
```

Return the number of concrete vertices in the graph.

```
virtual unsigned number_of_arcs() const;
```

Return the number of concrete arcs in the graph.

EXCEPTIONS

`Container_Error` —thrown by `set_first_vertex` and `set_second_vertex` if the arc and given vertex are not members of the same graph.

—thrown by `create_arc` if the given vertices are not members of the graph.

—thrown by `destroy_vertex` if the vertex is not a member of the graph.

—thrown by `destroy_arc` if the arc is not a member of the graph.

`Is_Null` —thrown by `set_item`, `item`, `set_first_vertex`, and `set_second_vertex` if the vertex or arc is null.

—thrown by `arity` if the vertex is null.

—thrown by `get_first_vertex` and `get_second_vertex` if the arc is null.

—thrown by `create_arc` if either or both given vertices are null.

—thrown by `destroy_vertex` if the vertex is null.

—thrown by `destroy_arc` if the arc is null.

`Overflow` —thrown by any bounded form member function when the static limits of the object are exceeded.

`Storage_Error` —thrown by any unbounded form member function when no more storage can be allocated.

—thrown by `clear` if the graph's concrete vertices and arcs have aliases.

—thrown by `destroy_vertex` if the vertex has aliases.

—thrown by `destroy_arc` if the arc has aliases.

OPTIONS

Undirected graphs are polylithic structures and so must be used cautiously in the presence of multiple threads of control. For this reason, we provide only the representation forms of undirected graphs:

- `Undirected_Vertex`

  `Undirected_Arc`

  `Undirected_Graph`

- `Unbounded_Undirected_Vertex`

  `Unbounded_Undirected_Arc`

  `Unbounded_Undirected_Graph`

- `Bounded_Undirected_Vertex`

  `Bounded_Undirected_Arc`

  `Bounded_Undirected_Graph`

We provide two sets of iterators, one for iterating across all the arcs associated with a vertex, and one for iterating across all the vertices in a graph. With these two sets of iterators, it is possible to visit every vertex and every arc in a graph.

The usual active and passive iterators are provided for the class `Undirected_Vertex`, with some simple variations. The vertex active iterator includes the member function `get_arc`, which sets the given arc to be an alias of the current concrete arc. Similarly, the signature of the apply function in the passive iterator requires an arc argument. Both forms of these iterators visit the arcs associated with self-loops only once (but note that the member function arity counts these arcs twice, because logically, a self-loop arc is attached to the same vertex at two points).

The usual active and passive iterators are provided for the class `Undirected_Vertex`, with some simple variations. The graph active iterator includes the member function `get_vertex`, which sets the given vertex to be an alias of the current concrete vertex. Similarly, the signature of the apply function in the passive iterator requires a vertex argument.

FILES

In the `undirected_graphs` class category:

```
ugraph      Undirected_Vertex
            Undirected_Arc
            Undirected_Graph
            Undirected_Vertex_Active_Iterator
            Undirected_Vertex_Passive_Iterator
            Undirected_Graph_Active_Iterator
            Undirected_Graph_Passive_Iterator
ugraph_u    Unbounded_Undirected_Vertex
            Unbounded_Undirected_Arc
            Unbounded_Undirected_Graph
ugraph_b    Bounded_Undirected_Vertex
            Bounded_Undirected_Arc
            Bounded_Undirected_Graph
```

SEE ALSO

Node (especially `Shared_Graph_Node`)

Heap (especially `Shared_Bounded_Graph_Node_Heap`)

Double_List

NAME

`Double_List`—A sequence of zero or more items, with links from one item to its previous and next items; structural sharing is permitted.

SYNOPSIS

```
template<class Item>
class Double_List {
public:

  Double_List();
  Double_List(Double_List<Item>&);
  virtual ~Double_List();

  virtual Double_List<Item>& operator=(Double_List<Item>&);
  virtual int operator==(Double_List<Item>&) const;
  virtual int operator!=(Double_List<Item>&) const;

  virtual Double_List<Item>& clear();
  virtual Double_List<Item>& construct(Item&);
```

Structures Class Strategy

```
    virtual Double_List<Item>& set_head(Item&);
    virtual Double_List<Item>& set_item(Item&, unsigned position);
    virtual Double_List<Item>& insert(Item&, unsigned before = 0);
    virtual Double_List<Item>& insert(Double_List<Item>&,
                                      unsigned before = 0);
    virtual Double_List<Item>& append(Item&, unsigned after = 0);
    virtual Double_List<Item>& append(Double_List<Item>&,
                                      unsigned after = 0);
    virtual Double_List<Item>& extract(Double_List<Item>&,
                                       unsigned count,
                                       unsigned position);
    virtual Double_List<Item>& share(Double_List<Item>&,
                                     unsigned position);
    virtual Double_List<Item>& share_head(Double_List<Item>&);
    virtual Double_List<Item>& share_foot(Double_List<Item>&);
    virtual Double_List<Item>& swap_tail(Double_List<Item>&);
    virtual Double_List<Item>& tail();
    virtual Double_List<Item>& predecessor();

    virtual unsigned length() const;
    virtual int is_null() const;
    virtual int is_shared() const;
    virtual Item& head() const;
    virtual Item& foot() const;
    virtual Item& nth(unsigned position);
};
```

DESCRIPTION

A double list denotes a sequence of zero or more items, with links from one item to its previous and next items. Lists are polylithic structures; hence, the semantics of copying, assignment, and equality involve structural sharing. Care must be taken in manipulating the same list named by more than one alias.

This abstraction has been carefully constructed to eliminate all storage leaks, except in the case of intentional abuses. When a list is manipulated, all items that become unreachable are automatically reclaimed. Furthermore, this design protects against dangling references: the node associated with an item is never reclaimed if an alias to it exists.

Unreachable items are those that belong to a list or a sublist whose head is not designated by any alias. For example, consider the list (A B C), with the head of the list designated by L1. L1 initially points to the head of the list, at item A. Invoking the member function tail on L1 now causes L1 to point to item B. Because A is now considered unreachable, the node associated with item A is reclaimed; the predecessor of B is now null. Similarly, consider the list (D E F), with the head of the list designated by both L1 and L2. Both L1 and L2 are aliases that initially point to the head of the list at item D. Invoking the member function `tail` on L1 now causes L1 to point to item E; L2 is unaffected. Suppose we now invoke the member function `clear` on L2. The semantics of this operation are such that only unreachable items are reclaimed. Thus, the node associated with item D is reclaimed, because it is no longer reachable; L2 is now null, and the predecessor of E is now null. Items E and F are not reclaimed, because they are reachable through L1.

An alternate abstraction would have been to consider items A and D reachable in these two circumstances. We explicitly rejected this design, to maintain consistency with the semantics of the singly linked list.

It is possible, but not generally desirable, to produce multiheaded lists. In such cases, the predecessor of the item at the neck of a multiheaded list points to the most recently attached head.

The class `Double_List` is defined independently of the singly linked list. Instances of the class `Double_List` are aliases of concrete nodes, but are themselves not the concrete nodes. For this reason, the semantics of `Double_List` involve structural sharing.

```
template<class Item>
```

The template item denotes the universe from which the list draws its items. The class `Item` may be either a primitive type or a user-defined class. If the latter, the class must provide a default constructor, copy constructor, assignment operator, and equality operator.

The template signature of the unbounded form requires a class `Container`, which must be a kind of `Shared_Double_Node`. The template signature of the bounded form requires an unsigned integer `Size`, representing the static size of all instances of the class. Additionally, the template signature of the guarded form requires a class `Guard` (such as the class `Semaphore`), and the template signature of the synchronized form requires a class `Monitor` (such as a kind of `Read_Write_Monitor`).

The representation of the bounded form of `Double_List` includes the static declaration of a bounded heap, from which all objects of this instantiation draw their storage. A client must provide a definition of this bounded heap, which must be a kind of `Shared_Bounded_Double_Node_Heap`.

```
Double_List();
```

Construct a null list.

```
Double_List(Double_List<Item>&);
```

If the given list is null, construct a null list. Otherwise, construct a list so that it structurally shares the concrete node denoted by the given list.

```
virtual ~Double_List();
```

Destroy the list. The concrete node (if not null) is no longer structurally shared by this alias, and the nodes associated with any unreachable items are reclaimed. For unbounded forms, individual items may or may not be destroyed, according to the semantics of the list's container. For bounded forms, individual items are not destroyed; such items are only destroyed when the associated bounded heap is destroyed, typically when its definition is no longer in scope.

```
virtual Double_List<Item>& operator=(Double_List<Item>&);
```

Clear the list. If the given list is not null, set the state of the list so that it structurally shares the concrete node denoted by the given list.

```
virtual int operator==(Double_List<Item>&) const;
```

Return 1 if and only if both lists are null or are an alias to the same concrete node.

```
virtual int operator!=(Double_List<Item>&) const;
```

Return the logical negation of operator==.

```
virtual Double_List<Item>& clear();
```

If the list is not null, remove this alias to the concrete node, make the list null, and reclaim the nodes associated with any unreachable items. For unbounded forms, individual items may or may not be destroyed, according to the semantics of the list's container. For bounded forms, individual items are not destroyed.

```
virtual Double_List<Item>& construct(Item&);
```

Create a new concrete node, whose successor is the concrete node designated by the list (which may be null). If this successor is not null, set its predecessor to be the newly created concrete node. Set the list to designate this new concrete node.

```
virtual Double_List<Item>& set_head(Item&);
```

If the list is null, throw the exception `Is_Null`. Otherwise, set the item of the associated concrete node.

```
virtual Double_List<Item>& set_item(Item&, unsigned position);
```

If the list is null, throw the exception `Is_Null`. Otherwise, set the item of the associated concrete node at the given ordinal position.

```
virtual Double_List<Item>& insert(Item&, unsigned before = 0);
```

If the ordinal position is larger than the length of the list, throw the exception `Invalid_Index`. Otherwise, insert the item before the given position. If the position is zero, the item is inserted at the beginning of the list, even if the list is null.

```
virtual Double_List<Item>& insert(Double_List<Item>&,
                                  unsigned before = 0);
```

If the ordinal position is larger than the length of the list, throw the exception `Invalid_Index`. Otherwise, insert the list before the given position. If the position is zero, the item is inserted at the beginning of the list, even if the list is null. The given list is structurally shared.

```
virtual Double_List<Item>& append(Item&, unsigned after = 0);
```

If the ordinal position is larger than the length of the list, throw the exception `Invalid_Index`. Otherwise, insert the item after the given position. If the position is zero, the item is inserted at the end of the list, even if the list is null.

```
virtual Double_List<Item>& append(Double_List<Item>&,
                                  unsigned after = 0);
```

If the ordinal position is larger than the length of the list, throw the exception `Invalid_Index`. Otherwise, insert the list after the given position. If the position is zero, the item is inserted at the end of the list, even if the list is null. The given list is structurally shared.

```
virtual Double_List<Item>& extract(Double_List<Item>&, unsigned
count, unsigned position);
```

If the ordinal position is zero or beyond the length of the list, if the list is null, or if the position plus the count is beyond the length of the list, throw the exception `Invalid_Index`. Otherwise, set the given list to the sublist starting at the given position, and continuing for count items, then remove that fragment from the list.

```
virtual Double_List<Item>& share(Double_List<Item>&,
                                 unsigned position);
```

If the ordinal position is zero or beyond the length of the given list, throw the exception `Invalid_Index`. Otherwise, clear the list and then set it to structurally share with the given list at the given ordinal position.

```
virtual Double_List<Item>& share_head(Double_List<Item>&);
```

If the ordinal position is zero or beyond the length of the given list, throw the exception `Invalid_Index`. Otherwise, clear the list and then set it to structurally share with the head of the given list.

`virtual Double_List<Item>& share_foot(Double_List<Item>&);`

If the ordinal position is zero or beyond the length of the given list, throw the exception `Invalid_Index`. Otherwise, clear the list and then set it to structurally share with the foot of the given list.

`virtual Double_List<Item>& swap_tail(Double_List<Item>&);`

If the list is null, throw the exception `Is_Null`. If the given list is not null, but does not represent the head of a list, throw the exception `Not_Root`. Otherwise, set the tail of the list (which may be null) to denote the given list (which may be null), and set the given list to the original tail of the list. If it is not null, the predecessor of the new tail of the list is set to be the head of the list. If it is not null, the predecessor of the new head of the given list is set to be null.

`virtual Double_List<Item>& tail();`

If the list is null, throw the exception `Is_Null`. Otherwise, set the list to now denote its tail (which may be null), and reclaim the nodes associated with any unreachable items. For unbounded forms, individual items may or may not be destroyed, according to the semantics of the list's container. For bounded forms, individual items are not destroyed.

`virtual Double_List<Item>& predecessor();`

If the list is null, throw the exception `Is_Null`. Otherwise, set the list to now denote its predecessor (which may be null), and reclaim the nodes associated with any unreachable items. For unbounded forms, individual items may or may not be destroyed, according to the semantics of the list's container. For bounded forms, individual items are not destroyed.

`virtual unsigned length() const;`

Return the number of items in the list.

`virtual int is_null() const;`

Return 1 if and only if the list does not denote any concrete node.

`virtual int is_shared() const;`

Return 1 if and only if the concrete node has an alias.

`virtual Item& head() const;`

If the list is null, throw the exception `Is_Null`. Otherwise, return a reference to the item of the designated concrete node.

```
virtual Item& foot() const;
```

If the list is null, throw the exception `Is_Null`. Otherwise, return a reference to the item of the designated concrete node at the foot of the list.

```
virtual Item& nth(unsigned position);
```

If the list is null, throw the exception `Is_Null`. If the given ordinal position is zero or beyond the length of the list, throw the exception `Invalid_Index`. Otherwise, return a reference to the item of the designated concrete node at the given ordinal position.

EXCEPTIONS

`Is_Null`	—thrown by `set_head`, `swap_tail`, `tail`, `predecessor`, and `head` if the list is null.
`Not_Root`	—thrown by `swap_tail` if the given list is not null, but does not represent the head of a list.
`Overflow`	—thrown by any bounded form member function when the static limits of the object are exceeded.
`Storage_Error`	—thrown by any unbounded form member function when no more storage can be allocated.

OPTIONS

Double lists are polylithic structures and so must be used cautiously in the presence of multiple threads of control. For this reason, we provide only the representation forms of double lists:

- `Double_List`
- `Unbounded_Double_List`
- `Bounded_Double_List`

We do not support the usual iterators, because lists already provide the member functions necessary for performing arbitrary traversals.

FILES

In the `double_lists` class category:

```
dlist      Double_List
dlist_u    Unbounded_Double_List
dlist_b    Bounded_Double_List
```

SEE ALSO

Node (especially Shared_Graph_Node)

Heap (especially Shared_Bounded_Double_Node_Heap)

SINGLE_LIST

NAME

Single_List—A sequence of zero or more items, with a link from one item to its following item; structural sharing is permitted.

SYNOPSIS

```
template<class Item>
class Single_List {
public:

  Single_List();
  Single_List(Single_List<Item>&);
  virtual ~Single_List();

  virtual Single_List<Item>& operator=(Single_List<Item>&);
  virtual int operator==(Single_List<Item>&) const;
  virtual int operator!=(Single_List<Item>&) const;

  virtual Single_List<Item>& clear();
  virtual Single_List<Item>& construct(Item&);
  virtual Single_List<Item>& set_head(Item&);
  virtual Single_List<Item>& set_item(Item&, unsigned position);
  virtual Single_List<Item>& insert(Item&, unsigned before = 0);
  virtual Single_List<Item>& insert(Single_List<Item>&,
                                    unsigned before = 0);
  virtual Single_List<Item>& append(Item&, unsigned after = 0);
  virtual Single_List<Item>& append(Single_List<Item>&,
                                    unsigned after = 0);
  virtual Single_List<Item>& extract(Single_List<Item>&,
                                     unsigned count,
                                     unsigned position);
  virtual Single_List<Item>& share(Single_List<Item>&,
                                   unsigned position);
```

```
    virtual Single_List<Item>& share_head(Single_List<Item>&);
    virtual Single_List<Item>& share_foot(Single_List<Item>&);
    virtual Single_List<Item>& swap_tail(Single_List<Item>&);
    virtual Single_List<Item>& tail();

    virtual unsigned length() const;
    virtual int is_null() const;
    virtual int is_shared() const;
    virtual Item& head() const;
    virtual Item& foot() const;
    virtual Item& nth(unsigned position);
};
```

DESCRIPTION

A single list denotes a sequence of zero or more items, with a link from one item to its following item. Lists are polylithic structures; hence, the semantics of copying, assignment, and equality involve structural sharing. Care must be taken in manipulating the same list named by more than one alias.

Items are indexed starting at one, up to the length of the list.

This abstraction has been carefully constructed to eliminate all storage leaks, except in the case of intentional abuses. When a list is manipulated, all items that become unreachable are automatically reclaimed. Furthermore, this design protects against dangling references: the node associated with an item is never reclaimed if an alias to it exists.

Unreachable items are those that belong to a list or a sublist whose head is not designated by any alias. For example, consider the list (A B C), with the head of the list designated by L1. L1 initially points to the head of the list, at item A. Invoking the member function `tail` on L1 now causes L1 to point to item B. Because A is now considered unreachable, the node associated with item A is reclaimed. Similarly, consider the list (D E F), with the head of the list designated by both L1 and L2. Both L1 and L2 are aliases that initially point to the head of the list at item D. Invoking the member function `tail` on L1 now causes L1 to point to item E; L1 is unaffected. Suppose we now invoke the member function `clear` on L2. The semantics of this operation are such that only unreachable items are reclaimed. Thus, the node associated with item D is reclaimed, because it is no longer reachable; L2 is now null. Items E and F are not reclaimed, because they are reachable through L1.

It is possible, but not generally desirable, to produce multiheaded lists.

The class `Single_List` is defined independently of the doubly linked list. Instances of the class `Single_List` are aliases of concrete nodes, but are themselves not the concrete nodes. For this reason, the semantics of `Single_List` involve structural sharing.

```
template<class Item>
```

The template item denotes the universe from which the list draws its items. The class `Item` may be either a primitive type or a user-defined class. If the latter, the class must provide a default constructor, copy constructor, assignment operator, and equality operator.

The template signature of the unbounded form requires a class `Container`, which must be a kind of `Shared_Node`. The template signature of the bounded form requires an unsigned integer `Size`, representing the static size of all instances of the class. Additionally, the template signature of the guarded form requires a class `Guard` (such as the class `Semaphore`), and the template signature of the synchronized form requires a class `Monitor` (such as a kind of `Read_Write_Monitor`).

The representation of the bounded form of `Single_List` includes the static declaration of a bounded heap, from which all objects of this instantiation draw their storage. A client must provide a definition of this bounded heap, which must be a kind of `Shared_Bounded_Node_Heap`.

```
Single_List();
Construct a null list.
```

```
Single_List(Single_List<Item>&);
```

If the given list is null, construct a null list. Otherwise, construct a list so that it structurally shares the concrete node denoted by the given list.

```
virtual ~Single_List();
```

Destroy the list. The concrete node (if not null) is no longer structurally shared by this alias, and the nodes associated with any unreachable items are reclaimed. For unbounded forms, individual items may or may not be destroyed, according to the semantics of the list's container. For bounded forms, individual items are not destroyed; such items are only destroyed when the associated bounded heap is destroyed, typically when its definition is no longer in scope.

```
virtual Single_List<Item>& operator=(Single_List<Item>&);
```

Clear the list. If the given list is not null, set the state of the list so that it structurally shares the concrete node denoted by the given list.

```
virtual int operator==(Single_List<Item>&) const;
```

Return 1 if and only if both lists are null or are an alias to the same concrete node.

```
virtual int operator!=(Single_List<Item>&) const;
```

Return the logical negation of `operator==`.

```
virtual Single_List<Item>& clear();
```

If the list is not null, remove this alias to the concrete node, make the list null, and reclaim the nodes associated with any unreachable items. For unbounded forms, individual items may or may not be destroyed, according to the semantics of the list's container. For bounded forms, individual items are not destroyed.

```
virtual Single_List<Item>& construct(Item&);
```

Create a new concrete node, whose successor is the concrete node designated by the list (which may be null). Set the list to designate this new concrete node.

```
virtual Single_List<Item>& set_head(Item&);
```

If the list is null, throw the exception `Is_Null`. Otherwise, set the item of the associated concrete node.

```
virtual Single_List<Item>& set_item(Item&, unsigned position);
```

If the list is null, throw the exception `Is_Null`. Otherwise, set the item of the associated concrete node at the given ordinal position.

```
virtual Single_List<Item>& insert(Item&, unsigned before = 0);
```

If the ordinal position is larger than the length of the list, throw the exception `Invalid_Index`. Otherwise, insert the item before the given position. If the position is zero, the item is inserted at the beginning of the list, even if the list is null.

```
virtual Single_List<Item>& insert(Single_List<Item>&,
                                  unsigned before = 0);
```

If the ordinal position is larger than the length of the list, throw the exception `Invalid_Index`. Otherwise, insert the list before the given position. If the position is zero, the item is inserted at the beginning of the list, even if the list is null. The given list is structurally shared.

```
virtual Single_List<Item>& append(Item&, unsigned after = 0);
```

If the ordinal position is larger than the length of the list, throw the exception `Invalid_Index`. Otherwise, insert the item after the given position. If the position is zero, the item is inserted at the end of the list, even if the list is null.

```
virtual Single_List<Item>& append(Single_List<Item>&,
                                  unsigned after = 0);
```

If the ordinal position is larger than the length of the list, throw the exception `Invalid_Index`. Otherwise, insert the list after the given position. If the position is zero, the item is inserted at the end of the list, even if the list is null. The given list is structurally shared.

```
virtual Single_List<Item>& extract(Single_List<Item>&, unsigned
count, unsigned position);
```

If the ordinal position is zero or beyond the length of the list, if the list is null, or if the position plus the count is beyond the length of the list, throw the exception `Invalid_Index`. Otherwise, set the given list to the sublist starting at the given position, and continuing for count items, then remove that fragment from the list.

```
virtual Single_List<Item>& share(Single_List<Item>&,
                                 unsigned position);
```

If the ordinal position is zero or beyond the length of the given list, throw the exception `Invalid_Index`. Otherwise, clear the list and then set it to structurally share with the given list at the given ordinal position.

```
virtual Single_List<Item>& share_head(Single_List<Item>&);
```

If the ordinal position is zero or beyond the length of the given list, throw the exception `Invalid_Index`. Otherwise, clear the list and then set it to structurally share with the head of the given list.

```
virtual Single_List<Item>& share_foot(Single_List<Item>&);
```

If the ordinal position is zero or beyond the length of the given list, throw the exception `Invalid_Index`. Otherwise, clear the list and then set it to structurally share with the foot of the given list.

```
virtual Single_List<Item>& swap_tail(Single_List<Item>&);
```

If the list is null, throw the exception `Is_Null`. If the given list is not null, but does not represent the head of a list, throw the exception `Not_Root`. Otherwise, set the tail of the list (which may be null) to denote the given list (which may be null), and set the given list to the original tail of the list.

```
virtual Single_List<Item>& tail();
```

If the list is null, throw the exception `Is_Null`. Otherwise, set the list to now denote its tail (which may be null), and reclaim the nodes associated with any unreachable items. For unbounded forms, individual items may or may not be destroyed, according to the semantics of the list's container. For bounded forms, individual items are not destroyed.

```
virtual unsigned length() const;
```

Return the number of items in the list.

```
virtual int is_null() const;
```

Return 1 if and only if the list does not denote any concrete node.

```
virtual int is_shared() const;
```

Return 1 if and only if the concrete node has an alias.

```
virtual Item& head() const;
```

If the list is null, throw the exception `Is_Null`. Otherwise, return a reference to the item of the designated concrete node at the head of the list.

```
virtual Item& foot() const;
```

If the list is null, throw the exception `Is_Null`. Otherwise, return a reference to the item of the designated concrete node at the foot of the list.

```
virtual Item& nth(unsigned position);
```

If the list is null, throw the exception `Is_Null`. If the given ordinal position is zero or beyond the length of the list, throw the exception `Invalid_Index`. Otherwise, return a reference to the item of the designated concrete node at the given ordinal position.

EXCEPTIONS

`Is_Null`	—thrown by `set_head`, `swap_tail`, `tail`, and `head` if the list is null.
`Not_Root`	—thrown by `swap_tail` if the given list is not null, but does not represent the head of a list.
`Overflow`	—thrown by any bounded form member function when the static limits of the object are exceeded.
`Storage_Error`	—thrown by any unbounded form member function when no more storage can be allocated.

OPTIONS

Single lists are polylithic structures and so must be used cautiously in the presence of multiple threads of control. For this reason, we provide only the representation forms of single lists:

- `Single_List`
- `Unbounded_Single_List`
- `Bounded_Single_List`

We do not support the usual iterators, because lists already provide the member functions necessary for performing arbitrary traversals.

FILES

In the `single_list` class category:

slist	Single_List
slist_u	Unbounded_Single_List
slist_b	Bounded_Single_List

SEE ALSO

Node (especially Shared_Graph_Node)

Heap (especially Shared_Bounded_Node_Heap)

MAP

NAME

Map—A collection forming a dictionary of domain/range pairs.

SYNOPSIS

```
template<class Item, class Value, unsigned int Buckets>
class Map {
public:

  Map();
  Map(unsigned (*hash)(Item&));
  Map(const Map<Item, Value, Buckets>&);
  virtual ~Map();

  Map<Item, Value, Buckets>& operator=(Map<Item, Value, Buckets>&);
  virtual int operator==(Map<Item, Value, Buckets>&) const;
  virtual int operator!=(Map<Item, Value, Buckets>&) const;

  virtual Map<Item, Value, Buckets>& clear();
  virtual Map<Item, Value, Buckets>& bind(Item&, Value&);
  virtual Map<Item, Value, Buckets>& rebind(Item&, Value&);
  virtual Map<Item, Value, Buckets>& unbind(Item&);
  virtual Map<Item, Value, Buckets>&
    set_hash_function(unsigned (*hash)(Item&));
```

```
virtual unsigned extent() const;
virtual int is_empty() const;
virtual int is_bound(Item&);
virtual Value& value(Item&);
```

```
};
```

DESCRIPTION

A map denotes a collection forming a dictionary of domain/range pairs. Maps are cached, so that the most recently accessed domain/range pair can be found on the order of `O(1)`.

`template<class Item, class Value, unsigned int Buckets>`

The template item denotes the universe from which the map draws its domain; the template value denotes the universe from which the map draws its range. The classes `Item` and `Value` typically represent different types, although they may represent the same types. Either may be a primitive type or a user-defined class. If the latter, the item must provide a default constructor, copy constructor, assignment operator, and equality operator; the value must provide a copy constructor and assignment operator.

In any case, the class `Item` must provide a hash function that returns an unsigned integer value. This value must not change during the lifetime of a given item. The range of hash values need not be constrained to the number of buckets in the map. This hash function may be set exactly once for each map at the time of the map's construction, or via the member function `set_hash_function`.

The hash function `h` must satisfy the condition that, for objects `A` and `B`, if `A == B`, then `h(A)` must equal `h(B)`. The hash function should attempt to spread the set of possible values uniformly across the number of buckets. The quality of the hash function has a significant impact on performance.

The template signature of the unbounded form requires a class `Container`, which must be a kind of `Association_Node`. The template signature of the bounded form requires an unsigned integer `Size`, representing the static size of all instances of the class. Additionally, the template signature of the guarded form requires a class `Guard` (such as the class `Semaphore`), and the template signature of the synchronized form requires a class `Monitor` (such as a kind of `Read_Write_Monitor`).

`Map();`

Construct an empty map, but do not set the hash function.

`Map(unsigned (*hash)(Item&));`

Construct an empty map with the given hash function.

```
Map(const Map<Item, Value, Buckets>&);
```

Copy the item/value pairs in the given map; items and values in the copied map are themselves copied.

```
virtual ~Map();
```

Destroy the map. For unbounded forms, individual items and values may or may not be destroyed, according to the semantics of the map's container. For bounded forms, individual items and values are destroyed.

```
Map<Item, Value, Buckets>& operator=(Map<Item, Value, Buckets>&);
```

Replace the state of the map with the item/value pairs in the given map; the map is initially cleared, and items and values (if any) in the given map are themselves copied. The cached item/value pair is cleared.

```
virtual int operator==(Map<Item, Value, Buckets>&) const;
```

Return 1 if and only if both maps have the same extent and the same item/value pairs; return 0 otherwise. Equality of items uses the default test for equality provided by the class Item. The cached item/value pair is unaffected.

```
virtual int operator!=(Map<Item, Value, Buckets>&) const;
```

Return the logical negation of operator==. The cached item/value pair is unaffected.

```
virtual Map<Item, Value, Buckets>& clear();
```

Empty the map of all item/value pairs. For unbounded forms, individual items and values may or may not be destroyed, according to the semantics of the map's container. For bounded forms, individual items and values are not destroyed. The cached item/value pair is cleared.

```
virtual Map<Item, Value, Buckets>& bind(Item&, Value&);
```

If there already exists a binding for the given item, throw the exception Duplicate. Otherwise, add the item/value pair to the map. The item and value themselves are copied. The cached item/value pair is set to this new binding.

```
virtual Map<Item, Value, Buckets>& rebind(Item&, Value&);
```

If the map is empty, throw the exception Underflow. If a binding for the given item is not found, throw the exception Not_Found. Otherwise, change the item's binding to the given value. The value itself is copied. The cached item/value pair is set to this new binding.

```
virtual Map<Item, Value, Buckets>& unbind(Item&);
```

If the map is empty, throw the exception `Underflow`. If a binding for the given item is not found, throw the exception `Not_Found`. Otherwise, remove the item/value binding. For unbounded forms, the item and value may or may not be destroyed, according to the semantics of the map's container. For bounded forms, the item and value are not destroyed. The cached item/value pair is cleared.

```
virtual Map<Item, Value, Buckets>&
  set_hash_function(unsigned (*hash)(Item&));
```

If the hash function is already set, throw the exception `Duplicate`. Otherwise, set the hash function to the given function.

```
virtual unsigned extent() const;
```

Return the number of item/value bindings in the map.

```
virtual int is_empty() const;
```

Return 1 if and only if there are no item/value bindings in the map.

```
virtual int is_bound(Item&);
```

Return 1 if and only if there is a binding for the given item in the map. The cached item/value pair is used to accelerate the search; if there is a cache hit, the time complexity of this operation is O(1).

```
virtual Value& value(Item&);
```

If there is no binding for the given item, throw the exception `Not_Found`. Otherwise, return a reference to the value bound to the given item. The cached item/value pair is used to accelerate the search; if there is a cache hit, the time complexity of this operation is O(1).

EXCEPTIONS

`Duplicate`	—thrown by `bind` if a binding already exists for the given item.
	—thrown by `set_hash_function` if the hash function is already set.
`Not_Found`	—thrown by `rebind`, `unbind`, and `value` if no binding exists for the given item.
`Overflow`	—thrown by any bounded form member function when the static limits of the object are exceeded.
`Storage_Error`	—thrown by any unbounded form member function when no more storage can be allocated.
`Underflow`	—thrown by `rebind` and `unbind` if the map is empty.

OPTIONS

Maps form a typical family of classes, supporting all the usual representation and process synchronization forms:

- Map
- Unbounded_Map
- Guarded_Unbounded_Map
- Synchronized_Unbounded_Map
- Bounded_Map
- Guarded_Bounded_Map
- Synchronized_Bounded_Map

Maps provide the usual active and passive iterators, with some simple variations. The map active iterator includes the member function value, which returns a pointer to the value part of the current binding. Similarly, the signature of the apply function in the passive iterator requires an argument for the value part of the current binding.

FILES

In the maps class category:

```
map        Map
           Map_Active_Iterator
           Map_Passive_Iterator
map_u      Unbounded_Map
map_ug     Guarded_Unbounded_Map
map_us     Synchronized_Unbounded_Map
map_b      Bounded_Map
map_bg     Guarded_Bounded_Map
map_bs     Synchronized_Bounded_Map
```

SEE ALSO

Node

Synch

Queue

NAME

Queue—A sequence in which items may be added from one end and removed from the opposite end.

SYNOPSIS

```
template<class Item>
class Queue {
public:

  Queue();
  Queue(const Queue<Item>&);
  virtual ~Queue();

  Queue<Item>& operator=(Queue<Item>&);
  virtual int operator==(Queue<Item>&) const;
  virtual int operator!=(Queue<Item>&) const;

  virtual Queue<Item>& clear();
  virtual Queue<Item>& add(Item&);
  virtual Queue<Item>& pop();

  virtual unsigned length() const;
  virtual int is_empty() const;
  virtual Item& front() const;

};
```

DESCRIPTION

A queue denotes a sequence of items in which items may be added from one end and removed from the opposite end of the sequence.

`template<class Item>`

The template item denotes the universe from which the queue draws its items. The class Item may be either a primitive type or a user-defined class. If the latter, the class must provide a default constructor, copy constructor, assignment operator, and equality operator.

The template signature of the unbounded form requires a class Container, which must be a kind of Node. The template signature of the bounded form requires an unsigned integer Size, representing the static size of all instances of the class. Additionally, the template signature of the guarded form requires a class

Structures Class Strategy

Guard (such as the class Semaphore), and the template signature of the synchronized form requires a class Monitor (such as a kind of Read_Write_Monitor).

```
Queue();
```

Construct an empty queue.

```
Queue(const Queue<Item>&);
```

Copy the items in the given queue, preserving their order; items in the copied queue are themselves copied.

```
virtual ~Queue();
```

Destroy the queue. For unbounded forms, individual items may or may not be destroyed, according to the semantics of the queue's container. For bounded forms, individual items are destroyed.

```
Queue<Item>& operator=(Queue<Item>&);
```

Replace the state of the queue with the items in the given queue, preserving their order; the queue is initially cleared, and items (if any) in the given queue are themselves copied.

```
virtual int operator==(Queue<Item>&) const;
```

Return 1 if and only if both queues have the same length and the same items in the same order; return 0 otherwise. Equality of items uses the default test for equality provided by the class Item.

```
virtual int operator!=(Queue<Item>&) const;
```

Return the logical negation of operator==.

```
virtual Queue<Item>& clear();
```

Empty the queue of all items. For unbounded forms, individual items may or may not be destroyed, according to the semantics of the queue's container. For bounded forms, individual items are not destroyed.

```
virtual Queue<Item>& add(Item&);
```

Add the item to the back of the queue; the item itself is copied.

```
virtual Queue<Item>& pop();
```

If the queue is empty, throw the exception Underflow. Otherwise, remove the item from the front of the queue. For unbounded forms, the removed item may or may not be destroyed according to the semantics of the queue's container. For bounded forms, the removed item is not destroyed.

```
virtual unsigned length() const;
```

Return the number of items in the queue.

`virtual int is_empty() const;`

Return 1 if and only if there are no items in the queue.

`virtual Item& front() const;`

If the queue is empty, throw the exception `Underflow`. Otherwise, return a reference to the item at the front of the queue.

EXCEPTIONS

`Overflow` —thrown by any bounded form member function when the static limits of the object are exceeded.

`Storage_Error` —thrown by any unbounded form member function when no more storage can be allocated.

`Underflow` —thrown by `pop` and `front` if the queue is empty.

Options

Queues form a typical family of classes, supporting all the usual representation and process synchronization forms:

- `Queue`
- `Unbounded_Queue`
- `Guarded_Unbounded_Queue`
- `Synchronized_Unbounded_Queue`
- `Bounded_Queue`
- `Guarded_Bounded_Queue`
- `Synchronized_Bounded_Queue`

Queues provide the usual active and passive iterators.

In addition to the core family of queue classes, there are three subclasses that provide variations on the theme:

- `Balking_Queue`
- `Priority_Queue`
- `Balking_Priority_Queue`

Each of these three abstractions provides the usual family of classes.

With the `Balking_Queue`, items may be removed from arbitrary positions in the queue. Items are numbered starting at the front of the queue, from 1 to the queue's length. `Balking_Queue` is a direct subclass of `Queue` and adds the following operations:

```
virtual Queue<Item>& remove(unsigned position);
```

If the given position is zero or greater than the length of the queue, throw the exception `Range_Error`. Otherwise, remove the item at the given ordinal position. For unbounded forms, the removed item may or may not be destroyed according to the semantics of the queue's container. For bounded forms, the removed item is not destroyed.

```
virtual unsigned position(Item&) const;
```

Return the ordinal position of the item in the queue. If the item does not exist in the queue, return 0. The test for existence of an item uses the default test for equality provided by the class `Item`.

With the priority form, items are ordered in the queue according to their priority, from highest to lowest priority. Priority is an integer, and the higher the number, the higher the priority; negative values are permitted. The class `Item` must provide a function that returns the priority of the item, which may be set exactly once for each queue, either at the time of the queue's construction, or via the member function `set_priority_function`. `Priority_Queue` is a direct subclass of `Queue`, and redefines one operation and adds one operation:

```
virtual Queue<Item>& add(Item&);
```

Add the item to the front of the queue in order of its priority; the item itself is copied. The item is added ahead of existing items with equal priority.

```
virtual Queue<Item>& set_priority_function(int (*priority)(Item&));
```

If the priority function is already set, throw the exception `Duplicate`. Otherwise, set the priority function to the given function.

`Balking_Priority_Queue` is a direct subclass of `Queue`, and adds the behavior of both the `Balking_Queue` and the `Priority_Queue`.

FILES

In the queue class category:

```
queue     Queue
          Queue_Active_Iterator
          Queue_Passive_Iterator
queue_u   Unbounded_Queue
```

```
queue_ug    Guarded_Unbounded_Queue
queue_us    Synchronized_Unbounded_Queue
queue_b     Bounded_Queue
queue_bg    Guarded_Bounded_Queue
queue_bs    Synchronized_Bounded_Queue
```

In the balking_queues class category:

```
bque        Balking_Queue
bque_u      Unbounded_Balking_Queue
bque_ug     Guarded_Unbounded_Balking_Queue
bque_us     Synchronized_Unbounded_Balking_Queue
bque_b      Bounded_Balking_Queue
bque_bg     Guarded_Bounded_Balking_Queue
bque_bs     Synchronized_Bounded_Balking_Queue
```

In the priority_queues class category:

```
pque        Priority_Queue
pque_u      Unbounded_Priority_Queue
pque_ug     Guarded_Unbounded_Priority_Queue
pque_us     Synchronized_Unbounded_Priority_Queue
pque_b      Bounded_Priority_Queue
pque_bg     Guarded_Bounded_Priority_Queue
pque_bs     Synchronized_Bounded_Priority_Queue
```

In the balking_priority_queues class category:

```
bpque       Balking_Priority_Queue
bpque_u     Unbounded_Balking_Priority_Queue
bpque_ug    Guarded_Unbounded_Balking_Priority_Queue
bpque_us    Synchronized_Unbounded_Balking_Priority_Queue
bpque_b     Bounded_Balking_Priority_Queue
bpque_bg    Guarded_Bounded_Balking_Priority_Queue
bpque_bs    Synchronized_Bounded_Balking_Priority_Queue
```

SEE ALSO

Node

Synch

RING

NAME

Ring—A sequence in which items may be added and removed from the top of a circular structure.

SYNOPSIS

```
enum Direction {FORWARD, REVERSE};

template<class Item>
class Ring {
public:

  Ring();
  Ring(const Ring<Item>&);
  virtual ~Ring();

  Ring<Item>& operator=(Ring<Item>&);
  virtual int operator==(Ring<Item>&) const;
  virtual int operator!=(Ring<Item>&) const;

  virtual Ring<Item>& clear();
  virtual Ring<Item>& insert(Item&);
  virtual Ring<Item>& pop();
  virtual Ring<Item>& rotate(Direction direction = FORWARD);
  virtual Ring<Item>& mark();
  virtual Ring<Item>& rotate_to_mark();

  virtual unsigned extent() const;
  virtual int is_empty() const;
  virtual Item& top() const;
  virtual int at_mark() const;

};
```

DESCRIPTION

A ring denotes a sequence in which items may be added and removed from the top of a circular structure. Because this structure has no beginning or ending, a client can mark one particular item to designate a point of reference in the structure.

```
enum Direction {FORWARD, REVERSE};
```

Direction is used by the member function `rotate` to denote the direction of rotation; FORWARD logically rotates the top of the ring clockwise; REVERSE logically rotates the top of the ring counterclockwise.

```
template<class Item>
```

The template item denotes the universe from which the ring draws its items. The class `UItem` may be either a primitive type or a user-defined class. If the latter, the class must provide a default constructor, copy constructor, assignment operator, and equality operator.

The template signature of the unbounded form requires a class `Container`, which must be a kind of `Double_Node`. The template signature of the bounded form requires an unsigned integer `Size`, representing the static size of all instances of the class. Additionally, the template signature of the guarded form requires a class `Guard` (such as the class `Semaphore`), and the template signature of the synchronized form requires a class `Monitor` (such as a kind of `Read_Write_Monitor`).

```
Ring();
```

Construct an empty ring; the mark is not set.

```
Ring(const Ring<Item>&);
```

Copy the items in the given ring, preserving their order, as well as the identity of the given ring's top and mark; items in the copied ring are themselves copied.

```
virtual ~Ring();
```

Destroy the ring. For unbounded forms, individual items may or may not be destroyed, according to the semantics of the ring's container. For bounded forms, individual items are destroyed.

```
Ring<Item>& operator=(Ring<Item>&);
```

Replace the state of the ring with the items in the given ring, preserving their order, as well as the identity of the given ring's top and mark. The ring is initially cleared, and items (if any) in the given ring are themselves copied.

```
virtual int operator==(Ring<Item>&) const;
```

Return 1 if and only if both rings have the same extent, and the same items in the same order; return 0 otherwise. The identity of the top and mark of both rings does not participate in this test of equality. Equality of distinct items uses the default test for equality provided by the class `Item`. The ring's top and mark are unaffected.

```
virtual int operator!=(Ring<Item>&) const;
```

Return the logical negation of `operator==`. The ring's top and mark are unaffected.

```
virtual Ring<Item>& clear();
```

Empty the ring of all items. For unbounded forms, individual items may or may not be destroyed, according to the semantics of the ring's container. For bounded forms, individual items are not destroyed. The mark is cleared.

```
virtual Ring<Item>& insert(Item&);
```

If the ring is empty, set the ring's mark to designate this item. Add the item to the top of the ring; the previous top item (if any) is now located clockwise adjacent to the new item; the old item is forward of the new one.

```
virtual Ring<Item>& pop();
```

If the ring is empty, throw the exception `Underflow`. Otherwise, remove the item from the top of the ring. The clockwise adjacent item (if any) is now designated as the ring's top. For unbounded forms, the removed item may or may not be destroyed according to the semantics of the ring's container. For bounded forms, the removed item is not destroyed. The test for membership of an item uses the default test for equality provided by the class `Item`. If the removed item had been marked, the ring's new top (which may be empty) is now designated as marked.

```
virtual Ring<Item>& rotate(Direction direction = FORWARD);
```

If the ring is empty, throw the exception `Is_Null`. Otherwise, rotate the top of the ring in the given direction. Rotating the ring in a forward direction moves the ring's top clockwise; rotating the ring in a reverse direction advances the ring's top counterclockwise. The ring's mark is unaffected. If there is exactly one item in the ring, rotating either direction always returns to the same item.

```
virtual Ring<Item>& mark();
```

Designate the item at the top of the ring (which may be empty) as marked.

```
virtual unsigned extent() const;
```

Return the number of items in the ring.

```
virtual int is_empty() const;
```

Return 1 if and only if there are no items in the ring.

```
virtual Item& top() const;
```

If the ring is empty, throw the exception `Underflow`. Otherwise, return a reference to the item at the top of the ring.

```
virtual int at_mark() const;
```

Return 1 if and only if the item at the top of the ring is marked. By implication, this member function will return 1 if the bag is empty, because the ring's top and mark both do not designate any item.

EXCEPTIONS

`Is_Null`	—thrown by rotate if the ring is empty.
`Overflow`	—thrown by any bounded form member function when the static limits of the object are exceeded.
`Storage_Error`	—thrown by any unbounded form member function when no more storage can be allocated.
`Underflow`	—thrown by pop and top if the ring is empty.

OPTIONS

Rings form a typical family of classes, supporting all the usual representation and process synchronization forms:

- `Ring`
- `Unbounded_Ring`
- `Guarded_Unbounded_Ring`
- `Synchronized_Unbounded_Ring`
- `Bounded_Ring`
- `Guarded_Bounded_Ring`
- `Synchronized_Bounded_Ring`

Rings provide the usual active and passive iterators.

FILES

In the rings class category:

```
ring     Ring
         Ring_Active_Iterator
         Ring_Passive_Iterator
ring_u   Unbounded_Ring
ring_ug  Guarded_Unbounded_Ring
ring_us  Synchronized_Unbounded_Ring
ring_b   Bounded_Ring
ring_bg  Guarded_Bounded_Ring
ring_bs  Synchronized_Bounded_Ring
```

SEE ALSO

Node (especially `Double_Node`)

Synch

Set

NAME

Set—A collection of items from some domain; may not contain duplicates.

SYNOPSIS

```
template<class Item>
class Set {
public:

  Set();
  Set(const Set<Item>&);
  virtual ~Set();

  Set<Item>& operator=(Set<Item>&);
  virtual int operator==(Set<Item>&) const;
  virtual int operator!=(Set<Item>&) const;

  virtual Set<Item>& clear();
  virtual Set<Item>& add(Item&);
  virtual Set<Item>& remove(Item&);
  virtual Set<Item>& set_union(Set<Item>&);
  virtual Set<Item>& intersection(Set<Item>&);
  virtual Set<Item>& difference(Set<Item>&);

  virtual unsigned extent() const;
  virtual int is_empty() const;
  virtual int is_member(Item&) const;
  virtual int is_subset(Set<Item>&) const;
  virtual int is_proper_subset(Set<Item>&) const;

};
```

DESCRIPTION

A set denotes a collection of items, drawn from some well-defined universe. Unlike a bag, a set may not contain duplicate items.

`template<class Item>`

The template item denotes the universe from which the set draws its items. The class `Item` may be either a primitive type or a user-defined class. If the latter, the class must provide a default constructor, copy constructor, assignment operator, and equality operator.

The template signature of the unbounded form requires a class `Container`, which must be a kind of `Node`. The template signature of the bounded form requires an unsigned integer `Size`, representing the static size of all instances of the class. Additionally, the template signature of the guarded form requires a class `Guard` (such as the class `Semaphore`), and the template signature of the synchronized form requires a class `Monitor` (such as a kind of `Read_Write_Monitor`).

```
Set();
```

Construct an empty set.

```
Set(const Set<Item>&);
```

Copy the given set; items in the copied set are themselves copied.

```
virtual ~Set();
```

Destroy the set. For unbounded forms, individual items may or may not be destroyed, according to the semantics of the set's container. For bounded forms, individual items are destroyed.

```
Set<Item>& operator=(Set<Item>&);
```

Replace the state of the set with the items in the given set; the set is initially cleared, and items (if any) in the given set are themselves copied.

```
virtual int operator==(Set<Item>&) const;
```

Return 1 if and only if both sets have the same number of items, and the same items themselves; return 0 otherwise. Equality of items uses the default test for equality provided by the class `Item`.

```
virtual int operator!=(Set<Item>&) const;
```

Return the logical negation of `operator==`.

```
virtual Set<Item>& clear();
```

Empty the set of all items. For unbounded forms, individual items may or may not be destroyed, according to the semantics of the set's container. For bounded forms, individual items are not destroyed.

```
virtual Set<Item>& add(Item&);
```

If the item is already a member of the set, throw the exception `Duplicate`. Otherwise, copy the item and add it to the set. The test for membership of an item uses the default test for equality provided by the class `Item`.

```
virtual Set<Item>& remove(Item&);
```

If the set is empty, throw the exception `Underflow`. If the item is not a member of the set, throw the exception `Not_Found`. Otherwise, remove the item from the set. For unbounded forms, the removed item may or may not be destroyed according to the semantics of the set's container. For bounded forms, the removed item is not destroyed. The test for membership of an item uses the default test for equality provided by the class `Item`.

```
virtual Set<Item>& set_union(Set<Item>&);
```

Perform a logical set union. At the completion of this operation, the set contains the items found in its original state combined with the given set (but without duplication). For each item in the given set, if the item is not already a distinct member of the set, copy the item and add it to the set. If the item already is a member, do nothing. The test for membership of an item uses the default test for equality provided by the class `Item`.

```
virtual Set<Item>& intersection(Set<Item>&);
```

Perform a logical set intersection. At the completion of this operation, the set contains the items found both in its original state and in the given set. For each item in the given set, if the item is not already a distinct member of the set, do nothing. If the item already is a member, do nothing. Items in the original set but not in the given set are also removed. For unbounded forms, the removed item may or may not be destroyed according to the semantics of the set's container. For bounded forms, the removed item is not destroyed. The test for membership of an item uses the default test for equality provided by the class `Item`.

```
virtual Set<Item>& difference(Set<Item>&);
```

Perform a logical set difference. At the completion of this operation, the set contains the items found in its original state, less those found in the given set. For each item in the given set, if the item is not already a distinct member of the set, do nothing. If the item already is a member, remove the item from the set. For unbounded forms, the removed item may or may not be destroyed according to the semantics of the set's container. For bounded forms, the removed item is not destroyed. The test for membership of an item uses the default test for equality provided by the class `Item`.

```
virtual unsigned extent() const;
```

Return the number of distinct items in the set.

```
virtual int is_empty() const;
```

Return 1 if and only if there are no items in the set.

```
virtual int is_member(Item&) const;
```

Return 1 if and only if the item exists in the set. The test for membership of an item uses the default test for equality provided by the class Item.

```
virtual int is_subset(Set<Item>&) const;
```

Return 1 if and only if the set has the same or fewer items than in the given set.

```
virtual int is_proper_subset(Set<Item>&) const;
```

Return 1 if and only if the set has fewer items than in the given set.

EXCEPTIONS

Duplicate	—thrown by add if the item is already a member of the set.
Not_Found	—thrown by remove if the item is not a member of the set.
Overflow	—thrown by any bounded form member function when the static limits of the object are exceeded.
UStorage_Error	—thrown by any unbounded form member function when no more storage can be allocated.
Underflow	—thrown by remove if the set is empty.

OPTIONS

Sets form a typical family of classes, supporting all the usual representation and process synchronization forms:

- Set
- Unbounded_Set
- Guarded_Unbounded_Set
- Synchronized_Unbounded_Set
- Bounded_Set
- Guarded_Bounded_Set
- Synchronized_Bounded_Set

Sets provide the usual active and passive iterators.

FILES

In the sets class category:

```
set   Set
      Set_Active_Iterator
      Set_Passive_Iterator
set_u     Unbounded_Set
```

set_ug	Guarded_Unbounded_Set
set_us	Synchronized_Unbounded_Set
set_b	Bounded_Set
set_bg	Guarded_Bounded_Set
set_bs	Synchronized_Bounded_Set

SEE ALSO

Node

Synch

STACK

NAME

Stack—A sequence in which items may be added and removed from one end.

SYNOPSIS

```
template<class Item>
class Stack {
public:

  Stack();
  Stack(const Stack<Item>&);
  virtual ~Stack();

  Stack<Item>& operator=(Stack<Item>&);
  virtual int operator==(Stack<Item>&) const;
  virtual int operator!=(Stack<Item>&) const;

  virtual Stack<Item>& clear();
  virtual Stack<Item>& push(Item&);
  virtual Stack<Item>& pop();

  virtual unsigned depth() const;
  virtual int is_empty() const;
  virtual Item& top() const;

};
```

DESCRIPTION

A stack denotes a sequence of items in which items may be added and removed from one end.

```
template<class Item>
```

The template item denotes the universe from which the stack draws its items. The class `Item` may be either a primitive type or a user-defined class. If the latter, the class must provide a default constructor, copy constructor, assignment operator, and equality operator.

The template signature of the unbounded form requires a class `Container`, which must be a kind of `Node`. The template signature of the bounded form requires an unsigned integer `Size`, representing the static size of all instances of the class. Additionally, the template signature of the guarded form requires a class `Guard` (such as the class `Semaphore`), and the template signature of the synchronized form requires a class `Monitor` (such as a kind of `Read_Write_Monitor`).

```
Stack();
```

Construct an empty stack.

```
Stack(const Stack<Item>&);
```

Copy the items in the given stack, preserving their order; items in the copied stack are themselves copied.

```
virtual ~Stack();
```

Destroy the stack. For unbounded forms, individual items may or may not be destroyed, according to the semantics of the stack's container. For bounded forms, individual items are destroyed.

```
Stack<Item>& operator=(Stack<Item>&);
```

Replace the state of the stack with the items in the given stack, preserving their order; the stack is initially cleared, and items (if any) in the given stack are themselves copied.

```
virtual int operator==(Stack<Item>&) const;
```

Return 1 if and only if both stacks have the same depth and the same items in the same order; return 0 otherwise. Equality of items uses the default test for equality provided by the class `Item`.

```
virtual int operator!=(Stack<Item>&) const;
```

Return the logical negation of `operator==`.

```
virtual Stack<Item>& clear();
```

Empty the stack of all items. For unbounded forms, individual items may or may not be destroyed, according to the semantics of the stack's container. For bounded forms, individual items are not destroyed.

```
virtual Stack<Item>& push(Item&);
```

Add the item to the top of the stack; the item itself is copied.

```
virtual Stack<Item>& pop();
```

If the stack is empty, throw the exception `Underflow`. Otherwise, remove the item from the top of the stack. For unbounded forms, the removed item may or may not be destroyed according to the semantics of the stack's container. For bounded forms, the removed item is not destroyed.

```
virtual unsigned depth() const;
```

Return the number of items in the stack.

```
virtual int is_empty() const;
```

Return 1 if and only if there are no items in the stack.

```
virtual Item& top() const;
```

If the stack is empty, throw the exception `Underflow`. Otherwise, return a reference to the item at the top of the stack.

EXCEPTIONS

- `Overflow` —thrown by any bounded form member function when the static limits of the object are exceeded.
- `Storage_Error` —thrown by any unbounded form member function when no more storage can be allocated.
- `Underflow` —thrown by `pop` and `top` if the stack is empty.

OPTIONS

Stacks form a typical family of classes, supporting all the usual representation and process synchronization forms:

- `Stack`
- `Unbounded_Stack`
- `Guarded_Unbounded_Stack`
- `Synchronized_Unbounded_Stack`
- `Bounded_Stack`
- `Guarded_Bounded_Stack`
- `Synchronized_Bounded_Stack`

Stacks provide the usual active and passive iterators.

FILES

In the stacks class category:

```
stack      Stack
           Stack_Active_Iterator
           Stack_Passive_Iterator
stack_u    Unbounded_Stack
stack_ug   Guarded_Unbounded_Stack
stack_us   Synchronized_Unbounded_Stack
stack_b    Bounded_Stack
stack_bg   Guarded_Bounded_Stack
stack_bs   Synchronized_Bounded_Stack
```

SEE ALSO

`Node`

`Synch`

Variable_String

NAME

`Variable_String`—A sequence of zero or more items.

SYNOPSIS

```cpp
template<class Item>
class Variable_String {
public:

  Variable_String();
  Variable_String(const Variable_String<Item>& s);
  virtual ~Variable_String();

  Variable_String<Item>& operator=(Variable_String<Item>&);
  virtual int operator==(Variable_String<Item>&) const;
  virtual int operator!=(Variable_String<Item>&) const;
  virtual Item& operator[](unsigned position);

  virtual Variable_String<Item>& clear();
  virtual Variable_String<Item>& insert(Item&, unsigned before = 0);
  virtual Variable_String<Item>& insert(Variable_String<Item>&,
                                        unsigned before = 0);
  virtual Variable_String<Item>& append(Item&, unsigned after = 0);
  virtual Variable_String<Item>& append(Variable_String<Item>&,
                                        unsigned after = 0);
```

```
    virtual Variable_String<Item>& remove(unsigned from, unsigned to);
    virtual Variable_String<Item>& preserve(unsigned from,
                                            unsigned to);
    virtual Variable_String<Item>& set_item(Item&, unsigned position);
    virtual Variable_String<Item>&
      set_substring(Variable_String<Item>&, unsigned position);
    virtual Variable_String<Item>& copy(Variable_String<Item>&,
                                        unsigned from, unsigned to);

    virtual unsigned length() const;
    virtual int is_null() const;

};
```

DESCRIPTION

A variable string denotes a sequence of zero or more items. The items in a string may be indexed, starting from 1 to the length of the string. A string may vary in length: it may grow and shrink, but it is always guaranteed to be sized exactly according to the number of items it currently contains. This class is named `Variable_String` to avoid conflict with the commonly used name `String`. As a template class, instances of `Variable_String` are not limited to strings of characters.

`template<class Item>`

The template item denotes the universe from which the string draws its items. The class `Item` may be either a primitive type or a user-defined class. If the latter, the class must provide a default constructor, copy constructor, assignment operator, and equality operator.

The template signature of the unbounded form requires a class `Container`, which must be a kind of `Node`. The template signature of the bounded form requires an unsigned integer `Size`, representing the static size of all instances of the class. Additionally, the template signature of the guarded form requires a class `Guard` (such as the class `Semaphore`), and the template signature of the synchronized form requires a class `Monitor` (such as a kind of `Read_Write_Monitor`).

`Variable_String();`

Construct a null string.

`Variable_String(const Variable_String<Item>& s);`

Copy the items in the given string, preserving their order; items in the copied string are themselves copied.

`virtual ~Variable_String();`

Destroy the string. For unbounded forms, individual items may or may not be destroyed, according to the semantics of the string's container. For bounded forms, individual items are destroyed.

```
Variable_String<Item>& operator=(Variable_String<Item>&);
```

Replace the state of the string with the items in the given string, preserving their order; the string is initially cleared, and items (if any) in the given string are themselves copied.

```
virtual int operator==(Variable_String<Item>&) const;
```

Return 1 if and only if both strings have the same length, and the same items in the same order; return 0 otherwise. Equality of items uses the default test for equality provided by the class Item.

```
virtual int operator!=(Variable_String<Item>&) const;
```

Return the logical negation of operator==.

```
virtual Item& operator[](unsigned position);
```

If the given position is zero or greater than the length of the string, throw the exception Range_Error. Otherwise, return a reference to the item at the given ordinal position.

```
virtual Variable_String<Item>& clear();
```

Empty the string of all items. For unbounded forms, individual items may or may not be destroyed, according to the semantics of the string's container. For bounded forms, individual items are not destroyed.

```
virtual Variable_String<Item>& insert(Item&, unsigned before = 0);
```

If before is larger than the length of the string, throw the exception Range_Error. Otherwise, expand the string by copying the item and inserting it ahead of the item at the given ordinal position; a value of 0 or 1 for before inserts the item at the first position in the string.

```
virtual Variable_String<Item>& insert(Variable_String<Item>&,
unsigned before = 0);
```

If the string and the given string denote the same object, throw the exception Duplicate. If before is larger than the length of the string, throw the exception Range_Error. Otherwise, expand the string by copying the items from the given string and inserting them, in order, ahead of the item at the given ordinal position; a value of 0 or 1 for before inserts the items at the first position in the string.

```
virtual Variable_String<Item>& append(Item&, unsigned after = 0);
```

If `after` is larger than the length of the string, throw the exception `Range_Error`. Otherwise, expand the string by copying the item and appending it after the item at the given ordinal position; a value of 0 for `after` appends the item to the end of the string.

```
virtual Variable_String<Item>& append(Variable_String<Item>&,
                                      unsigned after = 0);
```

If the string and the given string denote the same object, throw the exception `Duplicate`. If `after` is larger than the length of the string, throw the exception `Range_Error`. Otherwise, expand the string by copying the items from the given string and appending them in order, after the item at the given ordinal position; a value of 0 for `after` appends the items to the end of the string.

```
virtual Variable_String<Item>& remove(unsigned from, unsigned to);
```

If `from` or `to` is zero, or if `from` is larger than `to`, or if `from` or `to` is larger than the length of the string, throw the exception `Range_Error`. Otherwise, shorten the string by removing the items between `to` and `from`, inclusive. For unbounded forms, the removed item may or may not be destroyed according to the semantics of the string's container. For bounded forms, the removed item is not destroyed. The test for membership of an item uses the default test for equality provided by the class `Item`.

```
virtual Variable_String<Item>& preserve(unsigned from, unsigned to);
```

If `from` or `to` is zero, or if `from` is larger than `to`, or if `from` or `to` is larger than the length of the string, throw the exception `Range_Error`. Otherwise, shorten the string by removing all items except those between `to` and `from`, inclusive. For unbounded forms, the removed item may or may not be destroyed according to the semantics of the string's container. For bounded forms, the removed item is not destroyed. The test for membership of an item uses the default test for equality provided by the class `Item`.

```
virtual Variable_String<Item>& set_item(Item&, unsigned position);
```

If the position is zero or is larger than the length of the string, throw the exception `Range_Error`. Otherwise, set the item at the given ordinal position.

```
virtual Variable_String<Item>&
  set_substring(Variable_String<Item>&, unsigned position);
```

If the string and the given string denote the same object, throw the exception `Duplicate`. If the position is zero or is larger than the length of the string, less the length of the given string plus 1, throw the exception `Range_Error`. Otherwise, set the items starting at the given ordinal position with the items from the given string, in order.

```
virtual Variable_String<Item>& copy(Variable_String<Item>&,
unsigned from, unsigned to);
```

If the string and the given string denote the same object, throw the exception `Duplicate`. If `from` or `to` is zero, or if `from` is larger than `to`, or if `from` or `to` is larger than the length of the given string, throw the exception `Range_Error`. Otherwise, replace the state of the string with the items from the given string between `from` and `to`, inclusive, preserving their order; the string is initially cleared, and items in the given string are themselves copied.

```
virtual unsigned length() const;
```

Return the number of items in the string.

```
virtual int is_null() const;
```

Return 1 if and only if there are no items in the string.

EXCEPTIONS

`Duplicate`	—thrown by `insert`, `append`, `substring`, and `copy` if the string and the given string denote the same object.
`Overflow`	—thrown by any bounded form member function when the static limits of the object are exceeded.
`Range_Error`	—thrown by `operator[]`, `set_item`, and `substring` if the position is zero or beyond the length of the string.
	—thrown by `insert` and `append` if the position is beyond the length of the string.
	—thrown by `remove` and `preserve` if `from` or `to` is zero, if `from` is larger than `to`, or if `from` or `to` is larger than the string.
	—thrown by `copy` if `from` or `to` is zero, if `from` is larger than `to`, or if `from` or `to` is larger than the given string.
`Storage_Error`	—thrown by any unbounded form member function when no more storage can be allocated.

OPTIONS

Strings form a typical family of classes, supporting all the usual representation and process synchronization forms:

- `Variable_String`
- `Unbounded_Variable_String`
- `Guarded_Unbounded_Variable_String`
- `Synchronized_Unbounded_Variable_String`
- `Bounded_Variable_String`
- `Guarded_Bounded_Variable_String`
- `Synchronized_Bounded_Variable_String`

Strings provide the usual active and passive iterators.

FILES

In the strings class category:

```
vstring    Variable_String
           Variable_String_Active_Iterator
           Variable_String_Passive_Iterator
vstr_u     Unbounded_Variable_String
vstr_ug    Guarded_Unbounded_Variable_String
vstr_us    Synchronized_Unbounded_Variable_String
vstr_b     Bounded_Variable_String
vstr_bg    Guarded_Bounded_Variable_String
vstr_bs    Synchronized_Bounded_Variable_String
```

SEE ALSO

Node

Synch

ARBITRARY_TREE

NAME

`Arbitrary_Tree`—A rooted collection of nodes and arcs, where each node may have an arbitrary number of children; may not contain cycles or cross-references; structural sharing is permitted.

SYNOPSIS

```
template<class Item>
class Arbitrary_Tree {
public:

  Arbitrary_Tree();
  Arbitrary_Tree(Arbitrary_Tree<Item>&);
  virtual ~Arbitrary_Tree();

  virtual Arbitrary_Tree<Item>& operator=(Arbitrary_Tree<Item>&);
  virtual int operator==(Arbitrary_Tree<Item>&) const;
  virtual int operator!=(Arbitrary_Tree<Item>&) const;

  virtual Arbitrary_Tree<Item>& clear();
  virtual Arbitrary_Tree<Item>& construct(Item&);
  virtual Arbitrary_Tree<Item>& insert_child(Arbitrary_Tree<Item>&,
                                             unsigned before = 0);
  virtual Arbitrary_Tree<Item>& append_child(Arbitrary_Tree<Item>&,
                                             unsigned after = 0);
  virtual Arbitrary_Tree<Item>& remove_child(Arbitrary_Tree<Item>&);
  virtual Arbitrary_Tree<Item>& remove_child(unsigned child);
  virtual Arbitrary_Tree<Item>& set_item(Item&);
  virtual Arbitrary_Tree<Item>& swap_child(unsigned child,
                                           Arbitrary_Tree<Item>&);
  virtual Arbitrary_Tree<Item>& child(unsigned child);
  virtual Arbitrary_Tree<Item>& parent();

  virtual int is_null() const;
  virtual int is_shared() const;
  virtual Item& item() const;
  virtual unsigned arity() const;

};
```

DESCRIPTION

An arbitrary tree denotes a rooted collection of nodes and unidirectional arcs, where each node may have an arbitrary number of children, numbered starting at 1. A tree may not contain cycles or cross-references. Trees are polylithic structures; hence, the semantics of copying, assignment, and equality involve structural sharing. Care must be taken in manipulating the same tree named by more than one alias.

This abstraction has been carefully constructed to eliminate all storage leaks, except in the case of intentional abuses. When a tree is manipulated, all items that become unreachable are automatically reclaimed. Furthermore, this design protects against dangling references: the node associated with an item is never reclaimed if an alias to it exists.

Unreachable items are those that belong to a tree or a subtree whose root is not designated by any alias. For example, consider the tree (A (B C D (E F))), with the root of the tree designated by T1. T1 initially points to the root of the list, at item A. Invoking the member function `child(2)` on T1 now causes T1 to point to item C. Because A is now considered unreachable, the node associated with item A is reclaimed; the parent of C is now null. Additionally, the sibling subtrees rooted at B and D are also now unreachable and so are reclaimed (along with their children, and recursively so). Similarly, consider the same tree, with the root of the tree designated by both T1 and T2. Both T1 and T2 are aliases that initially point to the root of the tree, at item A. Invoking the member function `child(2)` on T1 now causes T1 to point to item C; T2 is unaffected. No nodes are reclaimed, because every element of the tree is still reachable. Suppose we now invoke the member function `clear` on T2. The semantics of this operation are such that only unreachable items are reclaimed. Thus, the node associated with item A is reclaimed, because it is no longer reachable; additionally, the siblings B and D (and recursively so, their children) are reclaimed, because they are also now unreachable; the subtree denoted by T1 is unaffected. T2 is now null, and the parent of C is now null.

It is possible, but not generally desirable, to produce multiheaded trees. In such cases, the parent of the item at the neck of a multiheaded tree points to the most recently attached head.

The class `Arbitrary_Tree` is defined independently of the binary tree. Instances of the class `Arbitrary_Tree` are aliases of concrete nodes, but are themselves not the concrete nodes. For this reason, the semantics of `Arbitrary_Tree` involve structural sharing.

```
template<class Item>
```

The template item denotes the universe from which the tree draws its items. The class `Item` may be either a primitive type or a user-defined class. If the latter, the class must provide a default constructor, copy constructor, assignment operator, and equality operator.

The template signature of the unbounded form requires a class `Container`, which must be a kind of `Shared_Tree_Node`. The template signature of the bounded form requires an unsigned integer `Size`, representing the static size of all instances of the class. Additionally, the template signature of the guarded form requires a class `Guard` (such as the class `Semaphore`), and the template signature of the synchronized form requires a class `Monitor` (such as a kind of `Read_Write_Monitor`).

The representation of the bounded form of `Arbitrary_Tree` includes the static declaration of a bounded heap, from which all objects of this instantiation draw their storage. A client must provide a definition of this bounded heap, which must be a kind of `Shared_Bounded_Tree_Node_Heap`.

```
Arbitrary_Tree();
```

Construct a null tree.

```
Arbitrary_Tree(Arbitrary_Tree<Item>&);
```

If the given tree is null, construct a null tree. Otherwise, construct a tree so that it structurally shares the concrete node denoted by the given tree.

```
virtual ~Arbitrary_Tree();
```

Destroy the tree. The concrete node (if not null) is no longer structurally shared by this alias, and the nodes associated with any unreachable items are reclaimed. For unbounded forms, individual items may or may not be destroyed, according to the semantics of the tree's container. For bounded forms, individual items are not destroyed; such items are only destroyed when the associated bounded heap is destroyed, typically when its definition is no longer in scope.

```
virtual Arbitrary_Tree<Item>& operator=(Arbitrary_Tree<Item>&);
```

Clear the tree. If the given tree is not null, set the state of the tree so that it structurally shares the concrete node denoted by given tree.

```
virtual int operator==(Arbitrary_Tree<Item>&) const;
```

Return 1 if and only if both trees are null or are an alias to the same concrete node.

```
virtual int operator!=(Arbitrary_Tree<Item>&) const;
```

Return the logical negation of `operator==`.

```
virtual Arbitrary_Tree<Item>& clear();
```

If the tree is not null, remove this alias to the concrete node, make the tree null, and reclaim the nodes associated with any unreachable items. For unbounded forms, individual items may or may not be destroyed, according to the semantics of the tree's container. For bounded forms, individual items are not destroyed.

```
virtual Arbitrary_Tree<Item>& construct(Item&);
```

Create a new concrete node, whose first and only child is the concrete node designated by the tree (which may be null). If this child is not null, set its parent to be the newly created concrete node. Set the tree to designate this new concrete node.

Structures Class Strategy

```
virtual Arbitrary_Tree<Item>& insert_child(Arbitrary_Tree<Item>&,
                                           unsigned before = 0);
```

If the tree or the given tree is null, throw the exception `Is_Null`. If the given tree is not null, but does not represent the root of a tree, throw the exception `Not_Root`. If the tree has no children and `before` is non-zero, throw the exception `Range_Error`. If `before` is larger than the last numbered child, throw the exception `Range_Error`. Otherwise, insert the given tree as a child of the tree, ahead of the child at the given ordinal position; a value of 0 or 1 for `before` inserts the tree at the first ordinal position among the children. The parent of the given tree is set to be the tree itself.

```
virtual Arbitrary_Tree<Item>& append_child(Arbitrary_Tree<Item>&,
                                           unsigned after = 0);
```

If the tree or the given tree is null, throw the exception `Is_Null`. If the given tree is not null, but does not represent the root of a tree, throw the exception `Not_Root`. If the tree has no children and `after` is non-zero, throw the exception `Range_Error`. If `after` is larger than the last numbered child, throw the exception `Range_Error`. Otherwise, append the given tree as a child of the tree, after the child at the given ordinal position; a value of 0 for `after` appends the tree after the last child. The parent of the given tree is set to be the tree itself.

```
virtual Arbitrary_Tree<Item>& remove_child(Arbitrary_Tree<Item>&);
```

If the tree or the given tree is null, throw the exception `Is_Null`. If the given tree is not a child of the tree, throw the exception `Not_Found`. Otherwise, remove the child; the parent of the child is set to be null, but the given tree still remains as an alias to the subtree.

```
virtual Arbitrary_Tree<Item>& remove_child(unsigned child);
```

If the tree is null, throw the exception `Is_Null`. If the given child is zero or is larger than the arity of the tree, throw the exception `Range_Error`. Otherwise, remove the child; the parent of the child is set to be null. The child is then cleared; if there are no aliases to the child, it becomes unreachable. For unbounded forms, individual items may or may not be destroyed, according to the semantics of the tree's container. For bounded forms, individual items are not destroyed.

```
virtual Arbitrary_Tree<Item>& set_item(Item&);
```

If the tree is null, throw the exception `Is_Null`. Otherwise, set the item of the associated concrete node.

```
virtual Arbitrary_Tree<Item>& swap_child(unsigned child,
                                         Arbitrary_Tree<Item>&);
```

If the tree is null or has no children, or if the given tree is null, throw the exception Is_Null. If the given tree is null, or does not represent the root of a tree, throw the exception Not_Root. If the given child is zero or is larger than the arity of the tree, throw the exception Range_Error. Otherwise, set the child of the tree (which may not be null) to denote the given tree (which may not be null), and set the given tree to the original child of the tree. The parent of the new child of the tree is set to be the tree itself. The parent of the new root of the given tree is set to be null.

```
virtual Arbitrary_Tree<Item>& child(unsigned child);
```

If the tree is null, throw the exception Is_Null. If the given child is zero or larger than the arity of the tree, throw the exception Range_Error. Otherwise, set the tree to now denote the given child (which may not be null), and reclaim the nodes associated with any unreachable items (which may include siblings). The parent of the tree is set to be null. For unbounded forms, individual items may or may not be destroyed, according to the semantics of the tree's container. For bounded forms, individual items are not destroyed.

```
virtual Arbitrary_Tree<Item>& parent();
```

If the tree is null, throw the exception Is_Null. Otherwise, set the list to now denote its parent (which may be null), and reclaim the nodes associated with any unreachable items. For unbounded forms, individual items may or may not be destroyed, according to the semantics of the tree's container. For bounded forms, individual items are not destroyed.

```
virtual int is_null() const;
```

Return 1 if and only if the tree does not denote any concrete node.

```
virtual int is_shared() const;
```

Return 1 if and only if the concrete node has an alias.

```
virtual Item& item() const;
```

If the tree is null, throw the exception Is_Null. Otherwise, return a reference to the item of the designated concrete node.

```
virtual unsigned arity() const;
```

If the tree is null, throw the exception Is_Null. Otherwise, return the number of direct children in the tree.

STRUCTURES CLASS STRATEGY

EXCEPTIONS

Is_Null —thrown by `insert_child`, `append_child`, and `remove_child` if the tree or given tree is null.

—thrown by `swap_child`, if the tree is null or has no children, or if the given tree is null.

—thrown by `set_item`, `child`, `parent`, `item`, and `arity` if the tree is null.

Not_Root —thrown by `insert_child`, `append_child`, `remove_child`, and `swap_child` if the given tree is not null, but does not represent the root of a tree.

Overflow —thrown by any bounded form member function when the static limits of the object are exceeded.

Range_Error —thrown by `insert_child` if the tree has no children and `before` is zero, or if `before` is larger than the last numbered child.

—thrown by `append_child` if the tree has no children and `after` is non-zero, or if `after` is larger than the last numbered child.

thrown by `remove_child`, `swap_child`, and `child` if the child number is zero or is larger than the arity of the tree.

Storage_Error —thrown by any unbounded form member function when no more storage can be allocated.

OPTIONS

Arbitrary trees are polylithic structures and so must be used cautiously in the presence of multiple threads of control. For this reason, we provide only the representation forms of arbitrary trees:

- Arbitrary_Tree
- Unbounded_Arbitrary_Tree
- Bounded_Arbitrary_Tree

We do not support the usual iterators, because trees already provide the member functions necessary for performing arbitrary traversals.

FILES

In the arbitrary_trees class category:

```
atree     Arbitrary_Tree
atree_u   Unbounded_Arbitrary_Tree
atree_b   Bounded_Arbitrary_Tree
```

SEE ALSO

Node (especially Shared_Tree_Node)

Heap (especially Shared_Bounded_Tree_Node_Heap)

BINARY_TREE

NAME

Binary_Tree—A rooted collection of nodes and arcs, where each node has two children; may not contain cycles or cross-references; structural sharing is permitted.

SYNOPSIS

```
enum Child {LEFT, RIGHT};

template<class Item>
class Binary_Tree {
public:

  Binary_Tree();
  Binary_Tree(Binary_Tree<Item>&);
  virtual ~Binary_Tree();

  virtual Binary_Tree<Item>& operator=(Binary_Tree<Item>&);
  virtual int operator==(Binary_Tree<Item>&) const;
  virtual int operator!=(Binary_Tree<Item>&) const;

  virtual Binary_Tree<Item>& clear();
  virtual Binary_Tree<Item>& construct(Item&, Child child);
  virtual Binary_Tree<Item>& set_item(Item&);
  virtual Binary_Tree<Item>& swap_child(Child child,
                                        Binary_Tree<Item>&);
  virtual Binary_Tree<Item>& child(Child child);
  virtual Binary_Tree<Item>& left_child();
  virtual Binary_Tree<Item>& right_child();
```

Structures Class Strategy

```
    virtual Binary_Tree<Item>& parent();

    virtual int is_null() const;
    virtual int is_shared() const;
    virtual Item& item() const;

};
```

DESCRIPTION

A binary tree denotes a rooted collection of nodes and unidirectional arcs, where each node has two children, named the left and right child, respectively. A tree may not contain cycles or cross-references. Trees are polylithic structures; hence, the semantics of copying, assignment, and equality involve structural sharing. Care must be taken in manipulating the same tree named by more than one alias.

This abstraction has been carefully constructed to eliminate all storage leaks, except in the case of intentional abuses. When a tree is manipulated, all items that become unreachable are automatically reclaimed. Furthermore, this design protects against dangling references: the node associated with an item is never reclaimed if an alias to it exists.

Unreachable items are those that belong to a tree or a subtree whose root is not designated by any alias. For example, consider the tree (A (B C (D E))), with the root of the tree designated by T1. T1 initially points to the root of the list, at item A. Invoking the member function right_child on T1 now causes T1 to point to item C. Because A is now considered unreachable, the node associated with item A is reclaimed; the parent of C is now null. Additionally, the sibling subtree rooted at B is also now unreachable and so is reclaimed (along with its children, and recursively so). Similarly, consider the same tree, with the root of the tree designated by both T1 and T2. Both T1 and T2 are aliases that initially point to the root of the tree at item A. Invoking the member function right_child on T1 now causes T1 to point to item C; T2 is unaffected. No nodes are reclaimed, because every element of the tree is still reachable. Suppose we now invoke the member function clear on T2. The semantics of this operation are such that only unreachable items are reclaimed. Thus, the node associated with item A is reclaimed, because it is no longer reachable; additionally, the sibling B (and recursively so, its children) is reclaimed, because it also is now unreachable; the subtree denoted by T1 is unaffected. T2 is now null, and the parent of C is now null.

It is possible, but not generally desirable, to produce multiheaded trees. In such cases, the parent of the item at the neck of a multiheaded tree points to the most recently attached head.

The class `Binary_Tree` is defined independently of the arbitrary tree. Instances of the class `Binary_Tree` are aliases of concrete nodes, but are themselves not the concrete nodes. For this reason, the semantics of `Binary_Tree` involve structural sharing.

```
template<class Item>
```

The template item denotes the universe from which the tree draws its items. The class `Item` may be either a primitive type or a user-defined class. If the latter, the class must provide a default constructor, copy constructor, assignment operator, and equality operator.

The template signature of the unbounded form requires a class `Container`, which must be a kind of `Shared_Tree_Node`. The template signature of the bounded form requires an unsigned integer `Size`, representing the static size of all instances of the class. Additionally, the template signature of the guarded form requires a class `Guard` (such as the class `Semaphore`), and the template signature of the synchronized form requires a class `Monitor` (such as a kind of `Read_Write_Monitor`).

The representation of the bounded form of `Binary_Tree` includes the static declaration of a bounded heap, from which all objects of this instantiation draw their storage. A client must provide a definition of this bounded heap, which must be a kind of `Shared_Bounded_Tree_Node_Heap`.

```
enum Child {LEFT, RIGHT};
```

Child is used by the member functions `construct`, `swap_child`, and `child` to specify a particular subtree to apply to the operation.

```
Binary_Tree();
```

Construct a null tree.

```
Binary_Tree(Binary_Tree<Item>&);
```

If the given tree is null, construct a null tree. Otherwise, construct a tree so that it structurally shares the concrete node denoted by the given tree.

```
virtual ~Binary_Tree();
```

Destroy the tree. The concrete node (if not null) is no longer structurally shared by this alias, and the nodes associated with any unreachable items are reclaimed. For unbounded forms, individual items may or may not be destroyed, according to the semantics of the tree's container. For bounded forms, individual items are not destroyed; such items are only destroyed when the associated bounded heap is destroyed, typically when its definition is no longer in scope.

```
virtual Binary_Tree<Item>& operator=(Binary_Tree<Item>&);
```

Clear the tree. If the given tree is not null, set the state of the tree so that it structurally shares the concrete node denoted by given tree.

`virtual int operator==(Binary_Tree<Item>&) const;`

Return 1 if and only if both trees are null or are an alias to the same concrete node.

`virtual int operator!=(Binary_Tree<Item>&) const;`

Return the logical negation of `operator==`.

`virtual Binary_Tree<Item>& clear();`

If the tree is not null, remove this alias to the concrete node, make the tree null, and reclaim the nodes associated with any unreachable items. For unbounded forms, individual items may or may not be destroyed, according to the semantics of the tree's container. For bounded forms, individual items are not destroyed.

`virtual Binary_Tree<Item>& construct(Item&, Child child);`

Create a new concrete node, whose designated child is set to be the original concrete node designated by the tree (which may be null). If this child is not null, set its parent to be the newly created concrete node. Set the tree to designate this new concrete node.

`virtual Binary_Tree<Item>& set_item(Item&);`

If the tree is null, throw the exception `Is_Null`. Otherwise, set the item of the associated concrete node.

`virtual Binary_Tree<Item>& swap_child(Child child,`
`                                     Binary_Tree<Item>&);`

If the tree is null, throw the exception `Is_Null`. If the given tree does not represent the root of a tree, throw the exception `Not_Root`. Otherwise, set the child of the tree (which may be null) to denote the given tree (which may be null), and set the given tree to the original child of the tree. If not null, the parent of the new child of the tree is set to be the tree itself. If not null, the parent of the new root of the given tree is set to be null.

`virtual Binary_Tree<Item>& child(Child child);`

If the tree is null, throw the exception `Is_Null`. Otherwise, set the tree to now denote the given child (which may be null), and reclaim the nodes associated with any unreachable items (which may include siblings). The parent of the tree is set to be null. For unbounded forms, individual items may or may not be destroyed, according to the semantics of the tree's container. For bounded forms, individual items are not destroyed.

`virtual Binary_Tree<Item>& left_child();`

Invoke the member function child(LEFT).

`virtual Binary_Tree<Item>& right_child();`

Invoke the member function child(RIGHT).

`virtual Binary_Tree<Item>& parent();`

If the tree is null, throw the exception Is_Null. Otherwise, set the list to now denote its parent (which may be null), and reclaim the nodes associated with any unreachable items. For unbounded forms, individual items may or may not be destroyed, according to the semantics of the tree's container. For bounded forms, individual items are not destroyed.

`virtual int is_null() const;`

Return 1 if and only if the tree does not denote any concrete node.

`virtual int is_shared() const;`

Return 1 if and only if the concrete node has an alias.

`virtual Item& item() const;`

If the tree is null, throw the exception Is_Null. Otherwise, return a reference to the item of the designated concrete node.

EXCEPTIONS

Is_Null	—thrown by set_item, swap_child, child, parent, and item if the tree is null.
Not_Root	—thrown by swap_child if the given tree is not null, but does not represent the root of a tree.
Overflow	—thrown by any bounded form member function when the static limits of the object are exceeded.
Storage_Error	—thrown by any unbounded form member function when no more storage can be allocated.

OPTIONS

Binary trees are polylithic structures and so must be used cautiously in the presence of multiple threads of control. For this reason, we provide only the representation forms of arbitrary trees:

- Binary_Tree
- Unbounded_Binary_Tree
- Bounded_Binary_Tree

We do not support the usual iterators, because trees already provide the member functions necessary for performing arbitrary traversals.

FILES

In the binary_trees class category:

```
btree     Binary_Tree
btree_u   Unbounded_Binary_Tree
btree_b   Bounded_Binary_Tree
```

See Also

    Node (especially Shared_Tree_Node)

    Heap (especially Shared_Bounded_Tree_Node_Heap)

Tools Class Category

Introduction

In the context of this library, a tool represents an agent responsible for some algorithmic abstraction. The C++ Booch Components provide classes for many domain-independent tools:

- Filter

    Input_Filter

    Lookahead_Input_Filter

    Output_Filter

    Lookbehind_Output_Filter

    Process_Filter

    Lookbehind_Process_Filter

C++ Programming PowerPack

- Pattern Matching

    Simple_Pattern_Match

    KMP_Pattern_Match

    BM_Pattern_Match

    Regular_Expression_Pattern_Match

- Searching

    Graph_Search

    Sequential_List_Search

    Ordered_Sequential_List_Search

    Arbitrary_Tree_Search

    Binary_Tree_Search

    Sequential_Search

    Ordered_Sequential_Search

    Binary_Search

- Sorting

    Graph_Sort

    Straight_Insertion_Sort

    Binary_Insertion_Sort

    Shell_Sort

    Bubble_Sort

    Shaker_Sort

    Quick_Sort

    Radix_Sort

    Straight_Selection_Sort

    Heap_Sort

- Utility

    Character_Utilities

    Float_Utilities

Integer_Utilities

String_Utilities

This section documents each of these tool classes, in the form of UNIX man pages.

INPUT_FILTER

NAME

Input_Filter—An agent that operates upon an input stream of data.

SYNOPSIS

```
template<class Item, class Source>
class Input_Filter {
public:

  Input_Filter();
  Input_Filter(Source& source, Item null_item);
  virtual ~Input_Filter();

  virtual Item get();
  virtual Input_Filter<Item, Source>& set_source(Source&);
  virtual Input_Filter<Item, Source>& set_null_item(Item&);

  virtual int is_done() const;

};
```

DESCRIPTION

An input filter denotes an agent that operates upon an input stream of data. The association between an input filter and its stream must be set at least once (during construction or via the member function set_source), but may be reset at any time. Similarly, the designation of a null item must be set at least once (during construction or via the member function set_null_item), but may be reset at any time.

`template<class Item, class Source>`

The template item denotes the universe upon which the input filter operates. The class Item may be either a primitive type or a user-defined class. If the latter, the class must provide a default constructor, copy constructor, and assignment operator. One such item is designated as the null item, which is returned by `get` when the input stream is empty. The class `Source` must be a pointer type whose designated class is a stream providing the functions `eof` (which returns 1 when the input stream is empty) and `get` (which returns the next item in the input stream).

```
Input_Filter();
```

Construct an input filter; its association with a particular input stream is left undefined, as is the definition of its null item.

```
Input_Filter(Source& source, Item null_item);
```

Construct an input filter, using the given input stream and definition of the null item.

```
virtual ~Input_Filter();
```

Destroy the input filter.

```
virtual Item get();
```

If the input stream is empty, return the null item. Otherwise, return the next item in the stream.

```
virtual Input_Filter<Item, Source>& set_source(Source&);
```

Set the association with the given input stream. This association may be reset at any time.

```
virtual Input_Filter<Item, Source>& set_null_item(Item&);
```

Set the definition of the null item. This definition may be reset at any time.

```
virtual int is_done() const;
```

Return 1 if and only if the input stream is empty.

EXCEPTIONS

No exceptions are raised by any member function. However, unpredictable behavior will result if the associated input stream is never set, or if the meaning of the null item is left undefined.

OPTIONS

In addition to the simple input filter, there is one subclass that provides a variation on the theme:

```
Lookahead_Input_Filter
```

With the `Lookahead_Input_Filter`, it is possible to look ahead in the input stream, up to some fixed number of items. This size is established at the time of template instantiation, via the unsigned integer template argument `Size`. The distance from the current position in the stream is numbered from 1 (the next item) to the value of `Size`. `Lookahead_Input_Filter` is a direct subclass of `Input_Filter` and adds the following operation:

```
virtual Item lookahead(unsigned distance);
```

If the given distance is zero or greater than `Size`, throw the exception `Range_Error`. Otherwise, return the item that is the given distance ahead in the input stream.

FILES

In the filters class category

```
filter_i  Input_Filter
    Lookahead_Input_Filter
```

OUTPUT_FILTER

NAME

`Output_Filter`—An agent that operates upon an output stream of data.

SYNOPSIS

```
emplate<class Item, class Destination>
class Output_Filter {
public:

  Output_Filter();
  Output_Filter(Destination&);
  virtual ~Output_Filter();

  virtual Output_Filter<Item, Destination>& put(Item);
  virtual Output_Filter<Item, Destination>&
    set_destination(Destination&);

};
```

DESCRIPTION

An output filter denotes an agent that operates upon an output stream of data. The association between an output filter and its stream must be set at least once (during construction or via the member function set_destination), but may be reset at any time.

```
template<class Item, class Destination>
```

The template item denotes the universe upon which the output filter operates. The class Item may be either a primitive type or a user-defined class. If the latter, the class must provide a default constructor, copy constructor, and assignment operator. The class Destination must be a pointer type whose designated class is a stream providing the function put (which puts the next item in the output stream).

```
Output_Filter();
```

Construct an output filter; its association with a particular output stream is left undefined.

```
Output_Filter(Destination&);
```

Construct an output filter, using the given output stream.

```
virtual ~Output_Filter();
```

Destroy the process filter.

```
virtual Output_Filter<Item, Destination>& put(Item);
```

Put the next item in the stream.

```
virtual Output_Filter<Item, Destination>&
  set_destination(Destination&);
```

Set the association with the given output stream. This association may be reset at any time.

EXCEPTIONS

No exceptions are raised by any member function. However, unpredictable behavior will result if the associated output stream is never set.

OPTIONS

In addition to the simple output filter, there is one subclass that provides a variation on the theme:

```
Lookbehind_Output_Filter
```

The `Lookbehind_Output_Filter` remembers the last several items placed on the output stream; it is possible to look behind in the output stream, up to some fixed number of items. This size is established at the time of template instantiation, via the unsigned integer template argument `Size`. The distance from the current position in the stream is numbered from 1 (the most recently placed item) to the value of `Size`. `Lookbehind_Output_Filter` is a direct subclass of `Output_Filter` and adds the following operation:

```
virtual Item lookbehind(unsigned distance);
```

If the given distance is zero or greater than `Size`, throw the exception `Range_Error`. Otherwise, return the item that is the given distance behind in the output stream.

FILES

In the filters class category

```
filter_o  Output_Filter
          Lookbehind_Output_Filter
```

PROCESS_FILTER

NAME

`Process_Filter`—An agent that transforms a stream of data.

SYNOPSIS

```
template<class Item_In, class Item_Out>
class Process_Filter {
public:

  Process_Filter();
  Process_Filter(Item_Out (*transform)(Item_In));
  virtual ~Process_Filter();

  virtual Item_Out transform(Item_In);
  virtual Process_Filter<Item_In, Item_Out>&
    set_transformation(Item_Out (*transform)(Item_In));

};
```

DESCRIPTION

A process filter denotes an agent that transforms a stream of data, by applying a function to items as they pass through.

```
template<class Item_In, class Item_Out>
```

The template items denote the universe upon which the process filter operates. `Item_In` represents the class of items input to the filter (upstream of transformation), and `Item_Out` represents the class of items output from the filter (downstream from transformation); these classes may be the same, although more commonly they are different. The classes `Item_In` and `Item_Out` may be either a primitive type or a user-defined class. If the latter, the class must provide a default constructor, copy constructor, and assignment operator.

```
Process_Filter();
```

Construct a process filter; its transformation function is left undefined.

```
Process_Filter(Item_Out (*transform)(Item_In));
```

Construct a process filter, using the transformation function.

```
virtual ~Process_Filter();
```

Destroy the process filter.

```
virtual Item_Out transform(Item_In);
```

Transform the given item.

```
virtual Process_Filter<Item_In, Item_Out>&
  set_transformation(Item_Out (*transform)(Item_In));
```

Set the transformation function. This function may be reset at any time.

EXCEPTIONS

No exceptions are raised by any member function. However, unpredictable behavior will result if the transformation function is never set.

OPTIONS

In addition to the simple process filter, there is one subclass that provides a variation on the theme:

```
Lookbehind_Process_Filter
```

The `Lookbehind_Process_Filter` remembers the last several items that have been transformed; it is possible to look behind in the process stream, up to some fixed number of items. This size is established at the time of template instantiation, via the unsigned integer template argument `Size`. The distance from the current position in the stream is numbered from 1 (the most recently transformed item) to the value of `Size`. `Lookbehind_Process_Filter` is a direct subclass of `Process_Filter` and adds the following operation:

```
virtual Item_In lookbehind(unsigned distance);
```

If the given distance is zero or greater than `Size`, throw the exception `Range_Error`. Otherwise, return the item that is the given distance behind in the process stream.

FILES

In the filters class category

```
filter_p  Process_Filter
          Lookbehind_Process_Filter
```

PATTERN_MATCH

NAME

`Pattern_Match`—An agent that searches vectors for a match against a sequence of items.

SYNOPSIS

```
template<class Item, class Sequence>
class Pattern_Match {
public:

  Pattern_Match();
  Pattern_Match(int (*is_equal)(Item& x, Item& y));
  virtual ~Pattern_Match();

  virtual unsigned match(Sequence& target, Sequence& pattern);
  virtual Pattern_Match<Item, Sequence>&
    set_is_equal_function(int (*is_equal)(Item& x, Item& y));

};
```

DESCRIPTION

A pattern matching agent searches vectors for a match against a sequence of items.

`template<class Item, class Sequence>`

The template items denote the universe upon which the pattern matching agent operates. The class `Item` may be either a primitive type or a user-defined class. If the latter, the class must provide a default constructor, copy constructor, assignment operator, and (indirectly) an equality operator. The class `Sequence` denotes an ordered collection of items and is used as the target of the search, as well as the pattern used for the search. `Sequence` must provide the function `operator[]`, whose index starts at 1.

`Pattern_Match();`

Construct a pattern matching agent; its equality function is left undefined.

`Pattern_Match(int (*is_equal)(Item& x, Item& y));`

Construct a pattern matching agent, using the equality function. This function may operate upon the item or, in the case of pointer items, upon the item designated by the pointer.

`virtual ~Pattern_Match();`

Destroy the pattern matching agent.

`virtual unsigned match(Sequence& target, Sequence& pattern);`

If the pattern is null, throw the exception `Illegal_Pattern`. Otherwise, if the pattern is not found in the target, return zero. Otherwise, return the index in the target where the match is found.

```
virtual Pattern_Match<Item, Sequence>&
  set_is_equal_function(int (*is_equal)(Item& x, Item& y));
```

Set the transformation function. This function may be reset at any time.

EXCEPTIONS

Unpredictable behavior will result if the equality function is never set.

`Illegal_Pattern` —thrown by match if the pattern is null.
`Storage_Error` —thrown by any member function when no more storage can be allocated.

OPTIONS

The class `Pattern_Match` is an abstract base class. There are three concrete classes that provide literal pattern matching:

- `Simple_Pattern_Match`
- `KMP_Pattern_Match`
- `BM_Pattern_Match`

Additionally, there is one concrete class that provides regular expression pattern matching:

`Regular_Expression_Pattern_Match`

The three literal pattern matching classes have the same class signature as the abstract base class `Pattern_Match`. However, each has slightly different time and space characteristics.

In the worst case, the `Simple_Pattern_Match` executes on the order O(pn), where p is the length of the pattern and n is the number of items being searched. Objects of this class consume no additional storage during matching.

The `KMP_Pattern_Match` uses the pattern matching algorithm developed by Knuth, Morris, and Pratt. On the average, the `KMP_Pattern_Match` is much faster, executing on the order of O(p + n). Objects of this class consume p additional storage during matching. Additionally, the search requires no backup, meaning that the index into the target sequence is always monotonically increasing.

The `BM_Pattern_Match` uses the pattern matching algorithm developed by Boyer and Moore. On the average, the performance of the `BM_Pattern_Match` is sublinear, meaning that the number of comparisons is on the order of c(p + n), where c < 1 and is inversely proportional to p. Except for extremely contrived cases, in the worst case, the performance of the Boyer-Moore algorithm is linear. Objects of this class consume p additional storage during matching. Additionally, the search requires backup in the sequence, meaning that this class is not suitable for consumable input streams.

The regular expression pattern matching class permits searching for limited regular expressions. Its patterns may include literals, arbitrary item matches (any item), negated matches (not item), closures (closure item), and sets of items (delimited by start and stop items). These special regular expression items are known as metaitems. A pattern may include a metaitem as a literal by preceding it with an escape item. This class has the same class signature as the abstract base class `Pattern_Match`, except that it adds the following operations:

```
Regular_Expression_Pattern_Match(Item& any_item, Item& escape_item,
Item& not_item, Item& closure_item,
Item& start, Item& stop);
```

Construct a pattern matching agent, using the given definition of regular expression metaitems; its equality function is left undefined.

```
Regular_Expression_Pattern_Match(int (*is_equal)(Item& x, Item& y),
Item& any_item, Item& escape_item,
Item& not_item, Item& closure_item,
Item& start, Item& stop);
```

Construct a pattern matching agent, using the given equality function and definition of regular expression metaitems; its equality function is left undefined.

```
virtual Pattern_Match<Item, Sequence>& set_metaitems
  (Item& any_item, Item& escape_item, Item& not_item,
   Item& closure_item, Item& start, Item& stop);
```

Set the regular expression metaitems; these items may be reset at any time.

Unpredictable behavior will result if the metaitems are never set. The member function match will throw the exception `Illegal_Pattern` if the regular expression is not well formed.

FILES

In the pattern matching class category

```
match_v   Simple_Pattern_Match
          KMP_Pattern_Match
          BM_Pattern_Match
          Regular_Expression_Pattern_Match
```

GRAPH_SEARCH

NAME

`Graph_Search`—An agent that traverses graphs in either a depth-first or a breadth-first manner.

SYNOPSIS

```
template<class Vertex, class Arc, class Graph,
         class Imp_Vertex_Iter, class Imp_Set,
         class Imp_Stack, class Imp_Queue>
class Graph_Search {
public:

  Graph_Search();
  virtual ~Graph_Search();

  virtual int
    depth(Graph& target, Vertex& start, int (*process)(Vertex&));
  virtual int
    breadth(Graph& target, Vertex& start, int (*process)(Vertex&));

};
```

DESCRIPTION

A graph search agent traverses graphs in either a depth-first or a breadth-first manner.

```
template<class Vertex, class Arc, class Graph,
            class Imp_Vertex_Iter, class Imp_Set,
            class Imp_Stack, class Imp_Queue>
```

The classes `Vertex`, `Arc`, and `Graph` denote the elements of a graph. The classes `Vertex` and `Arc` must provide a default constructor, copy constructor, assignment operator, and equality operator. The class `Graph` must provide the member function `is_member`. The vertex iterator, set, stack, and queue are implementation artifacts and exist to permit the client to determine the time/space characteristics of the tool. The class `Imp_Vertex_Iter` must provide a constructor and the member functions `reset`, `get_arc`, and `is_done`. The class `Imp_Set` must provide a default constructor and the member functions `add` and `is_member`. The class `Imp_Stack` must provide a default constructor and the member functions `push`, `pop`, and `is_empty`. The class `Imp_Queue` must provide a default constructor and the member functions `add`, `pop`, and `is_empty`.

```
Graph_Search();
```

Construct a graph search agent.

```
virtual ~Graph_Search();
```

Destroy the graph search agent.

```
virtual int
  depth(Graph& target, Vertex& start, int (*process)(Vertex&));
```

If the given vertex is null, throw the exception `Is_Null`; if the given vertex is not a member of the graph, throw the exception `Container_Error`. Otherwise, traverse the graph starting at the given vertex, in a depth-first fashion. For each vertex encountered, apply the given process. Return 0 if and only if the function was terminated before the traversal was completed.

```
virtual int
  breadth(Graph& target, Vertex& start, int (*process)(Vertex&));
```

If the given vertex is null, throw the exception `Is_Null`; if the given vertex is not a member of the graph, throw the exception `Container_Error`. Otherwise, traverse the graph starting at the given vertex, in a breadth-first fashion. For each vertex encountered, apply the given process. Return 0 if and only if the function was terminated before the traversal was completed.

EXCEPTIONS

`Container_Error`	—thrown by depth and breadth if the given vertex is not a member of the graph.
`Is_Null`	—thrown by depth and breadth if the given vertex is null.
`Storage_Error`	—thrown by any member function when no more storage can be allocated.

OPTIONS

None

FILES

In the searching class category

`search_g` `Graph_Search`

SEE ALSO

`Directed_Graph`

`Undirected_Graph`

List_Search

NAME

List_Search—An agent that searches lists for the first occurrence of a given item.

SYNOPSIS

```
template<class Item, class List>
class List_Search {
public:

  List_Search();
  List_Search(int (*is_equal)(Item& x, Item& y));
  virtual ~List_Search();

  virtual List location(List& target, Item& key);
  virtual List_Search<Item, List>&
    set_is_equal_function(int (*is_equal)(Item& x, Item& y));

};
```

DESCRIPTION

A list search agent searches lists for the first occurrence of a given item.

`template<class Item, class List>`

The template item denotes the universe from which the list draws its items. The class `Item` may be either a primitive type or a user-defined class. If the latter, the class must provide (indirectly) an equality function. The class `List` must provide the member functions `clear`, `tail`, `is_null`, and `head`.

`List_Search();`

Construct a list search agent; its equality function is left undefined.

`List_Search(int (*is_equal)(Item& x, Item& y));`

Construct a list search agent using the given equality function. This function may operate upon the item, or in the case of pointer items, upon the item designated by the pointer.

`virtual ~List_Search();`

Destroy the list search agent.

`virtual List location(List& target, Item& key);`

Search the list for the given item. If the item is not found in the target list, return a null list. Otherwise, return a list designating the head of the sublist where the item is found.

```
virtual List_Search<Item, List>&
  set_is_equal_function(int (*is_equal)(Item& x, Item& y));
```

Set the equality function. This function may be reset at any time.

EXCEPTIONS

No exceptions are raised by any member function. However, unpredictable behavior will result if the equality function is never set.

OPTIONS

The class List_Search is an abstract base class. There are two concrete classes that provide list searching:

- Sequential_List_Search
- Ordered_Sequential_List_Search

The two concrete classes have the same class signature as the abstract base class List_Search. However, each has slightly different time and space characteristics.

The Sequential_List_Search is simple, yet inefficient. In the worst case, a search executes on the order of O(n). Objects of this class make no assumptions about the order of items in the list.

The Ordered_Sequential_List_Search is faster (it executes on the order of O(n/2)), but assumes that items in the list are ordered. This class adds the following operations:

```
Ordered_Sequential_List_Search(int (*is_equal)(Item& x, Item& y),
                               int (*is_less_than)(Item& x, Item& y));
```

Construct a list search agent using the given equality function and less-than function. These functions may operate upon the item or, in the case of pointer items, upon the item designated by the pointer.

```
virtual List_Search<Item, List>&
  set_is_less_than_function(int (*is_less_than)(Item& x, Item& y));
```

Set the is-less-than function. This function may be reset at any time.

FILES

In the searching class category

```
search_l  List_Search
     Sequential_List_Search
     Ordered_Sequential_List_Search
```

SEE ALSO

> Double_List
>
> Single_List

EXAMPLE

In the tests directory, see searcht and its associated source file.

TREE_SEARCH

NAME

Tree_Search—An agent that traverses trees in a pre-order, in-order, or post-order manner.

SYNOPSIS

```
template<class Tree>
class Arbitrary_Tree_Search {
public:

  Arbitrary_Tree_Search();
  virtual ~Arbitrary_Tree_Search();

  virtual int pre_order(Tree& target, int (*process)(Tree&));
  virtual int post_order(Tree& target, int (*process)(Tree&));

};

template<class Tree>
class Binary_Tree_Search {
public:

  Binary_Tree_Search();
  virtual ~Binary_Tree_Search();

  virtual int pre_order(Tree& target, int (*process)(Tree&));
```

```
virtual int in_order(Tree& target, int (*process)(Tree&));
virtual int post_order(Tree& target, int (*process)(Tree&));
```

`};`

DESCRIPTION

A tree search agent traverses trees in a pre-order, in-order, or post-order manner. In-order traversal is not applicable to arbitrary trees, because they are not guaranteed to be symmetrical.

`template<class Tree>`

The class Tree denotes the elements of a tree. This class must provide a default constructor, copy constructor, assignment operator, and equality operator. For the binary tree, this class must also provide the functions left_child, right_child, and is_null. For the arbitrary tree, this class must provide the functions child, is_null, and arity.

```
Arbitrary_Tree_Search();
Binary_Tree_Search();
```

Construct a tree search agent.

```
virtual ~Arbitrary_Tree_Search();
virtual ~Binary_Tree_Search();
```

Destroy the tree search agent.

`virtual int pre_order(Tree& target, int (*process)(Tree&));`

Traverse the tree starting at the given node, in a pre-order fashion (first the node itself, then its children, and recursively so). Return 0 if and only if the function was terminated before the traversal was completed.

`virtual int in_order(Tree& target, int (*process)(Tree&));`

Applicable only to binary trees. Traverse the tree starting at the given node, in an in-order fashion (first the left child, then the node itself, then the right child, and recursively so). Return 0 if and only if the function was terminated before the traversal was completed.

`virtual int post_order(Tree& target, int (*process)(Tree&));`

Traverse the tree starting at the given node, in a post-order fashion (first the children, then the node itself, and recursively so). Return 0 if and only if the function was terminated before the traversal was completed.

EXCEPTIONS

No exceptions are raised by any member function.

OPTIONS

None

FILES

In the searching class category:

```
search_t  Arbitrary_Tree_Search
    Binary_Tree_Search
```

SEE ALSO

```
    Arbitrary_Tree

    Binary_Tree
```

SEARCH

NAME

Search—An agent that searches vectors for the first occurrence of a given item.

SYNOPSIS

```
template<class Item, class Sequence>
class Search {
public:

  Search();
  Search(int (*is_equal)(Item& x, Item& y));
  virtual ~Search();

  virtual unsigned location(Sequence& target, Item& key);
  virtual Search<Item, Sequence>&
    set_is_equal_function(int (*is_equal)(Item& x, Item& y));

};
```

DESCRIPTION

A vector search agent searches vectors for the first occurrence of a given item.

```
template<class Item, class Sequence>
```

The template item denotes the universe from which the search agent draws its items. The class Item may be either a primitive type or a user-defined class. If the latter, the class must provide (indirectly) an equality function. The class Sequence denotes an ordered collection of items and is used as the target of the search. Sequence must provide the function operator[], whose index starts at 1.

```
Search();
```

Construct a vector search agent; its equality function is left undefined.

```
Search(int (*is_equal)(Item& x, Item& y));
```

Construct a vector search agent using the given equality function. This function may operate upon the item, or in the case of pointer items, upon the item designated by the pointer.

```
virtual ~Search();
```

Destroy the vector search agent.

```
virtual unsigned location(Sequence& target, Item& key);
```

Search the vector for the given item. If the item is not found in the target list, return zero. Otherwise, return the index in the target where the item is found.

```
virtual Search<Item, Sequence>&
  set_is_equal_function(int (*is_equal)(Item& x, Item& y));
```

Set the equality function. This function may be reset at any time.

EXCEPTIONS

No exceptions are raised by any member function. However, unpredictable behavior will result if the equality function is never set.

OPTIONS

The class Search is an abstract base class. There are three concrete classes that provide vector searching:

- Sequential_Search
- Ordered_Sequential_Search
- Binary_Search

The three concrete classes have the same class signature as the abstract base class `Search`. However, each has slightly different time and space characteristics.

The `Sequential_Search` is simple, yet inefficient. In the worst case, a search executes on the order of O(n). Objects of this class make no assumptions about the order of items in the list.

The `Ordered_Sequential_Search` is faster (it executes on the order of O(n/2)), but assumes that items in the vector are ordered. This class adds the following operations:

```
Ordered_Sequential_Search(int (*is_equal)(Item& x, Item& y),
                          int (*is_less_than)(Item& x, Item& y));
```

Construct a vector search agent using the given equality function and less-than function. These functions may operate upon the item, or in the case of pointer items, upon the item designated by the pointer.

```
virtual Search<Item, List>&
   set_is_less_than_function(int (*is_less_than)(Item& x, Item& y));
```

Set the is-less-than function. This function may be reset at any time.

The `Binary_Search` is even faster (it executes on the order of O(log2n)), but assumes that items in the vector are ordered. This class adds the same operations as does `Ordered_Sequential_Search`.

FILES

In the searching class category

```
search_v  Search
     Sequential_Search
     Ordered_Sequential_Search
     Binary_Search
```

GRAPH_SORT

NAME

`Graph_Sort`—An agent that generates a topological sort of a graph.

SYNOPSIS

```
template<class Vertex, class Arc, class Graph,
         class Imp_Vertex_Iter, class Imp_Graph_Iter,
```

```
                 class Imp_Queue>
class Graph_Sort {
public:

  Graph_Sort();
  virtual ~Graph_Sort();

  virtual void sort(Graph& target,
                    int (*process_acyclic)(Vertex&),
                    int (*process_cyclic)(Vertex&),
                    int ignore_self_loops = 1);

};
```

DESCRIPTION

A graph sort agent generates a topological sort of a graph.

```
template<class Vertex, class Arc, class Graph,
         class Imp_Vertex_Iter, class Imp_Graph_Iter,
         class Imp_Queue>
```

The classes Vertex, Arc, and Graph denote the elements of a graph. The classes Vertex and Arc must provide a default constructor, copy constructor, assignment operator, and equality operator. The class Vertex must also provide the member functions clear and number_of_incoming_arcs. The class Graph must provide the member functions is_member and number_of_vertices. The vertex iterator, graph iterator, and queue are implementation artifacts and exist to permit the client to determine the time/space characteristics of the tool. The class Imp_Vertex_Iter must provide a constructor and the member functions reset, get_arc, and is_done. The class Imp_Graph_Iter must provide a constructor and the member functions reset, get_vertex, and is_done. The class Imp_Queue must provide a default constructor and the member functions add, pop, and is_empty.

`Graph_Sort();`

Construct a graph sorting agent.

`virtual ~Graph_Sort();`

Destroy the graph sorting agent.

```
virtual void sort(Graph& target,
                  int (*process_acyclic)(Vertex&),
                  int (*process_cyclic)(Vertex&),
                  int ignore_self_loops = 1);
```

Generate a topological sort of the given graph, applying the given functions to each vertex in order. First, all vertices that are not part of a cycle are visited, and the function `process_acyclic` is applied to each in turn; setting `ignore_self_loops` ignores the dependency a vertex may have upon itself directly. Next, visit all vertices that are part of a cycle, applying the function `process_cyclic` to each in turn. Return 0 if and only if the function was terminated before the sort was completed.

EXCEPTIONS

No exceptions are raised by any member function. However, unpredictable behavior will result if the equality function is never set.

OPTIONS

None

FILES

In the searching class category

sort_g   Graph_Sort

SEE ALSO

> Directed_Graph
>
> Undirected_Graph

EXAMPLE

In the tests directory, see `sortt` and its associated source file.

SORT

NAME

Sort—An agent that sorts vectors in place.

SYNOPSIS

```
template<class Item, class Sequence>
class Sort {
public:

  Sort();
  Sort(int (*is_less_than)(Item& x, Item& y));
```

```
virtual ~Sort();

virtual void sort(Sequence&);
virtual Sort<Item, Sequence>&
  set_is_less_than_function(int (*is_less_than)(Item& x, Item& y));
```
```
};
```

DESCRIPTION

A vector sort agent sorts vectors in place.

`template<class Item, class Sequence>`

The template item denotes the universe from which the sort agent draws its items. The class `Item` may be either a primitive type or a user-defined class. If the latter, the class must provide a default constructor, copy constructor, and assignment operator, plus (indirectly) a less-than function. The class `Sequence` denotes an ordered collection of items and is used as the target of the search. `Sequence` must provide the function `operator[]`, whose index starts at 1.

`Sort();`

Construct a vector sort agent; its less-than function is left undefined.

`Sort(int (*is_less_than)(Item& x, Item& y));`

Construct a vector sort agent using the given less-than function. This function may operate upon the item, or in the case of pointer items, upon the item designated by the pointer.

`virtual ~Sort();`

Destroy the vector sort agent.

`virtual void sort(Sequence&);`

Sort the vector in place. The ordering of items is established by the semantics of the given less-than function.

```
virtual Sort<Item, Sequence>&
  set_is_less_than_function(int (*is_less_than)(Item& x, Item& y));
```

Set the is-less-than function. This function may be reset at any time.

EXCEPTIONS

No exceptions are raised by any member function. However, unpredictable behavior will result if the less-than function is never set.

OPTIONS

The class Sort is an abstract base class. There are nine concrete classes that provide vector searching:

- Straight_Insertion_Sort
- Binary_Insertion_Sort
- Shell_Sort
- Bubble_Sort
- Shaker_Sort
- Quick_Sort
- Radix_Sort
- Straight_Selection_Sort
- Heap_Sort

These nine concrete classes have the same class signature as the abstract base class Search. However, each has slightly different time and space characteristics.

The Straight_Insertion_Sort is a stable sort, requiring an average number of comparisons on the order of $O(n^2)$ and an average number of moves on the order of $O(n^2)$.

The Binary_Insertion_Sort is a stable sort, requiring an average number of comparisons on the order of $O(n \log n)$ and an average number of moves on the order of $O(n^2)$.

The Shell_Sort is an unstable sort, requiring an average number of comparisons on the order of $O(n^{1.25})$ and an average number of moves on the order of $O(n^{1.25})$.

The Bubble_Sort is a stable sort, requiring an average number of comparisons on the order of $O(n^2)$ and an average number of moves on the order of $O(n^2)$.

The Shaker_Sort is a stable sort, requiring an average number of comparisons on the order of $O(n^2)$ and an average number of moves on the order of $O(n^2)$.

The Quick_Sort is an unstable sort, requiring an average number of comparisons on the order of $O(n \log n)$ and an average number of moves on the order of $O(n \log n)$.

The Straight_Selection_Sort is a stable sort, requiring an average number of comparisons on the order of O(n2) and an average number of moves on the order of O(n log n).

The Heap_Sort is an unstable sort, requiring an average number of comparisons on the order of O(n log n) and an average number of moves on the order of O(n log n).

The Radix_Sort is an unstable sort, requiring an average number of comparisons on the order of O(n log n) and an average number of moves on the order of O(n log n). For this class, the client must specify the number of bits in the item at the time of instantiation, via the unsigned integer template argument Byte_Size. This class adds the following operations:

```
Radix_Sort(int (*is_less_than)(Item& x, Item& y),
           int (*bit)(Item&, unsigned position));
```

Construct a vector sort agent using the given less-than function and bit extraction function. These functions may operate upon the item, or in the case of pointer items, upon the item designated by the pointer.

```
virtual Radix_Sort<Item, Sequence>&
  set_bit_function(int (*bit)(Item& x, Item& y));
```

Set the bit function. This function may be reset at any time.

FILES

In the sorting class category

```
sort_v    Sort
    Straight_Insertion_Sort
    Binary_Insertion_Sort
    Shell_Sort
    Bubble_Sort
    Shaker_Sort
    Quick_Sort
    Radix_Sort
    Straight_Selection_Sort
    Heap_Sort
```

Character_Utilities

NAME

Character_Utilities—A collection of nonmember functions operating upon characters.

TOOLS CLASS CATEGORY

SYNOPSIS

```
char uppercase(char c);
char lowercase(char c);

int is_alphanumeric(char c);
int is_alphabetic(char c);
int is_ascii(char c);
int is_control(char c);
int is_digit(char c);
int is_hex_digit(char c);
int is_graphic(char c);
int is_lowercase(char c);
int is_uppercase(char c);
int is_printable(char c);
int is_punctuation(char c);
int is_space(char c);

int is_equal(char, char, int case_sensitive = 1);
int is_less_than(char, char, int case_sensitive = 1);
int is_greater_than(char, char, int case_sensitive = 1);
```

DESCRIPTION

Character utilities provide a collection of useful nonmember functions operating upon characters.

`char uppercase(char c);`

If the character is a lowercase alphabetic character, return its uppercase equivalent. Otherwise, do nothing.

`char lowercase(char c);`

If the character is an uppercase alphabetic character, return its lowercase equivalent. Otherwise, do nothing.

`int is_alphanumeric(char c);`

Return 1 if and only if the given character is an alphabetic or numeric character. Otherwise, return 0.

`int is_alphabetic(char c);`

Return 1 if and only if the given character is a letter. Otherwise, return 0.

`int is_ascii(char c);`

Return 1 if and only if the given character is less than octal 0200. Otherwise, return 0.

`int is_control(char c);`

Return 1 if and only if the given character is octal 0177 or less than octal 0040. Otherwise, return 0.

```
int is_digit(char c);
```

Return 1 if and only if the given character is a decimal number (0 - 9). Otherwise, return 0.

```
int is_hex_digit(char c);
```

Return 1 if and only if the given character is a hexadecimal number (0 - 9, A - F, or a - f). Otherwise, return 0.

```
int is_graphic(char c);
```

Return 1 if and only if the given character is octal 0041 - 0176, inclusive. Otherwise, return 0.

```
int is_lowercase(char c);
```

Return 1 if and only if the given character is a lowercase letter. Otherwise, return 0.

```
int is_uppercase(char c);
```

Return 1 if and only if the given character is an uppercase letter. Otherwise, return 0.

```
int is_printable(char c);
```

Return 1 if and only if the given character is octal 0040 - 0176, inclusive. Otherwise, return 0.

```
int is_punctuation(char c);
```

Return 1 if and only if the given character is a punctuation character (that is, not a control or alphanumeric character). Otherwise, return 0.

```
int is_space(char c);
```

Return 1 if and only if the given character is a space character (that is, space, tab, carriage return, new line, vertical tab, or form feed). Otherwise, return 0.

```
int is_equal(char, char, int case_sensitive = 1);
```

Return 1 if and only if the two characters are equal in value; if `case_sensitive` is not set, the same letters with different case are considered equal. Otherwise, return 0.

```
int is_less_than(char, char, int case_sensitive = 1);
```

Return 1 if and only if the first character is smaller in value than the second; if `case_sensitive` is not set, the same letters with different case are considered equal. Otherwise, return 0.

```
int is_greater_than(char, char, int case_sensitive = 1);
```

Return 1 if and only if the first character is greater in value than the second; if case_sensitive is not set, the same letters with different case are considered equal. Otherwise, return 0.

EXCEPTIONS

No exceptions are raised by any member function.

OPTIONS

None

FILES

In the utilities class category

```
u_char      Character_Utilities
```

FLOAT_UTILITIES

NAME

Float_Utilities—A collection of nonmember functions operating upon floating point numbers.

SYNOPSIS

```
int integer_part(float);
float real_part(float);

int floor(float);
int ceiling(float);

float min(float, float);
float min(float[], unsigned count);

float max(float, float);
float max(float[], unsigned count);

int is_positive(float);
int is_natural(float);
```

```
int is_negative(float);
int is_zero(float);

float float_value(const char*, unsigned base = 10);
char* image(const float, unsigned base = 10,
            unsigned significant_digits = 6,
            int leading_sign = 0);
```

DESCRIPTION

Float utilities provide a collection of useful nonmember functions operating upon floating-point numbers.

`int integer_part(float);`

Return the signed integer part of the given floating-point number.

`float real_part(float);`

Return the unsigned fractional part of the given floating-point number.

`int floor(float);`

Return the nearest integer below the given floating-point number.

`int ceiling(float);`

Return the nearest integer above the given floating-point number.

`float min(float, float);`

Return the smallest of the two given floating-point numbers.

`float min(float[], unsigned count);`

Return the smallest of the given array of floating-point numbers; count specifies the number of items in the array.

`float max(float, float);`

Return the largest of the two given floating-point numbers.

`float max(float[], unsigned count);`

Return the largest of the given array of floating-point numbers; count specifies the number of items in the array.

`int is_positive(float);`

Return 1 if and only if the given floating-point number is greater than zero; otherwise, return 0.

`int is_natural(float);`

Return 1 if and only if the given floating point number is greater than one; otherwise, return 0.

```
int is_negative(float);
```

Return 1 if and only if the given floating point number is less than zero; otherwise, return 0.

```
int is_zero(float);
```

Return 1 if and only if the given floating point number is equal to zero; otherwise, return 0.

```
float float_value(const char*, unsigned base = 10);
```

If the given base is less than 2 or greater than 16, throw the exception `Math_Error`. If the given string does not contain a radix point, throw the exception `Lexical_Error`. If the given string contains a character that does not have an equivalent in the given base, throw the exception `Lexical_Error`. Otherwise, return the floating point equivalent of the string.

```
char* image(const float, unsigned base = 10,
            unsigned significant_digits = 6,
            int leading_sign = 0);
```

If the given base is less than 2 or greater than 16, throw the exception `Math_Error`. If the number of significant digits is zero, throw the exception `Math_Error`. Otherwise, return a string representing the floating point number, with the given number of significant digits after the radix point. If `leading_sign` is set, positive numbers are given a sign; otherwise, only negative numbers are signed.

EXCEPTIONS

`Lexical_Error` —thrown by `float_value` if the given string does not represent a well-formed number.

`Math_Error` —thrown by `float_value` and `image` if the given base is not between 2 and 16, inclusive.

—thrown by `image` if the number of significant digits is zero.

OPTIONS

None

FILES

In the utilities class category

u_float   Float_Utilities

INTEGER_UTILITIES

NAME

Integer_Utilities—A collection of nonmember functions operating upon integers.

SYNOPSIS

```
int min(int, int);
int min(int[], unsigned count);

int max(int, int);
int max(int[], unsigned count);

int is_positive(int);
int is_natural(int);
int is_negative(int);
int is_zero(int);
int is_odd(int);
int is_even(int);

int digit_value(const char c, unsigned base);
char digit_image(const int i);
int exponent(unsigned base, unsigned power);

int int_value(const char*, unsigned base = 10);
char* image(const int, unsigned base = 10, int leading_sign = 0);
```

DESCRIPTION

Integer utilities provide a collection of useful nonmember functions operating upon integers.

`int min(int, int);`

   Return the smallest of the two given integers.

`int min(int[], unsigned count);`

Return the smallest of the given array of integers; count specifies the number of items in the array.

```
int max(int, int);
```

Return the largest of the two given integers.

```
int max(int[], unsigned count);
```

Return the largest of the given array of integers; count specifies the number of items in the array.

```
int is_positive(int);
```

Return 1 if and only if the given integer is greater than zero; otherwise, return 0.

```
int is_natural(int);
```

Return 1 if and only if the given integer is greater than one; otherwise, return 0.

```
int is_negative(int);
```

Return 1 if and only if the given integer is less than zero; otherwise, return 0.

```
int is_zero(int);
```

Return 1 if and only if the given integer is equal to zero; otherwise, return 0.

```
int is_odd(int);
```

Return 1 if and only if the given integer is odd (not evenly divisible by 2); otherwise, return 0.

```
int is_even(int);
```

Return 1 if and only if the given integer is even (evenly divisible by 2); otherwise, return 0.

```
int digit_value(const char c, unsigned base);
```

If the given character does not have an equivalent in the given base, throw the exception Lexical_Error. Otherwise, return the integer equivalent of the character. This function assumes that base is in the range 0 - 15, inclusive.

```
char digit_image(const int i);
```

Return the character equivalent of the integer; this function assumes that i is in the range 0 - 15, inclusive.

```
int exponent(unsigned base, unsigned power);
```

Return the value of the base raised to the given power.

```
int int_value(const char*, unsigned base = 10);
```

If the given base is less than 2 or greater than 16, throw the exception `Math_Error`. Otherwise, return the integer equivalent of the string.

```
char* image(const int, unsigned base = 10, int leading_sign = 0);
```

If the given base is less than 2 or greater than 16, throw the exception `Math_Error`. Otherwise, return a string representing the integer. If `leading_sign` is set, positive numbers are given a sign; otherwise, only negative numbers are signed.

EXCEPTIONS

`Lexical_Error` —thrown by `digit_value` if the given character does not represent a well-formed number.

`Math_Error` —thrown by `int_value` and `image` if the given base is not between 2 and 16, inclusive.

OPTIONS

None

FILES

In the utilities class category

u_int   Integer_Utilities

STRING_UTILITIES

NAME

`String_Utilities`—A collection of nonmember functions operating upon null-terminated character strings.

SYNOPSIS

```
enum Elision {LEADING, TRAILING};

void apply_uppercase(char*);
void apply_lowercase(char*);
```

Tools Class Category

```
void apply_capitalize(char*);
void apply_uncapitalize(char*);
void apply_replace(char*, char old, char with,
                   int case_sensitive = 1);

char* uppercase(const char*);
char* lowercase(const char*);
char* capitalize(const char*);
char* uncapitalize(const char*);
char* replace(const char*, char old, char with,
              int case_sensitive = 1);

char* copy(const char*);
char* catenate(const char*, const char*);
char* strip(const char*, char, int case_sensitive = 1);
char* strip_leading(const char*, char, int case_sensitive = 1);
char* strip_trailing(const char*, char, int case_sensitive = 1);
char* center(const char*, unsigned width, char filler = ' ',
             Elision elision = TRAILING, char* ellipses = "...");
char* left_justify(const char*, unsigned width, char filler = ' ',
                   Elision elision = TRAILING,
                   char* ellipses = "...");
char* right_justify(const char*, unsigned width, char filler = ' ',
                    Elision elision = TRAILING,
                    char* ellipses = "...");

unsigned length(const char*);
unsigned count(const char*, char, int case_sensitive = 1);
unsigned count_leading(const char*, char, int case_sensitive = 1);
unsigned count_trailing(const char*, char, int case_sensitive = 1);

int is_alphanumeric(const char*);
int is_alphabetic(const char*);
int is_ascii(const char*);
int is_control(const char*);
int is_digit(const char*);
int is_hex_digit(const char*);
int is_graphic(const char*);
int is_lowercase(const char*);
int is_uppercase(const char*);
int is_printable(const char*);
int is_punctuation(const char*);
int is_space(const char*);

int is_equal(const char*, const char*, int case_sensitive = 1);
int is_less_than(const char*, const char*, int case_sensitive = 1);
int is_greater_than(const char*, const char*, int case_sensitive
                    = 1);
```

DESCRIPTION

String utilities provide a collection of useful nonmember functions operating upon null-terminated character strings.

Functions that return a char* allocate a new string, whose length is sized exactly to the number of characters generated by the function. The client is responsible for allocating these strings.

```
enum Elision {LEADING, TRAILING};
```

Elision is used by certain member functions to denote the direction of elision.

```
void apply_uppercase(char*);
```

In place, convert the string to uppercase.

```
void apply_lowercase(char*);
```

In place, convert the string to lowercase.

```
void apply_capitalize(char*);
```

In place, capitalize the first character of the string.

```
void apply_uncapitalize(char*);
```

In place, uncapitalize the first character of the string.

```
void apply_replace(char*, char old, char with,
                   int case_sensitive = 1);
```

In place, replace all occurrences of the given old character; if case_sensitive is not set, the same letters with different case are considered equal.

```
char* uppercase(const char*);
```

Return a new string, set as the uppercase value of the given string.

```
char* lowercase(const char*);
```

Return a new string, set as the lowercase value of the given string.

```
char* capitalize(const char*);
```

Return a new string, set as the capitalized value of the given string.

```
char* uncapitalize(const char*);
```

Return a new string, set as the uncapitalized value of the given string.

```
char* replace(const char*, char old, char with,
              int case_sensitive = 1);
```

Return a new string, with all occurrences of the given old character replaced; if case_sensitive is not set, the same letters with different case are considered equal.

```
char* copy(const char*);
```

Return a new string, equal in value to the old string.

```
char* catenate(const char*, const char*);
```

Return a new string, equal in value to the catenation of the two given strings.

```
char* strip(const char*, char, int case_sensitive = 1);
```

Return a new string, equal in value to the given string, stripped entirely of the given character; if case_sensitive is not set, the same letters with different case are considered equal.

```
char* strip_leading(const char*, char, int case_sensitive = 1);
```

Return a new string, equal in value to the given string, stripped of the leading given character; if case_sensitive is not set, the same letters with different case are considered equal.

```
char* strip_trailing(const char*, char, int case_sensitive = 1);
```

Return a new string, equal in value to the given string, stripped of the trailing given character; if case_sensitive is not set, the same letters with different case are considered equal.

```
char* center(const char*, unsigned width, char filler = ' ',
             Elision elision = TRAILING, char* ellipses = "...");
```

If the width is smaller than the size of the given string or the ellipses, throw the exception Lexical_Error. Otherwise, return a new string with the given string centered in the width. If needed, the filler character is used to pad the string. If the given string is larger than the width, elision applies in the given direction; elided characters are designated with the ellipses.

```
char* left_justify(const char*, unsigned width, char filler = ' ',
                   Elision elision = TRAILING,
                   char* ellipses = "...");
```

If the width is smaller than the size of the given string or the ellipses, throw the exception Lexical_Error. Otherwise, return a new string with the given string left-justified in the width. If needed, the filler character is used to pad the string. If the given string is larger than the width, elision applies in the given direction; elided characters are designated with the ellipses.

```
char* right_justify(const char*, unsigned width, char filler = ' ',
                    Elision elision = TRAILING,
                    char* ellipses = "...");
```

If the width is smaller than the size of the given string or the ellipses, throw the exception Lexical_Error. Otherwise, return a new string with the given string right-justified in the width. If needed, the filler character is used to pad the string. If the given string is larger than the width, elision applies in the given direction; elided characters are designated with the ellipses.

```
unsigned length(const char*);
```

Return the length of the string.

```
unsigned count(const char*, char, int case_sensitive = 1);
```

Return the number of occurrences of the given character in the string; if case_sensitive is not set, the same letters with different case are considered equal.

```
unsigned count_leading(const char*, char, int case_sensitive = 1);
```

Return the number of leading occurrences of the given character in the string; if case_sensitive is not set, the same letters with different case are considered equal.

```
unsigned count_trailing(const char*, char, int case_sensitive = 1);
```

Return the number of trailing occurrences of the given character in the string; if case_sensitive is not set, the same letters with different case are considered equal.

```
int is_alphanumeric(const char*);
```

Return 1 if and only if the given string consists entirely of alphabetic or numeric characters. Otherwise, return 0.

```
int is_alphabetic(const char*);
```

Return 1 if and only if the given string consists entirely of letters. Otherwise, return 0.

```
int is_ascii(const char*);
```

Return 1 if and only if the given string consists entirely of characters less than octal 0200. Otherwise, return 0.

```
int is_control(const char*);
```

Return 1 if and only if the given string consists entirely of characters equal to octal 0177 or less than octal 0040. Otherwise, return 0.

```
int is_digit(const char*);
```

Return 1 if and only if the given string consists entirely of decimal numbers (0 - 9). Otherwise, return 0.

```
int is_hex_digit(const char*);
```

Return 1 if and only if the given string consists entirely of hexadecimal numbers (0 - 9, A - F, or a - f). Otherwise, return 0.

```
int is_graphic(const char*);
```

Return 1 if and only if the given string consists entirely of characters between octal 0041 - 0176, inclusive. Otherwise, return 0.

```
int is_lowercase(const char*);
```

Return 1 if and only if the given string consists entirely of lowercase letters. Otherwise, return 0.

```
int is_uppercase(const char*);
```

Return 1 if and only if the given string consists entirely of uppercase letters. Otherwise, return 0.

```
int is_printable(const char*);
```

Return 1 if and only if the given string consists entirely of characters between octal 0040 - 0176, inclusive. Otherwise, return 0.

```
int is_punctuation(const char*);
```

Return 1 if and only if the given string consists entirely of punctuation characters (that is, not a control or alphanumeric character). Otherwise, return 0.

```
int is_space(const char*);
```

Return 1 if and only if the given string consists entirely of space characters (that is, space, tab, carriage return, new line, vertical tab, or form feed). Otherwise, return 0.

```
int is_equal(const char*, const char*, int case_sensitive = 1);
```

Return 1 if and only if the two strings are equal in value; if case_sensitive is not set, the same letters with different case are considered equal. Otherwise, return 0.

```
int is_less_than(const char*, const char*, int case_sensitive = 1);
```

Return 1 if and only if the first string is smaller in value than the second; if `case_sensitive` is not set, the same letters with different case are considered equal. Otherwise, return 0.

```
int is_greater_than(const char*, const char*, int case_sensitive = 1);
```

Return 1 if and only if the first string is greater in value than the second; if `case_sensitive` is not set, the same letters with different case are considered equal. Otherwise, return 0.

EXCEPTIONS

`Lexical_Error` —thrown by `center`, `left_justify`, and `right_justify` when the given width is too small to accommodate the string.

`Storage_Error` —thrown by any member function when no more storage can be allocated.

OPTIONS

None

FILES

In the utilities class category

`u_str`   `String_Utilities`

Support Class Category

The structures and tools that comprise the C++ Booch Components are all built from more primitive support abstractions. In general, application developers must only concern themselves with the higher-level abstractions of structures and tools. Library developers and power users, however, may wish to make use of the more primitive support abstractions, from which new structures and tools may be constructed, or through which the behavior of existing classes may be modified.

The C++ Booch Components provide the following support classes:

- `Bound`

  `Bounded_Simple_List`

  `Bounded_Simple_List_Active_Iterator`

  `Bounded_Simple_List_Passive_Iterator`

C++ Programming PowerPack

- Except

  Exception

  Duplicate

  Illegal_Pattern

  Is_Null

  Lexical_Error

  Math_Error

  Not_Found

  Not_Null

  Not_Root

  Overflow

  Position_Error

  Range_Error

  Storage_Error

  Underflow

- Free

  Storage_Manager

  Concurrent_Storage_Manager

  Managed

  Controlled

  Bounded_Storage_Manager

- Heap

  Bounded_Heap

  Bounded_Node_Heap

  Bounded_Double_Node_Heap

  Bounded_Tree_Node_Heap

  Bounded_Graph_Node_Heap

  Bounded_Counting_Node_Heap

Support Class Category

Bounded_Association_Node_Heap

Shared_Bounded_Node_Heap

Shared_Bounded_Double_Node_Heap

Shared_Bounded_Tree_Node_Heap

Shared_Bounded_Graph_Node_Heap

Shared_Bounded_Counting_Node_Heap

Shared_Bounded_Association_Node_Heap

- Node

Node

Double_Node

Tree_Node

Graph_Node

Counting_Node

Association_Node

Managed_Node

Managed_Double_Node

Managed_Tree_Node

Managed_Graph_Node

Managed_Counting_Node

Managed_Association_Node

Controlled_Node

Controlled_Double_Node

Controlled_Tree_Node

Controlled_Graph_Node

Controlled_Counting_Node

Controlled_Association_Node

Bounded_Node

Bounded_Double_Node

C++ Programming PowerPack

```
Bounded_Tree_Node

Bounded_Graph_Node

Bounded_Counting_Node

Bounded_Association_Node

Shared_Node

Shared_Double_Node

Shared_Tree_Node

Shared_Graph_Node

Shared_Counting_Node

Shared_Association_Node

Managed_Shared_Node

Managed_Shared_Double_Node

Managed_Shared_Tree_Node

Managed_Shared_Graph_Node

Managed_Shared_Counting_Node

Managed_Shared_Association_Node

Controlled_Shared_Node

Controlled_Shared_Double_Node

Controlled_Shared_Tree_Node

Controlled_Shared_Graph_Node

Controlled_Shared_Counting_Node

Controlled_Shared_Association_Node

Shared_Bounded_Node

Shared_Bounded_Double_Node

Shared_Bounded_Tree_Node

Shared_Bounded_Graph_Node

Shared_Bounded_Counting_Node

Shared_Bounded_Association_Node
```

Support Class Category

- Shared

    Counter

    Shared

- Synch

    Semaphore

    Read_Write_Monitor

    Single_Read_Write_Monitor

    Multiple_Read_Write_Monitor

    Lock

    Read_Lock

    Write_Lock

- Unbound

    Simple_List

    Simple_List_Active_Iterator

    Simple_List_Passive_Iterator

- Simple_Vector

    Simple_Vector

    Unsigned_Simple_Vector

This section documents each of these support classes, in the form of UNIX man pages.

Bounded_Simple_List

NAME

Bounded_Simple_List—A primitive linked list whose containers are stored on the stack.

SYNOPSIS

```
template<class Item, unsigned int Size>
class Bounded_Simple_List {
public:

  Bounded_Simple_List();
  Bounded_Simple_List(unsigned n);
  Bounded_Simple_List(Bounded_Heap<Item, Size>& heap,
                      unsigned n = 0);
  Bounded_Simple_List(const Bounded_Simple_List<Item, Size>&);
  ~Bounded_Simple_List();

  Bounded_Simple_List<Item, Size>& operator=
    (const Bounded_Simple_List<Item, Size>&);
  int operator==(const Bounded_Simple_List<Item, Size>&) const;
  int operator!=(const Bounded_Simple_List<Item, Size>&) const;

  Bounded_Simple_List<Item, Size>& clear (unsigned n);
  unsigned insert(unsigned n, unsigned before = 0);
  unsigned append(unsigned n, unsigned after = 0);
  unsigned remove(unsigned n = 0, unsigned count = 1);
  unsigned remove_nth(unsigned position);
  Bounded_Simple_List<Item, Size>&
    set_heap(Bounded_Heap<Item, Size>& heap);

  unsigned length() const;
  unsigned front() const;
  unsigned last() const;
  unsigned nth(unsigned position) const;
  unsigned find(Item&) const;
  unsigned position(Item&) const;

};
```

DESCRIPTION

A bounded simple list is a primitive linked list whose containers are stored on the stack. This is a low-level abstraction: the client is responsible for storage management and for establishing a policy to govern structural sharing.

A bounded simple list is not a polylithic abstraction. The semantics of copying, assignment, and equality do not involve structural sharing.

This class relies on the polymorphic behavior of bounded heaps. Every bounded simple list instance must be associated with a bounded heap (either at the time of the list's construction or, explicitly, via the member function set_heap). It is from this heap that the list draws its containers. Each list instance may have its own heap, but more commonly several different lists share the same heap. It is not required that all instances of the same instantiation share the same heap.

Because bounded simple lists are stack-based, individual containers are identified by an unsigned integer tag. As is the convention with pointers, a value of zero represents a null structure.

This class is not intended to be subclassed, and so it provides no virtual member functions.

This class is used by bounded maps and all bounded polylithic structures.

```
template<class Item, unsigned int Size>
```

The template item denotes the universe from which the list draws its items. The class `Item` may be either a primitive type or a user-defined class. If the latter, the class must provide a default constructor, copy constructor, assignment operator, and equality operator.

The template argument `Size` signifies the static (and therefore bounded) number of containers available to the list.

```
Bounded_Simple_List();
```

Construct a null list. The list's association with a particular bounded heap is left undefined.

```
Bounded_Simple_List(unsigned n);
```

Construct a list whose head is the given container. A value of 0 represents a null list. The list's association with a particular bounded heap is left undefined.

```
Bounded_Simple_List(Bounded_Heap<Item, Size>& heap,
                    unsigned n = 0);
```

Construct a list whose head is the given container. A value of 0 (the default) represents a null list. The list's association with a particular bounded heap is established.

```
Bounded_Simple_List(const Bounded_Simple_List<Item, Size>&);
```

If the given list is null, construct a null list. Otherwise, construct a list so that it is a complete copy of the given list. This operation relies on the polylithic behavior of `copy_state` for bounded nodes.

```
~Bounded_Simple_List();
```

Destroy the list. All containers associated with the list are reclaimed. Individual items are not destroyed; such items are only destroyed when the associated bounded heap is destroyed, typically when its definition is no longer in scope.

```
Bounded_Simple_List<Item, Size>& operator=
  (const Bounded_Simple_List<Item, Size>&);
```

Clear the list. If the given list is not null, set the state of the list so that it is a complete copy of the given list. This operation relies on the polylithic behavior of copy_state for bounded nodes.

```
int operator==(const Bounded_Simple_List<Item, Size>&) const;
```

Return 1 if and only if both lists are null or have the same number of containers and the same item for each container. This operation relies on the polylithic behavior of is_equal for bounded nodes.

```
int operator!=(const Bounded_Simple_List<Item, Size>&) const;
```

Return the logical negation of operator==.

```
Bounded_Simple_List<Item, Size>& clear (unsigned n);
```

If the designated container is not an element of the list, throw the exception Not_Found. Otherwise, reclaim all the containers associated with the sublist whose head is the given node, and make the list null. Individual items are not destroyed.

```
unsigned insert(unsigned n, unsigned before = 0);
```

If n is 0, throw the exception Is_Null. If before does not designate a container that is an element of the list, throw the exception Not_Found. Otherwise, insert the given container before the designated list element. If before is 0 (the default), the given container is inserted at the head of the list.

```
unsigned append(unsigned n, unsigned after = 0);
```

If n is 0, throw the exception Is_Null. If after does not designate a container that is an element of the list, throw the exception Not_Found. Otherwise, append the given container after the designated list element. If after is 0 (the default), the given container is inserted at the end of the list.

```
unsigned remove(unsigned n = 0, unsigned count = 1);
```

If the list is null, throw the exception Is_Null. If n does not designate a container that is an element of the list, throw the exception Not_Found. Otherwise, remove the given container from the list. If count is 1 (the default), only the given container is reclaimed. Otherwise, exactly count number of containers are reclaimed, starting with the given container. If count is larger than the length of the sublist starting with the given container, the entire sublist is reclaimed.

```
unsigned remove_nth(unsigned position);
```

If the list is null, throw the exception `Is_Null`. If `position` is 0, or larger than the length of the list, throw the exception `Range_Error`. Otherwise, remove the nth container in the list (designated by the given position) and reclaim it. Containers are numbered from the head of the list, starting at 1, up to the length of the list.

```
Bounded_Simple_List<Item, Size>&
  set_heap(Bounded_Heap<Item, Size>& heap);
```

Set the association with the given heap. This association may be reset at any time.

```
unsigned length() const;
```

Return the number of items in the list.

```
unsigned front() const;
```

Return the tag of the container at the head of the list. If the list is null, return 0.

```
unsigned last() const;
```

Return the tag of the container at the end of the list. If the list is null, return 0.

```
unsigned nth(unsigned position) const;
```

If `position` is 0, return the tag of the container at the head of the list (if the list is null, return 0). If `position` is larger than the length of the list, throw the exception `Range_Error`. Otherwise, return the tag of the nth container in the list (designated by the given position). Containers are numbered from the head of the list, starting at 1, up to the length of the list.

```
unsigned find(Item&) const;
```

Return the tag of the first container whose item is equal to the given item. If no such container is found, return 0.

```
unsigned position(Item&) const;
```

Return the position of the first container whose item is equal to the given item. If no such container is found, return 0. Containers are numbered from the head of the list, starting at 1, up to the length of the list.

EXCEPTIONS

Unpredictable behavior will result if the list's heap is never set.

Not_Found	—thrown by clear, insert, append, and remove if the given container is not an element of the list.
Is_Null	—thrown by insert, append, remove, and remove_nth if the given list is null.
Range_Error	—thrown by remove_nth and nth if the given position is 0 or larger than the length of the list.
Storage_Error	—thrown by any member function when no more storage can be allocated from the heap.

OPTIONS

Bounded simple lists provide the usual active and passive iterators.

FILES

In the support class category

bound	Bounded_Simple_List Bounded_Simple_List_Active_Iterator Bounded_Simple_List_Passive_Iterator

SEE ALSO

Node (especially bounded nodes)

Heap

EXCEPTION

NAME

Exception—A primitive abstraction of an event that causes suspension of normal program execution.

SYNOPSIS

```
class Exception {
public:

  Exception(const char* name, const char* who, const char* what);
  virtual ~Exception();

  virtual void display(ostream&) const;
```

SUPPORT CLASS CATEGORY

```
const char* name() const;
const char* who() const;
const char* what() const;
};
```

DESCRIPTION

An exception represents a primitive abstraction of an event that causes suspension of normal program execution. The class `Exception` supports the C++ exception handling mechanism. Instances of this class and its subclasses serve as agents that carry information from the point at which the exception is thrown to the agent that ultimately handles the exception.

`Exception(const char* name, const char* who, const char* what);`

Construct an exception: `name` denotes the name of the exception; `who` denotes the agent that threw the exception; and `what` denotes the nature of or reason for the exception. The given strings are copied.

`virtual ~Exception();`

Destroy the exception.

`virtual void display(ostream&) const;`

Display the exception on the given stream.

`const char* name() const;`

Return the name of the exception.

`const char* who() const;`

Return a designation of the agent that threw the exception.

`const char* what() const;`

Return a designation of the nature of or reason for the exception.

EXCEPTIONS

No exceptions are raised by exceptions themselves.

OPTIONS

In addition to the base class `Exception`, there are 13 subclasses.

- `Duplicate`
- `Illegal_Pattern`

- Is_Null
- Lexical_Error
- Math_Error
- Not_Found
- Not_Null
- Not_Root
- Overflow
- Position_Error
- Range_Error
- Storage_Error
- Underflow

These classes have the same class signature as the base class Exception. The class Math_Error adds a constructor and display member function to manipulate an error number, representative of the exceptional value in question.

The library also provides several constants, which are used to provide standard reasons for why an exception was thrown (the what element of an exception).

- _DISJOINT;
- _DUPLICATE;
- _EMPTY;
- _FULL;
- _ILLEGAL;
- _INVALID_INDEX;
- _INVALID_NUMBER;
- _MISSING;
- _NOT_EMPTY;
- _NOT_ROOT;
- _NULL;
- _OUT_OF_MEMORY;

- `_TOO_LARGE;`
- `_TOO_SMALL;`

The library also provides several nonmember functions, which may be used to handle exceptions in the absence of a complete C++ exception facility.

```
extern void _catch(const Exception&);
```

Catch the given exception. In the absence of a complete C++ exception facility, all calls to `throw` are redefined to be calls to `_catch`. The default behavior of `_catch` displays the exception on the standard error stream and then calls `terminate`.

```
typedef void (*PFV)();
extern PFV set_terminate(PFV);
```

Set the helping function called by `terminate`; this function may be reset at any time as a means of customizing the response to a `_catch` call.

```
extern void terminate();
```

Call the helping function (if it is defined) and exit the program.

FILES

In the support class category

```
except    Exception
          Duplicate
          Illegal_Pattern
          Is_Null
          Lexical_Error
          Math_Error
          Not_Found
          Not_Null
          Not_Root
          Overflow
          Position_Error
          Range_Error
          Storage_Error
          Underflow
```

STORAGE_MANAGER

NAME

`Storage_Manager`—A primitive facility for managing storage on a free list.

SYNOPSIS

```
class Storage_Manager {
public:

  Storage_Manager();
  virtual ~Storage_Manager();

  virtual void* allocate(unsigned size);
  virtual void free(void*, unsigned size);

};

template<unsigned int Size>
class Bounded_Storage_Manager {
public:

  Bounded_Storage_Manager();
  virtual ~Bounded_Storage_Manager();

  virtual unsigned allocate();
  virtual void free(unsigned);

  unsigned available() const;

};
```

DESCRIPTION

A storage manager provides a primitive facility for managing storage on a free list. Storage managers collaborate with nodes, so that nodes are allocated and reclaimed to the free list in a manner that is transparent to all node clients.

The library provides two major variations of storage managers, Storage_Manager, which operates upon the heap, and Bounded_Storage_Manager, which operates upon the stack (more precisely, instances of Bounded_Heap).

The semantics of the class Storage_Manager are guaranteed only in the presence of a single thread of control. The subclass Concurrent_Storage_Manager has the same signature as the class Storage_Manager, but its semantics are guaranteed in the presence of multiple threads of control.

The class Storage_Manager is used with the class Managed to provide a managed storage management policy. Managed is a mix-in class that uses a storage manager instance and defines the member functions new and delete to operate with the given free list. In a similar manner, the mix-in class Controlled uses a concurrent storage manager instance. Every client within the same application shares the same managed or controlled free list. Alternate semantics would be for each client to have its own free list, but this can easily lead to fragmentation.

The class `Bounded_Storage_Manager` collaborates with bounded heaps to manage stack-based heap storage.

For the `Storage_Manager` class, the following behavior applies:

```
Storage_Manager();
```

Construct a storage manager; the free list is initially empty.

```
virtual ~Storage_Manager();
```

Destroy the storage manager. All storage associated with the free list is reclaimed to the heap, and individual items are, in turn, destroyed.

```
virtual void* allocate(unsigned size);
```

If the free list contains storage of the given size, remove the storage from the free list and return a pointer to it. Otherwise, allocate the storage from the heap. If the allocation fails, throw the exception `Storage_Error`.

```
virtual void free(void*, unsigned size);
```

Return the storage to the free list. Storage is retained on the free list, sorted by size. This member function may throw the exception `Storage_Error`; `free` occasionally must allocate nodes to manage the free list itself, and if such allocation fails, the exception is thrown.

For the `Bounded_Storage_Manager` class, the following behavior applies:

```
template<unsigned int Size>
```

The template argument `Size` signifies the static (and therefore bounded) number of containers available in the free list.

```
Bounded_Storage_Manager();
```

Construct a bounded storage manager; the free list is set to indicate that the entire bounded heap space is initially available.

```
virtual ~Bounded_Storage_Manager();
```

Destroy the bounded storage manager. Individual items are not destroyed; such items are only destroyed when the associated bounded heap is destroyed, typically when its definition is no longer in scope.

```
virtual unsigned allocate();
```

If the free list is empty, throw the exception `Storage_Error` (because no other storage is available). Otherwise, remove the storage from the free list and return a tag to it.

```
virtual void free(unsigned);
```

Return the storage to the free list. The item is not destroyed; such items are only destroyed when the associated bounded heap is destroyed, typically when its definition is no longer in scope.

```
unsigned available() const;
```

Return the amount of available storage in the free list.

EXCEPTIONS

`Storage_Error` —thrown by any member function when no more storage can be allocated from the heap.

OPTIONS

None

FILES

In the support class category

```
free_u    Storage_Manager
          Concurrent_Storage_Manager
free_m    Managed
free_c    Controlled
free_b    Bounded_Storage_Manager
```

SEE ALSO

`Node`

`Heap`

BOUNDED_HEAP

NAME

`Bounded_Heap`—A primitive abstraction of a stack-based heap.

SYNOPSIS

```
template<class Item, unsigned int Size>
class Bounded_Heap : public Bounded_Storage_Manager<Size> {
public:

  Bounded_Heap();
  virtual ~Bounded_Heap();

  virtual Bounded_Node<Item>* element(const unsigned) const;

};

template<class Item, unsigned int Size>
class Bounded_Node_Heap : public Bounded_Heap<Item, Size> {
public:

  Bounded_Node_Heap();
  virtual ~Bounded_Node_Heap();

  virtual Bounded_Node<Item>& operator[](const unsigned);

  virtual Bounded_Node<Item>* element(const unsigned) const;

protected:

  Bounded_Node<Item> rep_heap[Size];

};
```

DESCRIPTION

A bounded heap is a primitive abstraction of a stack-based heap. Bounded heaps collaborate with bounded storage managers, so that nodes are allocated and reclaimed to the free list in a manner that is transparent to all node clients.

The responsibility of the class `Bounded_Heap` is to manage the free list; the responsibility of the class `Bounded_Node_Heap` (and its sibling classes) is to provide the actual heap storage managed by the `Bounded_Heap`.

Ultimately, bounded heaps are constructed using arrays, and so we cannot rely on the polymorphic behavior of their items (because we must store values, not references). For this reason, we provide several sibling classes of `Bounded_Node_Heap`, one for each kind of bounded node. The class `Bounded_Heap` serves to provide the behavior common to all concrete heaps, as well as provide a common protocol for extracting bounded nodes from the heap (a protocol that the `Bounded_Storage_Manager` mechanism relies on). The concrete subclasses, on the other hand, add operations for extracting nodes from the heap according to the particular kind of node in the heap (a protocol that clients of the bounded heap rely on, to avoid casting).

For the Bounded_Heap, the following behavior applies:

```
template<class Item, unsigned int Size>
```

The template item denotes the universe from which the heap draws its items. The class Item may be either a primitive type or a user-defined class. If the latter, the class must provide a default constructor, copy constructor, assignment operator, and equality operator.

The template argument Size signifies the static (and therefore bounded) number of items in the heap.

```
Bounded_Heap();
```

Construct a bounded heap.

```
virtual ~Bounded_Heap();
```

Destroy the bounded heap.

```
virtual Bounded_Node<Item>* element(const unsigned) const;
```

This operation must be redefined by subclasses of Bounded_Heap to return a pointer to the designated element in the heap; items in the heap are numbered from 1 to Size.

For the Bounded_Node_Heap, the following behavior applies:

```
template<class Item, unsigned int Size>
```

The template item denotes the universe from which the heap draws its items. The class Item may be either a primitive type or a user-defined class. If the latter, the class must provide a default constructor, copy constructor, assignment operator, and equality operator.

The template argument Size signifies the static (and therefore bounded) number of items in the heap.

```
Bounded_Node_Heap();
```

Construct a bounded node heap.

```
virtual ~Bounded_Node_Heap();
```

Destroy the bounded node heap; individual items are, in turn, destroyed.

```
virtual Bounded_Node<Item>& operator[](const unsigned);
```

Return a reference to the indexed element in the heap; items in the heap are numbered from 1 to `Size`.

```
virtual Bounded_Node<Item>* element(const unsigned) const;
```

Return a pointer to the designated element in the heap; items in the heap are numbered from 1 to `Size`.

EXCEPTIONS

No exceptions are raised by any member function.

OPTIONS

There are 12 concrete heap classes (in addition to the base class `Bounded_Heap`) that provide the actual heap storage for every kind of bounded node.

- `Bounded_Node_Heap`
- `Bounded_Double_Node_Heap`
- `Bounded_Tree_Node_Heap`
- `Bounded_Graph_Node_Heap`
- `Bounded_Counting_Node_Heap`
- `Bounded_Association_Node_Heap`
- `Shared_Bounded_Node_Heap`
- `Shared_Bounded_Double_Node_Heap`
- `Shared_Bounded_Tree_Node_Heap`
- `Shared_Bounded_Graph_Node_Heap`
- `Shared_Bounded_Counting_Node_Heap`
- `Shared_Bounded_Association_Node_Heap`

The signature of each of these classes is the same, except that the member function `operator[]` returns a reference to the specific kind of bounded node stored in the heap.

FILES

In the support class category

heap_b	Bounded_Heap
	Bounded_Node_Heap
	Bounded_Tree_Node_Heap
	Bounded_Graph_Node_Heap
	Bounded_Counting_Node_Heap
	Bounded_Association_Node_Heap
sheap_b	Shared_Bounded_Node_Heap
	Shared_Bounded_Double_Node_Heap
	Shared_Bounded_Tree_Node_Heap
	Shared_Bounded_Graph_Node_Heap
	Shared_Bounded_Counting_Node_Heap
	Shared_Bounded_Association_Node_Heap

SEE ALSO

Node

Free

NODE

NAME

Node—A primitive container of items.

SYNOPSIS

```
template<class Item>
class Node {
public:

  Node(Item& item, Node<Item>* next = 0);
  Node(const Node<Item>&);
  virtual ~Node();

  virtual Node<Item>* clone();

  virtual int is_equal(const Node<Item>&) const;
  Item& item();
  Node<Item>*& next();

};
```

Support Class Category

```
template<class Item>
class Bounded_Node {
public:

  Bounded_Node();
  Bounded_Node(Item& item, unsigned next = 0);
  Bounded_Node(const Bounded_Node<Item>&);
  virtual ~Bounded_Node();

  virtual void copy_state(const Bounded_Node<Item>&);

  virtual is_equal(const Bounded_Node<Item>&) const;
  Item& item();
  unsigned& next();

};
```

DESCRIPTION

A node is a primitive container of items. Nodes store item values, not references.

A node consists of an item and a link to the next node. The class Node is the base class of all containers for unbounded forms; such nodes live on the heap, and so their links are pointers. The class Bounded_Node is the base class of all containers for bounded forms; such nodes live on the stack (more precisely, on instances of Bounded_Heap), and so their links are unsigned integers.

Nodes collaborate with simple lists to provide the essential representation of all monolithic structures. Nodes are used directly in the representation of all polylithic structures.

Nodes also collaborate with storage managers to implement the library's various storage management policies.

For all node classes, the member functions operator=, operator==, and operator!= are private. This requires clients to explicitly use the member functions clone and is_equal for the class Node, and the member functions copy_state and is_equal for the class Bounded_Node. We require this protocol to increase the readability of clients that rely on the polymorphic behavior of nodes.

For the class Node, the following behavior applies:

template<class Item>

The template item denotes the universe from which the node draws its items. The class Item may be either a primitive type or a user-defined class. If the latter, the class must provide a default constructor, copy constructor, assignment operator, and equality operator.

```
Node(Item& item, Node<Item>* next = 0);
```

Construct a node with the given item; set the next link of the node to the given node (whose default is null).

```
Node(const Node<Item>&);
```

Construct a node with a copy of the given item and next link.

```
virtual ~Node();
```

Destroy the node; the item itself is also destroyed.

```
virtual Node<Item>* clone();
```

Allocate a new node, using a copy of the given node's item; all links are set to denote null.

```
virtual int is_equal(const Node<Item>&) const;
```

Return 1 if and only if both nodes have the same item values.

```
Item& item();
```

Return a reference to the node's item.

```
Node<Item>*& next();
```

Return a reference to the node's link to the next node.

For the Bounded_Node, the following behavior applies:

```
template<class Item>
```

The template item denotes the universe from which the node draws its items. The class Item may be either a primitive type or a user-defined class. If the latter, the class must provide a default constructor, copy constructor, assignment operator, and equality operator.

```
Bounded_Node();
```

Construct a node; the item is left undefined, and the next link of the node is set to 0. This constructor exists to permit the declaration of arrays of bounded nodes.

```
Bounded_Node(Item& item, unsigned next = 0);
```

Construct a node with the given item; set the next link of the node to the given node (whose default is 0).

```
Bounded_Node(const Bounded_Node<Item>&);
```

Construct a node with a copy of the given item and next link.

```
virtual ~Bounded_Node();
```

Destroy the node; the item itself is also destroyed.

```
virtual void copy_state(const Bounded_Node<Item>&);
```

Copy the given node's item; all links are set to denote 0.

```
virtual is_equal(const Bounded_Node<Item>&) const;
```

Return 1 if and only if both nodes have the same item values.

```
Item& item();
```

Return a reference to the node's item.

```
unsigned& next();
```

Return a reference to the node's link to the next node.

EXCEPTIONS

No exceptions are raised by any member function.

OPTIONS

There are six major variations of the class `Node`, each containing at least one item plus additional state (primarily links to other nodes):

- Node
- Double_Node
- Tree_Node
- Graph_Node
- Counting_Node
- Association_Node

Structures and tools are designed to use the smallest node necessary, so that no storage is wasted.

The class `Double_Node` is a kind of `Node`, but adds a link back to the previous node. The signature of this class is the same as for `Node`, but adds the following operations:

```
Double_Node(Item& item, Node<Item>* next = 0,
            Node<Item>* previous = 0);
```

Construct a node with the given item; set the links of the node to the given values (whose defaults are 0).

```
Node<Item>*& previous();
```

Return a reference to the node's link to the previous node.

The class `Tree_Node` is a kind of `Double_Node`, but adds one link and redefines the meaning of the existing links. The signature of this class is the same as for `Double_Node`, but adds the following operations:

```
Tree_Node(Item& item, Node<Item>* left = 0,
         Node<Item>* right = 0,
         Node<Item>* parent = 0);
```

Construct a node with the given item; set the links of the node to the given values (whose defaults are 0).

```
Node<Item>*& left();
```

Return a reference to the node's link to the left node. This member function redefines the meaning of the next link for binary trees.

```
Node<Item>*& right();
```

Return a reference to the node's link to the right node. This member function redefines the meaning of the previous link for binary trees.

```
Node<Item>*& parent();
```

Return a reference to the node's link to the parent node.

```
Node<Item>*& child();
```

Return a reference to the node's link to the child node. This member function redefines the meaning of the next link for arbitrary trees.

```
Node<Item>*& sibling();
```

Return a reference to the node's link to the sibling node. This member function redefines the meaning of the previous link for arbitrary trees.

The class `Graph_Node` is a kind of `Tree_Node`, but adds one link and redefines the meaning of existing links. The signature of this class is the same as for `Tree_Node`, but adds the following operations:

```
Graph_Node(Item& item, Node<Item>* next = 0,
           Node<Item>* previous = 0,
           Node<Item>* to_node = 0,
           Node<Item>* from_node = 0);
```

Construct a node with the given item; set the links of the node to the given values (whose defaults are 0).

`Node<Item>*& to_node();`

Return a reference to the node's link to the next outgoing node. This member function redefines the meaning of the parent link.

`Node<Item>*& from_node();`

Return a reference to the node's link to the next incoming node.

The class `Counting_Node` is a kind of `Node`, but mixes in the class `Counter` to add an unsigned integer counter to the state of the node. The signature of this class is the same as for `Node`; no new operations are added, but `clone` and `is_equal` are redefined to account for this additional state.

The class `Association_Node` is a kind of `Node`, but includes a value as part of its state. In this manner, an instance of this class represents item/value pairs. The signature of this class is the same as for `Node`; `clone` and `is_equal` are redefined to account for its additional state. This class requires a slightly different template signature, plus one new operation:

`template<class Item, class Value>`

The template item and value denote the universe from which the node draws its items. The classes `Item` and `Value` may be either a primitive type or a user-defined class. If the latter, the class must provide a default constructor, copy constructor, assignment operator, and equality operator.

`Value& value();`

Return a reference to the node's value.

There exist the same six variations for the class `Bounded_Node`. This leaves us with a total of 12 node classes.

To support the semantics of structural sharing in polylithic structures, we introduce the mechanism of reference counting, as provided by the class `Share`. We form a subclass of each of the six basic classes (for both unbounded and bounded nodes), by mixing in the class `Share`. In this manner, the signature of these new classes is the same as their base node class, but now includes a reference counter, which keeps track of the number of aliases to that node. This leaves us with a total of 24 node classes.

For the unbounded nodes only, we must consider support for different storage management policies. The design of the library's structures and tools permits the use of many different such policies. In this library, we provide the implementation of two of the most common policies.

To support the semantics of managed storage management, in which unused nodes are drawn from a free list, we apply the mix-in class Managed. We form a subclass of each of the six basic classes (and similarly for their shared variations), by mixing in the class Managed. In this manner, the signature of these new classes is the same as their base node class, but now includes the new and delete semantics that operate upon a free list. This adds 12 more classes to our total.

To support the semantics of controlled storage management, in which the semantics of the free list are guaranteed in the presence of multiple threads of control, we apply the mix-in class Controlled. We form a subclass of each of the six basic classes (and similarly for their shared variations), by mixing in the class Controlled. In this manner, the signature of these new classes is the same as their base node class, but now includes the new and delete semantics that operate upon a concurrent free list. This adds 12 more classes to our total.

This leaves us with 36 classes for unbounded nodes and 12 classes for bounded nodes, for a total of 48 node classes.

FILES

In the support class category:

```
node_u    Node
          Double_Node
          Tree_Node
          Graph_Node
          Counting_Node
          Association_Node
node_m    Managed_Node
          Managed_Double_Node
          Managed_Tree_Node
          Managed_Graph_Node
          Managed_Counting_Node
          Managed_Association_Node
node_c    Controlled_Node
          Controlled_Double_Node
          Controlled_Tree_Node
          Controlled_Graph_Node
          Controlled_Counting_Node
          Controlled_Association_Node
node_b    Bounded_Node
          Bounded_Double_Node
          Bounded_Tree_Node
          Bounded_Graph_Node
          Bounded_Counting_Node
          Bounded_Association_Node
snode_u   Shared_Node
```

	Shared_Double_Node
	Shared_Tree_Node
	Shared_Graph_Node
	Shared_Counting_Node
	Shared_Association_Node
snode_m	Managed_Shared_Node
	Managed_Shared_Double_Node
	Managed_Shared_Tree_Node
	Managed_Shared_Graph_Node
	Managed_Shared_Counting_Node
	Managed_Shared_Association_Node
snode_c	Controlled_Shared_Node
	Controlled_Shared_Double_Node
	Controlled_Shared_Tree_Node
	Controlled_Shared_Graph_Node
	Controlled_Shared_Counting_Node
	Controlled_Shared_Association_Node
snode_b	Shared_Bounded_Node
	Shared_Bounded_Double_Node
	Shared_Bounded_Tree_Node
	Shared_Bounded_Graph_Node
	Shared_Bounded_Counting_Node
	Shared_Bounded_Association_Node

SEE ALSO

Free

Heap

Shared

COUNTER, SHARED

NAME

Counter—A primitive mix-in class, used for counting items.

Shared—A primitive mix-in class, used for reference counting.

SYNOPSIS

```
class Counter {
public:

  Counter();
  Counter(const Counter&);
  ~Counter();
```

```
    Counter& operator=(Counter&);

    unsigned increment(const unsigned count = 1);
    unsigned decrement(const unsigned count = 1);
    unsigned set_count(const unsigned count = 1);

    unsigned count() const;

};

class Shared {
public:

    Shared();
    Shared(const Shared&);
    ~Shared();

    Shared& operator=(Shared&);

    unsigned share(const unsigned count = 1);
    unsigned unshare(const unsigned count = 1);
    unsigned set_count(const unsigned count = 1);

    int is_shared() const;
    unsigned count() const;

};
```

DESCRIPTION

The class `Counter` is a primitive mix-in class that provides an unsigned integer value, used for counting items. This class supports the semantics of bags.

The class `Share` is a primitive mix-in class that provides an unsigned integer value, used for reference counting. This class supports the storage management policies for all polylithic forms.

The semantics of these two classes are sufficiently different to warrant making them sibling classes, rather than relating them through an inheritance hierarchy.

For the `Counter` class, the following behavior applies:

`Counter();`

Construct a counter; its count is set to 1.

`Counter(const Counter&);`

Construct a counter with a copy of the given count.

`~Counter();`

Destroy the counter.

`Counter& operator=(Counter&);`

Assign the count to the given count.

`unsigned increment(const unsigned count = 1);`

Increment the count by the given value (default is 1).

`unsigned decrement(const unsigned count = 1);`

Decrement the count by the given value (default is 1).

`unsigned set_count(const unsigned count = 1);`

Set the count to the given value (default is 1).

`unsigned count() const;`

Return the value of the count.

For the `Shared` class, the following behavior applies:

`Shared();`

Construct a reference counter; its count is set to 1.

`Shared(const Shared&);`

Construct a reference counter; its count is set to 1.

`~Shared();`

If the reference count is not 0, throw the exception `Storage_Error`. Otherwise, destroy the reference counter.

`Shared& operator=(Shared&);`

Set the reference count to 1.

`unsigned share(const unsigned count = 1);`

Increment the reference count by the given value (default is 1).

`unsigned unshare(const unsigned count = 1);`

Decrement the reference count by the given value (default is 1).

`unsigned set_count(const unsigned count = 1);`

Set the reference count to the given value (default is 1).

`int is_shared() const;`

Return 1 if and only if the reference count is greater than 0.

`unsigned count() const;`

Return the value of the count.

EXCEPTIONS

`Storage_Error` —thrown by ~Shared when the reference count is not 0.

OPTIONS

None

FILES

In the support class category

```
shared     Counter
           Shared
```

SEE ALSO

```
Node
```

Semaphore, Monitor, Lock

NAME

`Semaphore`—A primitive facility for process synchronization with single readers and writers.

`Read_Write_Monitor`—A primitive facility for process synchronization, with multiple readers and writers.

`Lock`—A primitive facility for forming critical regions.

SYNOPSIS

```
class Semaphore {
public:

  Semaphore(const unsigned = 0);
  virtual ~Semaphore();

  virtual void seize();
  virtual void release();

  unsigned none_pending() const;

};
```

```
class Read_Write_Monitor : public Semaphore {
public:

  Read_Write_Monitor();
  virtual ~Read_Write_Monitor();

  virtual void seize_for_reading() = 0;
  virtual void seize_for_writing() = 0;
  virtual void release_from_reading() = 0;
  virtual void release_from_writing() = 0;

};

class Lock {
public:

  Lock(const Semaphore&);
  ~Lock();

};
```

DESCRIPTION

The class `Semaphore` provides a primitive facility for process synchronization with single readers and writers. Library developers must provide an implementation to this class that relies on the local implementation of concurrency mechanisms. The library's only dependencies on the local implementation are intentionally isolated in the implementation of this class.

The class `Read_Write_Monitor` provides a primitive facility for process synchronization with multiple readers and writers. This class builds upon the facilities of the class `Semaphore`.

The class `Lock` provides a primitive facility for forming critical regions. Instances of this class collaborate with semaphores and monitors, such that member functions that use locks act as atomic actions.

For the `Semaphore` class, the following behavior applies:

```
Semaphore(const unsigned = 0);
```

Construct a new counting semaphore; by default, its state is initially not seized.

```
virtual ~Semaphore();
```

Destroy the semaphore.

```
virtual void seize();
```

Seize the semaphore. If the semaphore is already seized, the agent that called this member function blocks until the semaphore is no longer seized.

```
virtual void release();
```

Release the semaphore. The next waiting agent (if any) is allowed to proceed.

```
unsigned none_pending();
```

Return 1 if and only if there are no agents waiting on the semaphore.

An implementation of a semaphore class using the AT&T task library is described in [Stroustrup/Shopiro 87].

For the `Read_Write_Monitor` class, the following behavior applies:

```
Read_Write_Monitor();
```

Construct a new monitor; by default, its state is initially not seized.

```
virtual ~Read_Write_Monitor();
```

Destroy the monitor.

```
virtual void seize_for_reading();
```

Seize the monitor for reading. All readers block if there is an active writer; otherwise, the readers may proceed.

```
virtual void seize_for_writing();
```

Seize the monitor for writing. If there is an active writer, then block. Otherwise, block all other waiting agents and then proceed when all active readers are finished.

```
virtual void release_from_reading();
```

Release the monitor from reading. The next waiting writer (if any) is allowed to proceed; otherwise, any waiting readers are allowed to proceed.

```
virtual void release_from_writing();
```

Release the monitor from writing. The next waiting writer (if any) is allowed to proceed; otherwise, any waiting readers are allowed to proceed.

```
unsigned none_pending() const;
```

Return 1 if and only if there are no agents waiting on the semaphore.

This class implements the readers-writers algorithm described in [Holt et al. 78].

The semantics of the class `ULock` relies on the semantics of constructors and destructors for locally declared objects. For the `Lock` class, the following behavior applies:

`Lock(const Semaphore&);`

Construct a new lock using the given semaphore.

`~Lock();`

Destroy the lock.

This class implements the critical region mechanism described in [Shopiro 87].

EXCEPTIONS

No exceptions are raised by any member function.

OPTIONS

The class `Read_Write_Monitor` is an abstract base class. There are two concrete subclasses of this class:

- `Single_Read_Write_Monitor`
- `Multiple_Read_Write_Monitor`

The signature of these two classes is the same as for `Read_Write_Monitor`. The class `Single_Read_Write_Monitor` supports a single reader or a single writer. The class `Multiple_Read_Write_Monitor` supports multiple simultaneous readers and a single writer, and so permits the largest degree of parallelism.

The class `Lock` is a base class; its instances do not distinguish between readers and writers. To facilitate protecting critical regions for readers or writers, we have the following two subclasses of the class `Lock`:

- `Read_Lock`
- `Write_Lock`

The signature of these two classes is the same as for the class `Lock`, except that their constructors require a monitor, not a semaphore.

FILES

In the support class category

```
synch     Semaphore
          Read_Write_Monitor
          Single_Read_Write_Monitor
          Multiple_Read_Write_Monitor
          Lock
          Read_Lock
          Write_Lock
```

Simple_List

NAME

Simple_List—A primitive linked list whose containers are stored on the heap.

SYNOPSIS

```cpp
template<class Item>
class Simple_List {
public:

  Simple_List();
  Simple_List(Node<Item>* n);
  Simple_List(const Simple_List<Item>&);
  ~Simple_List();

  Simple_List<Item>& operator=(const Simple_List<Item>&);
  int operator==(const Simple_List<Item>&) const;
  int operator!=(const Simple_List<Item>&) const;

  Simple_List<Item>& clear (Node<Item>* n);
  Node<Item>* insert(Node<Item>* n, Node<Item>* before = 0);
  Node<Item>* append(Node<Item>* n, Node<Item>* after = 0);
  Node<Item>* remove(Node<Item>* n = 0, unsigned count = 1);
  Node<Item>* remove_nth(unsigned position);

  unsigned length() const;
  Node<Item>* front() const;
  Node<Item>* last() const;
  Node<Item>* nth(unsigned position) const;
  Node<Item>* find(Item&) const;
  unsigned position(Item&) const;

};
```

DESCRIPTION

A simple list is a primitive linked list whose containers are stored on the heap. This is a low-level abstraction: the client is responsible for storage management and for establishing a policy to govern structural sharing.

A simple list is not a polylithic abstraction. The semantics of copying, assignment, and equality do not involve structural sharing.

This class relies on the polymorphic behavior of nodes, especially with regard to their semantics for `clone` and `is_equal`.

Because simple lists are heap-based, individual containers are identified by a pointer. A value of zero represents a null structure.

This class is not intended to be subclassed, and so it provides no virtual member functions.

This class is used by all unbounded monolithic structures.

```
template<class Item>
```

The template item denotes the universe from which the list draws its items. The class `Item` may be either a primitive type or a user-defined class. If the latter, the class must provide a default constructor, copy constructor, assignment operator, and equality operator.

```
Simple_List();
```

Construct a null list.

```
Simple_List(Node<Item>* n = 0);
```

Construct a list whose head is the given container. A value of 0 represents a null list.

```
Simple_List(const Simple_List<Item>&);
```

If the given list is null, construct a null list. Otherwise, construct a list so that it is a complete copy of the given list. This operation relies on the polylithic behavior of `clone` for unbounded nodes.

```
~Simple_List();
```

Destroy the list. Individual items may or may not be destroyed, according to the semantics of the list's containers.

```
Simple_List<Item>& operator=(const Simple_List<Item>&);
```

Clear the list. If the given list is not null, set the state of the list so that it is a complete copy of the given list. This operation relies on the polylithic behavior of `clone` for unbounded nodes.

```
int operator==(const Simple_List<Item>&) const;
```

Return 1 if and only if both lists are null or have the same number of containers and the same item for each container. This operation relies on the polylithic behavior of `is_equal` for unbounded nodes.

```
int operator!=(const Simple_List<Item>&) const;
```

Return the logical negation of `operator==`.

```
Simple_List<Item>& clear (Node<Item>* n);
```

If the designated container is not an element of the list, throw the exception `Not_Found`. Otherwise, reclaim all the containers associated with the sublist whose head is the given node, and make the list null. Individual items may or may not be destroyed, according to the semantics of the list's containers.

```
Node<Item>* insert(Node<Item>* n, Node<Item>* before = 0);
```

If n is null, throw the exception `Is_Null`. If `before` does not designate a container that is an element of the list, throw the exception `Not_Found`. Otherwise, insert the given container before the designated list element. If `before` is null (the default), the given container is inserted at the head of the list.

```
Node<Item>* append(Node<Item>* n, Node<Item>* after = 0);
```

If n is null, throw the exception `Is_Null`. If `after` does not designate a container that is an element of the list, throw the exception `Not_Found`. Otherwise, append the given container after the designated list element. If `after` is null (the default), the given container is inserted at the end of the list.

```
Node<Item>* remove(Node<Item>* n = 0, unsigned count = 1);
```

If the list is null, throw the exception `Is_Null`. If n does not designate a container that is an element of the list, throw the exception `Not_Found`. Otherwise, remove the given container from the list. If count is 1 (the default), only the given container is reclaimed. Otherwise, exactly count number of containers are reclaimed, starting with the given container. If count is larger than the length of the sublist starting with the given container, the entire sublist is reclaimed.

```
Node<Item>* remove_nth(unsigned position);
```

If the list is null, throw the exception `Is_Null`. If position is 0, or larger than the length of the list, throw the exception `Range_Error`. Otherwise, remove the nth container in the list (designated by the given position) and reclaim it. Containers are numbered from the head of the list, starting at 1, up to the length of the list.

`unsigned length() const;`

Return the number of items in the list.

`Node<Item>* front() const;`

Return a pointer to the container at the head of the list. If the list is null, return 0.

`Node<Item>* last() const;`

Return a pointer to the container at the end of the list. If the list is null, return 0.

`Node<Item>* nth(unsigned position) const;`

If `position` is 0, return a pointer to the container at the head of the list (if the list is null, return 0). If `position` is larger than the length of the list, throw the exception `Range_Error`. Otherwise, return a pointer to the nth container in the list (designated by the given position). Containers are numbered from the head of the list, starting at 1, up to the length of the list.

`Node<Item>* find(Item&) const;`

Return a pointer to the container whose item is equal to the given item. If no such container is found, return 0.

`unsigned position(Item&) const;`

Return the position of the first container whose item is equal to the given item. If no such container is found, return 0. Containers are numbered from the head of the list, starting at 1, up to the length of the list.

EXCEPTIONS

Not_Found	—thrown by `clear`, `insert`, `append`, and `remove` if the given container is not an element of the list.
Is_Null	—thrown by `insert`, `append`, `remove`, and `remove_nth` if the given list is null.
Range_Error	—thrown by `remove_nth` and `nth` if the given position is 0 or larger than the length of the list.
Storage_Error	—thrown by any member function when no more storage can be allocated from the heap.

OPTIONS

Unbounded simple lists provide the usual active and passive iterators.

FILES

In the support class category

```
unbound    Simple_List
    Simple_List_Active_Iterator
    Simple_List_Passive_Iterator
```

SEE ALSO

Node

SIMPLE_VECTOR

NAME

Simple_Vector—A primitive sequence whose items are stored on the stack.

SYNOPSIS

```
template<class Item, unsigned int Size>
class Simple_Vector {
public:

  Simple_Vector ();
  Simple_Vector (const Simple_Vector <Item, Size>&);
  Simple_Vector ();

  Simple_Vector <Item, Size>&
    operator=(const Simple_Vector <Item, Size>&);
  int operator==(const Simple_Vector <Item, Size>&) const;
  int operator!=(const Simple_Vector <Item, Size>&) const;
  Item& operator[](const unsigned);

  Simple_Vector <Item, Size>& clear();
  Simple_Vector <Item, Size>& insert(Item&, unsigned before = 0);
  Simple_Vector <Item, Size>& append(Item&, unsigned after = 0);
  Simple_Vector <Item, Size>& remove_nth(unsigned at);

  unsigned length() const;
  Item* item(unsigned at) const;
  unsigned find(Item&) const;

};
```

SUPPORT CLASS CATEGORY

DESCRIPTION

A vector is a primitive sequence whose items are stored on the stack. This is a low-level abstraction: the client is responsible for establishing a policy to govern structural sharing.

A vector is not a polylithic abstraction. The semantics of copying, assignment, and equality do not involve structural sharing.

The operations of inserting, appending, and removing items are implemented such that, in the worst case, their time complexity is on the order of O(n/2).

Because vectors are stack-based, individual items are identified by an unsigned integer index. Items are indexed starting at 1, up to the length of the vector.

This class is not intended to be subclassed, and so it provides no virtual member functions.

This class is used by all bounded monolithic structures.

```
template<class Item, unsigned int Size>
```

The template item denotes the universe from which the vector draws its items. The class Item may be either a primitive type or a user-defined class. If the latter, the class must provide a default constructor, copy constructor, assignment operator, and equality operator.

The template argument Size signifies the static (and therefore bounded) number of items available to the vector.

```
Simple_Vector();
```

Construct a vector, whose length is initially 0.

```
Simple_Vector(const Simple_Vector<Item, Size>&);
```

If the given vector is empty, construct an empty vector. Otherwise, construct a vector so that it is a complete copy of the given vector.

```
Simple_Vector();
```

Destroy the vector; individual items are also destroyed.

```
Simple_Vector<Item, Size>& operator=(const Simple_Vector<Item, Size>&);
```

Clear the vector. If the given vector is not empty, set the state of the vector so that it is a complete copy of the given vector.

```
int operator==(const Simple_Vector<Item, Size>&) const;
```

Return 1 if and only if both vectors are empty or have the same number of items and the same value for each item.

```
int operator!=(const Simple_Vector<Item, Size>&) const;
```

Return the logical negation of `operator==`.

```
Item& operator[](const unsigned);
```

If the given index is 0 or larger than the length of the vector, throw the exception `Range_Error`. Otherwise, return a reference to the item at the given index.

```
Simple_Vector<Item, Size>& clear();
```

Clear the vector and set its length to 0; individual items are not destroyed.

```
Simple_Vector<Item, Size>& insert(Item&, unsigned before = 0);
```

If the vector is already full, throw the exception `Overflow`. If `before` is larger than the length of the vector, throw the exception `Range_Error`. Otherwise, insert the item before the item at the given index. If `before` is 0 (the default), insert the item at the start of the vector.

```
Simple_Vector<Item, Size>& append(Item&, unsigned after = 0);
```

If the vector is already full, throw the exception `Overflow`. If `after` is larger than the length of the vector, throw the exception `Range_Error`. Otherwise, append the item after the item at the given index. If `after` is 0 (the default), append the item at the end of the vector.

```
Simple_Vector<Item, Size>& remove_nth(unsigned at);
```

If the vector is empty, throw the exception `Underflow`. If `at` is 0 or greater than the length of the vector, throw the exception `Range_Error`. Otherwise, remove the item at the given index.

```
unsigned length() const;
```

Return the number of items in the vector.

```
Item* item(unsigned at) ;
```

Return a pointer to the item at the given index. No range checking is provided.

```
unsigned find(Item&) const;
```

Return the index of the first occurrence of the item; if no such item is found, return 0.

EXCEPTIONS

Range_Error —thrown by operator[], insert, append, and remove_nth if the given index is larger than the length of the vector.

Overflow —thrown by insert and append if the vector is already full.

Underflow —thrown by remove_nth if the vector is empty.

OPTIONS

There exists one subclass of Simple_Vector:

- Unsigned_Simple_Vector

This class provides a vector of unsigned integers.

FILES

In the support class category

```
vector    Simple_Vector
          Unsigned_Simple_Vector
```

SEE ALSO

Node (especially bounded nodes)

Heap

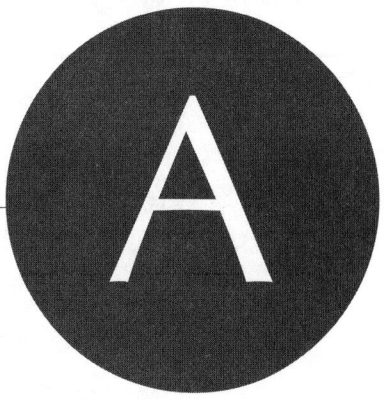

Source Code Listings

This appendix lists the source code for the example program in Chapter 1, "Using the PowerPack," including the source for the C++ Booch Components included by the program. Note that the source file suffixes vary, depending on the platform.

Example Source Code

example.[c,cpp,cp]

```
#include <stdlib.h> // for EXIT_SUCCESS, EXIT_FAILURE
#include <fstream.h>    // for ifstream
#include <iomanip.h>    // for setw
#include "str.h"        // for simple String class
#include "bag_b.h"  // for Bounded_Bag template
```

```cpp
        // typedefs cause template instantiation for Borland, tpl:
        typedef Bag<String>              bag;
        typedef Simple_Vector<String, 100U>    _vec;
        typedef Unsigned_Vector<100U>          _uvec;
        typedef Bounded_Bag<String, 100U> Collect;
        typedef Bag_Active_Iterator<String>    Iterator;

        // Local definitions:

        static void error(const char* const);

        class Include : public String {
        public:
          Include(const char* const);       // parse an #include directive
        };

        static Include includes(ifstream&);    // find Includes in file
                                  // returns "" String at eof()

        main(int argc, char* argv[])   // list #included files
        {
          Collect bag;      // collect up the #included filenames

          cout << "Files and their includes:" << endl;
          for (int i=1; i<argc; ++i) {
            const String file = argv[i];
            cout << file << ':' << endl;
            ifstream f = argv[i];     if (!f) error(argv[i]);

            Include s = includes(f);
            while ( s ) {
              cout << '\t' << s << endl;
              bag.add(s);
              s = includes(f);
            }
          }

          cout << "\nSummary:" << endl;
          for (Iterator iter(bag); !iter.is_done(); iter.next() ) {
            cout << setw(15) << *iter.item() << " included "
                 << setw(2)  << iter.size() << " times" << endl;
          }
          return EXIT_SUCCESS;
        }

        // Auxiliary support:

        static void error(const char* const s)
        {
```

```cpp
    cerr << "Error: " << s << endl;
    exit(EXIT_FAILURE);
}

#include <string.h> // for strchr
#include <stddef.h> // for ptrdiff_t

Include::Include(const char* const s)
// parses the string s to find the text between <> or ""
// examples:   #include <iostream> ==> iostream
//             #include "mine.h"   ==> mine.h
{
    if (s) {
        const char* start = s;
        const char* end = start;
        register const char* p = strchr(s,'<');
        if (p) {
            start = p+1;
            p = strchr(start, '>');
            if (!p) error("Include");
            end = p-1;
        } else {
            p = strchr(s, '"');
            if (!p) error("Include");
            start = p+1;
            p = strchr(start, '"');
            if (!p) error("Include");
            end = p-1;
        }
        ptrdiff_t len = (end>=start) ? end-start+1 : start-end+1;
        if (len) assign(start, len);    // inherited
    }
}

static Include includes(ifstream& f)
// iterate over the file a line at a time, looking for lines
// of the form "#include ..." => return the include filename
{
    static char buf[120];           // wimpy, but effective
    static const String include = "#include";

    while (f.good() && f.getline(buf, sizeof buf)) {
        if (include.matches(buf)) {
            Include line = buf;     // do the parsing
            return line;            // return the file name
        }
    }
    return 0;                       // return null string @ eof
```

STR.H

```cpp
// str.h
#ifndef STR_H
#define STR_H 1

class ostream;

class String {
public:
  String();
  String(const char* const);
  String(const String&);
  ~String();

  String& operator=(const char* const);
  String& operator=(const String&);

  int operator==(const char* const) const;
  int operator==(const String&) const;
  int operator!=(const char* const) const;
  int operator!=(const String&) const;
  int operator<=(const String&) const;
  int matches(const char* const) const;
  int matches(const String&) const;
  operator int() const;              // non-null test

  friend ostream& operator<<(ostream&, const String&);
protected:
  void assign(const char* const s, unsigned sz);
private:
  unsigned size;
  char* rep;
};

#endif
```

STR.[C,CPP,CP]

```cpp
#include "str.h"
#include <string.h>
#include <iostream.h>

ostream& operator<<(ostream& out, const String& s)
{
  return out << s.rep;
}

void String::assign(const char* const s, unsigned sz)
{
```

```cpp
  if (rep) delete [] rep;
  size = sz;
  rep = new char[size+1];
  strncpy(rep,s,size);
  rep[size] = '\0';
}

String::String() : size(0), rep(0) {}

String::String(const char* const s)
  : size(0), rep(0)
{
  if (s) assign(s,strlen(s));
}

String::String(const String& s)
  : size(0), rep(0)
{
  if (s.size) assign(s.rep, s.size);
}

String::~String()
{
  if (rep) { delete[] rep; rep = 0; size = 0; }
}

String& String::operator=(const char* const s)
{
  if (s) assign(s, strlen(s));
  return *this;
}

String& String::operator=(const String& s)
{
  if (this != &s) assign(s.rep, s.size);
  return *this;
}

int String::operator==(const char* const s) const
{
  return (!s && !rep) || !strcmp(rep, s);
}

int String::operator==(const String& s) const
{
  return (size == s.size) && operator==(s.rep);
}

int String::operator!=(const char* const s) const
{
```

```
    return !operator==(s);
}

int String::operator!=(const String& s) const
{
    return !operator==(s);
}

int String::operator<=(const String& s) const
{
    return strcmp(rep,s.rep) <= 0;
}

int String::matches(const char* const s) const
{
    return (!s && !rep) || !strncmp(rep, s, size);
}

int String::matches(const String& s) const
{
    return matches(s.rep);
}

String::operator int() const
{
    return size>0;
}
```

SUPPORT.[CPP,CP]

This file is not needed by C++ implementation environments that support Automatic Template Instantiation (ATI).

```
// support file to trick non-cfront implementations into template
// instantiations

#include "str.h"    // for simple String class

#if macintosh
#include "svector.cp"   // for Simple_Vector template
#include "bag.cp"       // for Bag template
#include "bag_b.cp" // for Bounded_Bag template
#endif

#if __BORLANDC__
#include "svector.cpp"
#include "bag.cpp"
#include "bag_b.cpp"
```

```
typedef Simple_Vector<String, 100U> _vector1;
typedef Unsigned_Vector<100U> _vector2;
typedef Bag<String> _string_bag;
typedef Bounded_Bag<String, 100U> _string_bag2;
typedef Bag_Active_Iterator<String> _iter1;
typedef Bag_Passive_Iterator<String> _iter2;
#endif
```

SUPPORT2.[CPP,CP]

This file is not needed by C++ implementation environments that support Automatic Template Instantiation (ATI).

```
// support file to trick non-cfront implementations into template
// instantiations

#if macintosh
#include "svector.cp"      // for Simple_Vector template
#endif

#if __BORLANDC__
#include "svector.cpp"

typedef Simple_Vector<unsigned, 100U> _vector;
#endif
```

COMPONENTS—STRUCTURES

BAG.H

```
//  The C++ Booch Components (Version 1.4.7)
//  (C) Copyright 1990-1992 Grady Booch. All Rights Reserved.
//
//  bag.h
//
//  This file contains the declaration of the bag abstract base
//  class and its iterators.

#ifndef _BAG_H
#define _BAG_H 1

template<class Item>
class Bag_Active_Iterator;

template<class Item>
class Bag_Passive_Iterator;
```

```cpp
// Bag abstract base class

template<class Item>
class Bag {
public:

  Bag();
  Bag(const Bag<Item>&);
  virtual ~Bag();

  Bag<Item>& operator=(Bag<Item>&);
  virtual int operator==(Bag<Item>&) const;
  virtual int operator!=(Bag<Item>&) const;

  virtual Bag<Item>& clear();
  virtual Bag<Item>& add(const Item&);
  virtual Bag<Item>& remove(const Item&);
  virtual Bag<Item>& bag_union(Bag<Item>&);
  virtual Bag<Item>& intersection(Bag<Item>&);
  virtual Bag<Item>& difference(Bag<Item>&);

  virtual unsigned extent() const;
  virtual unsigned size() const;
  virtual unsigned number(const Item&) const;
  virtual int is_empty() const;
  virtual int is_member(const Item&) const;
  virtual int is_subset(Bag<Item>&) const;
  virtual int is_proper_subset(Bag<Item>&) const;

protected:

  unsigned rep_extent;
  unsigned rep_size;

  virtual void purge();
  virtual void append(const Item&, unsigned count);
  virtual void expunge(void*, unsigned count);
  virtual void increment(void*, unsigned count);
  virtual void decrement(void*, unsigned count);
  virtual void* exists(const Item&) const = 0;

  virtual void lock_argument();
  virtual void unlock_argument();

  virtual void* iter_first() const = 0;
  virtual void* iter_next(void*) const = 0;
  virtual int iter_is_done(void*) const = 0;
  virtual Item* iter_item(void*) const = 0;
  virtual unsigned iter_size(void*) const = 0;
```

```cpp
private:

  friend class Bag_Active_Iterator<Item>;
  friend class Bag_Passive_Iterator<Item>;

};

// Bag iterators

template <class Item>
class Bag_Active_Iterator {
public:

  Bag_Active_Iterator(const Bag<Item>&);
  virtual ~Bag_Active_Iterator();

  virtual void reset();
  virtual int next();

  virtual int is_done();
  virtual Item* item();
  virtual unsigned size();

protected:

  const Bag<Item>& rep_bag;
  void* rep_current;

};

template <class Item>
class Bag_Passive_Iterator {
public:

  Bag_Passive_Iterator(const Bag<Item>&);
  virtual ~Bag_Passive_Iterator();

  virtual int apply(int (*)(Item*, unsigned));

protected:

  const Bag<Item>& rep_bag;

};

#endif
```

BAG.[C,CPP,CP]

```cpp
//  The C++ Booch Components (Version 1.4.7)
//  (C) Copyright 1990-1992 Grady Booch. All Rights Reserved.
//
//  Restricted Rights Legend
//  Use, duplication, or disclosure is subject to restrictions as
//  set forth in subdivision (c)(1)(ii) of the Rights in Technical
//  Data and Computer Software clause at DFARS 252.227-7013.
//
//  bag.c
//
//  This file contains the definitions for the bag abstract base
//  class and its iterators.

#include "except.h"
#include "bag.h"

template<class Item>
Bag<Item>::Bag()
  : rep_extent(0), rep_size(0) {}

template<class Item>
Bag<Item>::Bag(const Bag<Item>& b)
  : rep_extent(b.rep_extent), rep_size(b.rep_size) {}

template<class Item>
Bag<Item>::~Bag() {}

template<class Item>
Bag<Item>& Bag<Item>::operator=(Bag<Item>& b)
{
  if (this == &b)
    return *this;
  b.lock_argument();
  purge();
  Bag_Active_Iterator<Item> iter(b);
  while (!iter.is_done()) {
    append(*iter.item(), iter.size());
    iter.next();
  }
  b.unlock_argument();
  return *this;
}

template<class Item>
int Bag<Item>::operator==(Bag<Item>& b) const
{
  if (this == &b)
    return 1;
```

```
    b.lock_argument();
    if ((rep_extent != b.rep_extent) || (rep_size != b.rep_size)) {
      b.unlock_argument();
      return 0;
    }
    Bag_Active_Iterator<Item> iter(b);
    while (!iter.is_done()) {
      void* i = exists(*iter.item());
      if ((i == 0) || (iter_size(i) != iter.size()))  {
        b.unlock_argument();
        return 0;
      }
      iter.next();
    }
    b.unlock_argument();
    return 1;
}

template<class Item>
int Bag<Item>::operator!=(Bag<Item>& b) const
{
  return !operator==(b);
}

template<class Item>
Bag<Item>& Bag<Item>::clear()
{
  purge();
  return *this;
}

template<class Item>
Bag<Item>& Bag<Item>::add(const Item&)
{
  rep_extent++;
  rep_size++;
  return *this;
}

template<class Item>
Bag<Item>& Bag<Item>::remove(const Item&)
{
  if (rep_extent == 0)
    throw(Underflow("Bag<Item>::remove()", _EMPTY));
  --rep_extent;
  --rep_size;
  return *this;
}

template<class Item>
```

```cpp
Bag<Item>& Bag<Item>::bag_union(Bag<Item>& b)
{
  if (this == &b)
    return *this;
  b.lock_argument();
  Bag_Active_Iterator<Item> iter(b);
  while (!iter.is_done()) {
    void* i = exists(*iter.item());
    if (!i)
      append(*iter.item(), iter.size());
    else
      increment(i, iter.size());
    iter.next();
  }
  b.unlock_argument();
  return *this;
}

template<class Item>
Bag<Item>& Bag<Item>::intersection(Bag<Item>& b)
{
  if (this == &b)
    return *this;
  b.lock_argument();
  void* i = iter_first();
  while (!iter_is_done(i)) {
    void* j = b.exists(*iter_item(i));
    if (!j) {
      void* temp = iter_next(i);
      expunge(i, iter_size(i));
      i = temp;
    } else {
      int delta = iter_size(i) - b.iter_size(j);
      if (delta > 0)
        decrement(i, delta);
      i = iter_next(i);
    }
  }
  b.unlock_argument();
  return *this;
}

template<class Item>
Bag<Item>& Bag<Item>::difference(Bag<Item>& b)
{
  if (this == &b) {
    purge();
    return *this;
  }
  b.lock_argument();
```

```cpp
  Bag_Active_Iterator<Item> iter(b);
  while (!iter.is_done()) {
    void* i;
    if ((i = exists(*iter.item())) != 0) {
      int delta = iter_size(i) - iter.size();
      if (delta > 0)
        decrement(i, iter.size());
      else
        expunge(i, iter_size(i));
    }
    iter.next();
  }
  b.unlock_argument();
  return *this;
}

template<class Item>
unsigned Bag<Item>::extent() const
{
  return rep_extent;
}

template<class Item>
unsigned Bag<Item>::size() const
{
  return rep_size;
}

template<class Item>
unsigned Bag<Item>::number(const Item& item) const
{
  void* i = exists(item);
  if (!i)
    return 0;
  else
    return iter_size(i);
}

template<class Item>
int Bag<Item>::is_empty() const
{
  return (rep_extent == 0);
}

template<class Item>
int Bag<Item>::is_member(const Item& item) const
{
  return (exists(item) != 0);
}
```

```cpp
template<class Item>
int Bag<Item>::is_subset(Bag<Item>& b) const
{
  if (this == &b)
    return 1;
  b.lock_argument();
  if ((rep_extent > b.rep_extent) || (rep_size > b.rep_size)) {
    b.unlock_argument();
    return 0;
  }
  Bag_Active_Iterator<Item> iter(*this);
  while (!iter.is_done()) {
    void* i = b.exists(*iter.item());
    if ((!i) || (iter.size() > b.iter_size(i))) {
      b.unlock_argument();
      return 0;
    }
    iter.next();
  }
  b.unlock_argument();
  return 1;
}

template<class Item>
int Bag<Item>::is_proper_subset(Bag<Item>& b) const
{
  if (this == &b)
    return 0;
  b.lock_argument();
  if ((rep_extent >= b.rep_extent) || (rep_size >= b.rep_size)) {
    b.unlock_argument();
    return 0;
  }
  Bag_Active_Iterator<Item> iter(*this);
  while (!iter.is_done()) {
    void* i = b.exists(*iter.item());
    if ((!i) || (iter.size() > b.iter_size(i))) {
      b.unlock_argument();
      return 0;
    }
    iter.next();
  }
  b.unlock_argument();
  return 1;
}

template<class Item>
void Bag<Item>::purge()
{
  rep_extent = 0;
```

```cpp
    rep_size = 0;
}

template<class Item>
void Bag<Item>::append(const Item&, unsigned count)
{
  rep_extent++;
  rep_size += count;
}

template<class Item>
void Bag<Item>::expunge(void*, unsigned count)
{
  --rep_extent;
  rep_size -= count;
}

template<class Item>
void Bag<Item>::increment(void*, unsigned count)
{
  rep_size += count;
}

template<class Item>
void Bag<Item>::decrement(void*, unsigned count)
{
  rep_size -= count;
}

template<class Item>
void Bag<Item>::lock_argument()
{
}

template<class Item>
void Bag<Item>::unlock_argument()
{
}

template<class Item>
Bag_Active_Iterator<Item>::Bag_Active_Iterator(const Bag<Item>& b)
  : rep_bag(b), rep_current(b.iter_first()) {}

template<class Item>
Bag_Active_Iterator<Item>::~Bag_Active_Iterator() {}

template<class Item>
void Bag_Active_Iterator<Item>::reset()
{
  rep_current = rep_bag.iter_first();
}
```

```cpp
template<class Item>
int Bag_Active_Iterator<Item>::next()
{
  if (rep_current)
    rep_current = rep_bag.iter_next(rep_current);
  return (!rep_bag.iter_is_done(rep_current));
}

template<class Item>
int Bag_Active_Iterator<Item>::is_done()
{
  return rep_bag.iter_is_done(rep_current);
}

template<class Item>
Item* Bag_Active_Iterator<Item>::item()
{
  return (!rep_current) ? 0 : rep_bag.iter_item(rep_current);
}

template<class Item>
unsigned Bag_Active_Iterator<Item>::size()
{
  return rep_bag.iter_size(rep_current);
}

template<class Item>
Bag_Passive_Iterator<Item>::Bag_Passive_Iterator(const Bag<Item>& b)
  : rep_bag(b) {}

template<class Item>
Bag_Passive_Iterator<Item>::~Bag_Passive_Iterator() {}

template<class Item>
int Bag_Passive_Iterator<Item>::apply(int (*f)(Item*, unsigned))
{
  void * i = rep_bag.iter_first();
  while (!rep_bag.iter_is_done(i)) {
    if (!f(rep_bag.iter_item(i), rep_bag.iter_size(i)))
      return 0;
    i = rep_bag.iter_next(i);
  }
  return 1;
}
```

BAG_B.H

```
// The C++ Booch Components (Version 1.4.7)
// (C) Copyright 1990-1992 Grady Booch. All Rights Reserved.
//
```

```cpp
//  bag_b.h
//
//  This file contains the declaration of the bounded bag.

#ifndef _BAG_B_H
#define _BAG_B_H 1

#include "svector.h"
#include "bag.h"

// Bounded bag

template<class Item, unsigned int Size>
class Bounded_Bag : private Simple_Vector<Item, Size>,
                    public Bag<Item> {
public:

  Bounded_Bag();
  Bounded_Bag(const Bounded_Bag<Item, Size>&);
  virtual ~Bounded_Bag();

  Bounded_Bag<Item, Size>& operator=(Bounded_Bag<Item, Size>&);
  virtual int operator==(Bag<Item>&) const;
  virtual int operator!=(Bag<Item>&) const;

  virtual Bag<Item>& clear();
  virtual Bag<Item>& add(const Item&);
  virtual Bag<Item>& remove(const Item&);

  virtual unsigned available() const;

protected:

  Unsigned_Vector<Size> rep_count;

  virtual void purge();
  virtual void append(const Item&, unsigned);
  virtual void expunge(void*, unsigned);
  virtual void increment(void*, unsigned);
  virtual void decrement(void*, unsigned);
  virtual void* exists(const Item&) const;

  virtual void* iter_first() const;
  virtual void* iter_next(void*) const;
  virtual int iter_is_done(void*) const;
  virtual Item* iter_item(void*) const;
  virtual unsigned iter_size(void*) const;

};

#endif
```

BAG_B.[C,CPP,CP]

```cpp
//  The C++ Booch Components (Version 1.4.7)
//  (C) Copyright 1990-1992 Grady Booch. All Rights Reserved.
//
//  Restricted Rights Legend
//  Use, duplication, or disclosure is subject to restrictions as
//  set forth in subdivision (c)(1)(ii) of the Rights in Technical
//  Data and Computer Software clause at DFARS 252.227-7013.
//
//  bag_b.cp
//
//  This file contains the definitions for the bounded bag.

#include "except.h"
#include "bag_b.h"

template<class Item, unsigned int Size>
Bounded_Bag<Item, Size>::Bounded_Bag() {}

template<class Item, unsigned int Size>
Bounded_Bag<Item, Size>::
  Bounded_Bag(const Bounded_Bag<Item, Size>& b)
    : Bag<Item>(b), Simple_Vector<Item, Size>(b),
rep_count(b.rep_count) {}

template<class Item, unsigned int Size>
Bounded_Bag<Item, Size>::~Bounded_Bag() {}

template<class Item, unsigned int Size>
Bounded_Bag<Item, Size>& Bounded_Bag<Item, Size>::
  operator=(Bounded_Bag<Item, Size>& b)
{
  Bag<Item>::operator=(b);
  return *this;
}

template<class Item, unsigned int Size>
int Bounded_Bag<Item, Size>::operator==(Bag<Item>& b) const
{
  return Bag<Item>::operator==(b);
}

template<class Item, unsigned int Size>
int Bounded_Bag<Item, Size>::operator!=(Bag<Item>& b) const
{
  return Bag<Item>::operator!=(b);
}

template<class Item, unsigned int Size>
```

```cpp
Bag<Item>& Bounded_Bag<Item, Size>::clear()
{
  Bag<Item>::clear();
  return *this;
}

template<class Item, unsigned int Size>
Bag<Item>& Bounded_Bag<Item, Size>::add(const Item& item)
{
  unsigned n = find(item);
  if (n) {
    rep_count[n] += 1;
    rep_size++;
  } else {
    Bag<Item>::add(item);
    Simple_Vector<Item, Size>::insert(item);
    rep_count.insert(1);
  }
  return *this;
}

template<class Item, unsigned int Size>
Bag<Item>& Bounded_Bag<Item, Size>::remove(const Item& item)
{
  unsigned n = find(item);
  if (!n)
    throw(Not_Found("Bounded_Bag<Item, Size>::remove()", _MISSING));
  if (rep_count[n] -= 1)
    --rep_size;
  else {
    Bag<Item>::remove(item);
    Simple_Vector<Item, Size>::remove_nth(n);
    rep_count.remove_nth(n);
  }
  return *this;
}

template<class Item, unsigned int Size>
unsigned Bounded_Bag<Item, Size>::available() const
{
  return (Size - rep_extent);
}

template<class Item, unsigned int Size>
void Bounded_Bag<Item, Size>::purge()
{
  Bag<Item>::purge();
  Simple_Vector<Item, Size>::clear();
  rep_count.clear();
}
```

```cpp
template<class Item, unsigned int Size>
void Bounded_Bag<Item, Size>::append(const Item& item, unsigned count)
{
  Bag<Item>::append(item, count);
  Simple_Vector<Item, Size>::append(item);
  rep_count.append(count);
}

template<class Item, unsigned int Size>
void Bounded_Bag<Item, Size>::expunge(void* ptr, unsigned count)
{
  Bag<Item>::expunge(ptr, count);
  Simple_Vector<Item, Size>::remove_nth(rep_extent - (unsigned)ptr + 2);
  rep_count.remove_nth(rep_extent - (unsigned)ptr + 2);
}

template<class Item, unsigned int Size>
void Bounded_Bag<Item, Size>::increment(void* ptr, unsigned count)
{
  Bag<Item>::increment(ptr, count);
  rep_count[rep_extent - (unsigned)ptr + 1] += count;
}

template<class Item, unsigned int Size>
void Bounded_Bag<Item, Size>::decrement(void* ptr, unsigned count)
{
  Bag<Item>::decrement(ptr, count);
  rep_count[rep_extent - (unsigned)ptr + 1] -= count;
}

template<class Item, unsigned int Size>
void* Bounded_Bag<Item, Size>::exists(const Item& item) const
{
  unsigned l = find(item);
  return (l == 0) ? 0 : (void*)(rep_extent + 1 - l);
}

template<class Item, unsigned int Size>
void* Bounded_Bag<Item, Size>::iter_first() const
{
  return (void*)rep_extent;
}

template<class Item, unsigned int Size>
void* Bounded_Bag<Item, Size>::iter_next(void* ptr) const
{
  return (void*)((unsigned)ptr - 1);
}
```

```cpp
template<class Item, unsigned int Size>
int Bounded_Bag<Item, Size>::iter_is_done(void* ptr) const
{
  return (ptr == 0);
}

template<class Item, unsigned int Size>
Item* Bounded_Bag<Item, Size>::iter_item(void* ptr) const
{
  return (ptr == 0) ? 0 : (item(rep_extent - (unsigned)ptr + 1));
}

template<class Item, unsigned int Size>
unsigned Bounded_Bag<Item, Size>::iter_size(void* ptr) const
{
  return *rep_count.item(rep_extent - (unsigned)ptr + 1);
}
```

Components—Support

SVECTOR.H

```cpp
//  The C++ Booch Components (Version 1.4.7)
//  (C) Copyright 1990-1992 Grady Booch. All Rights Reserved.
//
//  svector.h
//
//  This file contains the declaration of the vector class
//  used in bounded storage management.

#ifndef _SVECTOR_H
#define _SVECTOR_H 1

template<class Item, unsigned int Size>
  class Simple_Vector_Active_Iterator;
template<class Item, unsigned int Size>
  class Simple_Vector_Passive_Iterator;

// Vector class for storage management in bounded classes

template<class Item, unsigned int Size>
class Simple_Vector {
public:

  Simple_Vector();
  Simple_Vector(const Simple_Vector<Item, Size>&);
  ~Simple_Vector();
```

```cpp
  Simple_Vector<Item, Size>& operator=(const Simple_Vector<Item,
                                       Size>&);
  int operator==(const Simple_Vector<Item, Size>&) const;
  int operator!=(const Simple_Vector<Item, Size>&) const;
  Item& operator[](const unsigned);

  Simple_Vector<Item, Size>& clear();
  Simple_Vector<Item, Size>& insert(const Item&, unsigned before = 0);
  Simple_Vector<Item, Size>& append(const Item&, unsigned after = 0);
  Simple_Vector<Item, Size>& remove_nth(unsigned at);

  unsigned length() const;
  Item* item(unsigned at) const;
  unsigned find(const Item&) const;

protected:

  Item rep[Size];
  unsigned rep_start;
  unsigned rep_stop;

  unsigned expand_left(unsigned from);
  unsigned expand_right(unsigned from);
  void shrink_left(unsigned from);
  void shrink_right(unsigned from);

private:

  friend class Simple_Vector_Active_Iterator<Item, Size>;
  friend class Simple_Vector_Passive_Iterator<Item, Size>;

};

// Vector iterators

template<class Item, unsigned int Size>
class Simple_Vector_Active_Iterator {
public:

  Simple_Vector_Active_Iterator(const Simple_Vector<Item, Size>&);
  virtual ~Simple_Vector_Active_Iterator();

  virtual void reset();
  virtual int next();

  virtual int is_done();
  virtual Item* item();

protected:
```

```cpp
    const Simple_Vector<Item, Size>& rep_vector;
    unsigned rep_current;
    unsigned rep_limit;

};

template<class Item, unsigned int Size>
class Simple_Vector_Passive_Iterator {
public:

    Simple_Vector_Passive_Iterator(const Simple_Vector<Item, Size>&);
    virtual ~Simple_Vector_Passive_Iterator();

    virtual int apply(int (*)(Item*));

protected:

    const Simple_Vector<Item, Size>& rep_vector;
    unsigned rep_limit;

};

// Unsigned vector class

template<unsigned int Size>
class Unsigned_Vector: public Simple_Vector<unsigned, Size> {
public:

    Unsigned_Vector();
    virtual ~Unsigned_Vector();

};

#endif
```

SVECTOR.[C,CPP,CP]

```
//  The C++ Booch Components (Version 1.4.7)
//  (C) Copyright 1990-1992 Grady Booch. All Rights Reserved.
//
//  Restricted Rights Legend
//  Use, duplication, or disclosure is subject to restrictions as
//  set forth in subdivision (c)(1)(ii) of the Rights in Technical
//  Data and Computer Software clause at DFARS 252.227-7013.
//
//  svector.c
//
//  This file contains the definitions for the classes supporting
//  bounded storage management.
```

```cpp
#include "except.h"
#include "svector.h"

template<class Item, unsigned int Size>
Simple_Vector<Item, Size>::Simple_Vector()
  : rep_start(0), rep_stop(0) {}

template<class Item, unsigned int Size>
Simple_Vector<Item, Size>::Simple_Vector(const Simple_Vector<Item,
Size>& v)
  : rep_start(v.rep_start), rep_stop(v.rep_stop)
{
  unsigned i;
  if (rep_start)
    if (rep_start <= rep_stop)
      for (i = rep_start; (i <= rep_stop); i++)
        rep[i - 1] = v.rep[i - 1];
    else {
      for (i = rep_start; (i <= Size); i++)
        rep[i - 1] = v.rep[i - 1];
      for (i = 1; (i <= rep_stop); i++)
        rep[i - 1] = v.rep[i - 1];
    }
}

template<class Item, unsigned int Size>
Simple_Vector<Item, Size>::~Simple_Vector() {}

template<class Item, unsigned int Size>
Simple_Vector<Item, Size>& Simple_Vector<Item, Size>::operator=(const
Simple_Vector<Item, Size>& v)
{
  unsigned i;
  rep_start = v.rep_start;
  rep_stop = v.rep_stop;
  if (rep_start)
    if (rep_start <= rep_stop)
      for (i = rep_start; (i <= rep_stop); i++)
        rep[i - 1] = v.rep[i - 1];
    else {
      for (i = rep_start; (i <= Size); i++)
        rep[i - 1] = v.rep[i - 1];
      for (i = 1; i <= rep_stop; i++)
        rep[i - 1] = v.rep[i - 1];
    }
  return *this;
}

template<class Item, unsigned int Size>
int Simple_Vector<Item, Size>::operator==(const Simple_Vector<Item,
Size>& v) const
{
```

Source Code Listings

```cpp
  unsigned n = length();
  if (n == v.length()) {
    for (register unsigned i = 1; (i <= n); i++)
      if (*item(i) != *(v.item(i)))
        return 0;
    return 1;
  } else
    return 0;
}

template<class Item, unsigned int Size>
int Simple_Vector<Item, Size>::operator!=(const Simple_Vector<Item, Size>& v) const
{
  return !operator==(v);
}

template<class Item, unsigned int Size>
Item& Simple_Vector<Item, Size>::operator[](const unsigned index)
{
  if ((index == 0) || (index > length()))
    throw(Range_Error("Simple_Vector<Item, Size>::operator[]",
                      _INVALID_INDEX));
  return *item(index);
}

template<class Item, unsigned int Size>
Simple_Vector<Item, Size>& Simple_Vector<Item, Size>::clear () {
  rep_start = rep_stop = 0;
  return *this;
}

template<class Item, unsigned int Size>
Simple_Vector<Item, Size>& Simple_Vector<Item, Size>::insert(const Item& item, unsigned before)
{
  unsigned n = length();
  if (n == Size)
    throw(Overflow("Simple_Vector<Item, Size>::insert()", _FULL));
  if (before > n)
    throw(Range_Error("Simple_Vector<Item, Size>::insert()",
                      _INVALID_INDEX));
  if ((before == 0) && (n > 0))
    before = 1;
  if (before > 0)
    if (rep_start <= rep_stop)
      if (before <= (rep_stop - rep_start - before + 2)) {
        unsigned x = expand_left(rep_start + before - 2) - 1;
        rep[x] = (Item&)item;
```

```cpp
      } else {
        unsigned p = rep_start + before - 1;
        expand_right(p);
        rep[p - 1] = (Item&)item;
      }
    else
      if (before <= (Size - rep_start + 1))
        rep[expand_left(rep_start + before - 2) - 1] = (Item&)item;
      else
        rep[expand_right(rep_start + before - 1 - Size) - 1]
                            = (Item&)item;
  else {
    rep_start = rep_stop = 1;
    rep[rep_start - 1] = (Item&)item;
  }
  return *this;
}

template<class Item, unsigned int Size>
Simple_Vector<Item, Size>& Simple_Vector<Item, Size>::append(const Item&
item, unsigned after)
{
  unsigned n = length();
  if (n == Size)
    throw(Overflow("Simple_Vector<Item, Size>::append()", _FULL));
  if (after > n)
    throw(Range_Error("Simple_Vector<Item, Size>::append()",
                      _INVALID_INDEX));
  if ((after == 0) && (n > 0))
    after = n;
  if (after > 0)
    if (rep_start <= rep_stop)
      if (after < (rep_stop - rep_start - after + 2)) {
        unsigned p = rep_start + after - 1;
        expand_left(p);
        rep[p - 1] = (Item&)item;
      } else
        rep[expand_right(rep_start + after) - 1] = (Item&)item;
    else
      if (after <= (Size - rep_start + 1))
        rep[expand_left(rep_start + after - 1) - 1] = (Item&)item;
      else
        rep[expand_right(rep_start + after - Size) - 1] = (Item&)item;
  else {
    rep_start = rep_stop = 1;
    rep[rep_start - 1] = (Item&)item;
  }
  return *this;
}
```

```cpp
template<class Item, unsigned int Size>
Simple_Vector<Item, Size>& Simple_Vector<Item,
Size>::remove_nth(unsigned at)
{
  unsigned n = length();
  if (n == 0)
    throw(Underflow("Simple_Vector<Item, Size>::remove_nth()",
_EMPTY));
  if ((at > n) || (at == 0))
    throw(Range_Error("Simple_Vector<Item, Size>::remove_nth()",
_INVALID_INDEX));
  if (rep_start <= rep_stop)
    if (at <= (rep_stop - rep_start - at + 2))
      shrink_left(rep_start + at - 1);
    else
      shrink_right(rep_start + at - 1);
  else
    if (at <= (Size - rep_start + 1))
      shrink_left(rep_start + at - 1);
    else
      shrink_right(rep_start + at - 1 - Size);
  if (n == 1)
    rep_start = rep_stop = 0;
  return *this;
}

template<class Item, unsigned int Size>
unsigned Simple_Vector<Item, Size>::length() const
{
  if (rep_start)
    if (rep_start <= rep_stop)
      return (rep_stop - rep_start + 1);
    else
      return (Size - rep_start + rep_stop + 1);
  else
    return 0;
}

template<class Item, unsigned int Size>
Item* Simple_Vector<Item, Size>::item(unsigned at) const
{
  Item* ptr;
  if (rep_start <= rep_stop)
    ptr = (Item*)(&rep[rep_start + at - 2]);
  else {
    unsigned n = rep_start + at - 1;
    if (n > Size)
      n -= Size;
    ptr = (Item*)(&rep[n - 1]);
  }
```

```cpp
    return ptr;
}

template<class Item, unsigned int Size>
unsigned Simple_Vector<Item, Size>::find(const Item& it) const
{
  unsigned n = length();
  for (register unsigned i = 1; i <= length(); ++i)
    if (*item(i) == (Item&)it)
      return i;
  return 0;
}

template<class Item, unsigned int Size>
unsigned Simple_Vector<Item, Size>::expand_left(unsigned from)
{
  unsigned i = rep_start;
  if (i == 1) {
    i++;
    if (from)
      rep[Size - 1] = rep[0];
  }
  for (; i <= from; i++)
    rep[i - 2] = rep[i - 1];
  if (rep_start == 1)
    rep_start = Size;
  else
    rep_start--;
  return (from) ? from : Size;
}

template<class Item, unsigned int Size>
unsigned Simple_Vector<Item, Size>::expand_right(unsigned from)
{
  unsigned i = rep_stop;
  if (i == Size) {
    i--;
    if (from)
      rep[0] = rep[Size - 1];
  }
  for (; i >= from; i--)
    rep[i] = rep[i - 1];
  if (rep_stop == Size)
    rep_stop = 1;
  else
    rep_stop++;
  return (from > Size) ? 1 : from;
}
```

```cpp
template<class Item, unsigned int Size>
void Simple_Vector<Item, Size>::shrink_left(unsigned from)
{
  for (register unsigned i = from; i > rep_start; i--)
    rep[i - 1] = rep[i - 2];
  if (rep_start == Size)
    rep_start = 1;
  else
    rep_start++;
}

template<class Item, unsigned int Size>
void Simple_Vector<Item, Size>::shrink_right(unsigned from)
{
  for (register unsigned i = from; i < rep_stop; i++)
    rep[i - 1] = rep[i];
  if (rep_stop == 1)
    rep_stop = Size;
  else
    rep_stop--;
}

template<class Item, unsigned int Size>
Simple_Vector_Active_Iterator<Item, Size>::
  Simple_Vector_Active_Iterator(const Simple_Vector<Item, Size>& v)
    : rep_vector(v), rep_current(1), rep_limit(v.length()) {}

template<class Item, unsigned int Size>
Simple_Vector_Active_Iterator<Item,
Size>::~Simple_Vector_Active_Iterator () {}

template<class Item, unsigned int Size>
void Simple_Vector_Active_Iterator<Item, Size>::reset()
{
  rep_current = 1;
}

template<class Item, unsigned int Size>
int Simple_Vector_Active_Iterator<Item, Size>::next()
{
  if (rep_current <= rep_limit)
    rep_current++;
  return (rep_current <= rep_limit);
}

template<class Item, unsigned int Size>
int Simple_Vector_Active_Iterator<Item, Size>::is_done()
{
  return (rep_current > rep_limit);
}
```

```cpp
template<class Item, unsigned int Size>
Item* Simple_Vector_Active_Iterator<Item, Size>::item()
{
  return (rep_current > rep_limit) ? 0 : &(rep_vector[rep_current]);
}

template<class Item, unsigned int Size>
Simple_Vector_Passive_Iterator<Item, Size>::
  Simple_Vector_Passive_Iterator(const Simple_Vector<Item, Size>& v)
    : rep_vector(v), rep_limit(v.length()) {}

template<class Item, unsigned int Size>
Simple_Vector_Passive_Iterator<Item,
Size>::~Simple_Vector_Passive_Iterator() {}

template<class Item, unsigned int Size>
int Simple_Vector_Passive_Iterator<Item, Size>::apply(register int
(*f)(Item*))
{
  for (register i = 1; i <= rep_limit; i++)
    if (!f(&rep_vector[i])) return 0;
  return 1;
}

template<unsigned int Size>
Unsigned_Vector<Size>::Unsigned_Vector() {}

template<unsigned int Size>
Unsigned_Vector<Size>::~Unsigned_Vector() {}
```

Except.h

```cpp
//  The C++ Booch Components (Version 1.4.7)
//  (C) Copyright 1990-1992 Grady Booch. All Rights Reserved.
//
//  except.h
//
//  This file contains the declaration of the classes and
//  functions associated with exception handling.

#ifndef _EXCEPT_H
#define _EXCEPT_H 1

class ostream;

// Exception base class

class Exception {
public:
```

Source Code Listings

```cpp
    Exception(const char* name, const char* who, const char* what);
    virtual ~Exception();

    virtual void display(ostream&) const;

    const char* name() const;
    const char* who() const;
    const char* what() const;

protected:

    enum { MAX = 63 };

    char rep_name[MAX+1];
    char rep_who [MAX+1];
    char rep_what[MAX+1];

private:

    friend ostream& operator<<(ostream&, const Exception&);

};

// Predefined global exceptions

class Duplicate : public Exception {
public:

    Duplicate(const char* who, const char* what);
    virtual ~Duplicate();

};

class Container_Error : public Exception {
public:

    Container_Error(const char* who, const char* what);
    virtual ~Container_Error();

};

class Illegal_Pattern : public Exception {
public:

    Illegal_Pattern(const char* who, const char* what);
    virtual ~Illegal_Pattern();

};

class Is_Null : public Exception {
public:
```

```cpp
  Is_Null(const char* who, const char* what);
  virtual ~Is_Null();

};

class Lexical_Error : public Exception {
public:

  Lexical_Error(const char* who, const char* what);
  virtual ~Lexical_Error();

};

class Math_Error : public Exception {
public:

 Math_Error(const char* who, const char* what, int errno);
 virtual ~Math_Error();

 virtual void display(ostream&) const;

protected:

   int rep_err;

};

class Not_Found : public Exception {
public:

  Not_Found(const char* who, const char* what);
  virtual ~Not_Found();

};

class Not_Null : public Exception {
public:

  Not_Null(const char* who, const char* what);
  virtual ~Not_Null();

};

class Not_Root : public Exception {
public:

  Not_Root(const char* who, const char* what);
  virtual ~Not_Root();

};
```

```cpp
class Overflow : public Exception {
public:

  Overflow(const char* who, const char* what);
  virtual ~Overflow();

};

class Position_Error : public Exception {
public:

  Position_Error(const char* who, const char* what);
  virtual ~Position_Error();

};

class Range_Error : public Exception {
public:

  Range_Error(const char* who, const char* what);
  virtual ~Range_Error();

};

class Storage_Error : public Exception {
public:

  Storage_Error(const char* who, const char* what);
  virtual ~Storage_Error();

};

class Underflow : public Exception {
public:

  Underflow(const char* who, const char* what);
  virtual ~Underflow();

};

// Common exceptions

extern const char* _DISJOINT;
extern const char* _DUPLICATE;
extern const char* _EMPTY;
extern const char* _FULL;
extern const char* _ILLEGAL;
extern const char* _INVALID_INDEX;
extern const char* _INVALID_NUMBER;
extern const char* _MISSING;
```

```
extern const char* _NOT_EMPTY;
extern const char* _NOT_ROOT;
extern const char* _NULL;
extern const char* _OUT_OF_MEMORY;
extern const char* _TOO_LARGE;
extern const char* _TOO_SMALL;

// Exception handler

extern void _catch(const Exception&);

// Termination operations

typedef void (*PFV)();

extern PFV set_terminate(PFV);

extern void terminate();

#endif
```

EXCEPT.[C,CPP,CP]

```
//  The C++ Booch Components (Version 1.4.7)
//  (C) Copyright 1990-1992 Grady Booch. All Rights Reserved.
//
//  Restricted Rights Legend
//  Use, duplication, or disclosure is subject to restrictions as
//  set forth in subdivision (c)(1)(ii) of the Rights in Technical
//  Data and Computer
//  Software clause at DFARS 252.227-7013.
//
//  except.c
//
//  This file contains the definitions for the classes and
//  functions associated with exception handling.

#include <stdlib.h>
#include <string.h>
#include <iostream.h>
#include "except.h"

const char* _DISJOINT = "objects are members of different
                         structures";
const char* _DUPLICATE = "object already exists";
const char* _EMPTY = "object is empty";
const char* _FULL = "the object is full";
const char* _ILLEGAL = "illegal pattern";
const char* _INVALID_INDEX = "index is out of range";
```

```cpp
const char* _INVALID_NUMBER = "string does not denote a valid number";
const char* _MISSING = "object does not exist";
const char* _NULL = "object is null";
const char* _NOT_EMPTY = "object is not empty";
const char* _NOT_ROOT = "object is not at root of structure";
const char* _OUT_OF_MEMORY = "heap storage exhausted";
const char* _TOO_LARGE = "object is too large";
const char* _TOO_SMALL = "object is too small";

static const char EOS = '\0';

Exception::Exception(const char* name, const char* who,
                     const char* what)
{
  rep_name[0] = rep_who [0] = rep_what[0] = EOS;
  if (name)
    strncpy(rep_name, name, MAX);
  if (who)
    strncpy(rep_who,  who , MAX);
  if (what)
    strncpy(rep_what, what, MAX);
  rep_name[MAX] = rep_who [MAX] = rep_what[MAX] = EOS;
}

Exception::~Exception() {}

void Exception::display(ostream& out) const
{
  out << rep_name << " (Who: " << rep_who << ",
                     What: " << rep_what << ")";
}

const char* Exception::name() const
{
  return rep_name;
}

const char* Exception::who()  const
{
  return rep_who;
}

const char* Exception::what() const
{
  return rep_what;
}

Container_Error::Container_Error(const char* who, const char* what)
  : Exception("Container error", who, what) {}
```

```cpp
Container_Error::~Container_Error() {}

Duplicate::Duplicate(const char* who, const char* what)
  : Exception("Duplicate", who, what) {}

Duplicate::~Duplicate() {}

Illegal_Pattern::Illegal_Pattern(const char* who, const char* what)
  : Exception("Not_Found", who, what) {}

Illegal_Pattern::~Illegal_Pattern() {}

Is_Null::Is_Null(const char* who, const char* what)
  : Exception("Is_Null", who, what) {}

Is_Null::~Is_Null() {}

Lexical_Error::Lexical_Error(const char* who, const char* what)
  : Exception("Lexical_Error", who, what) {}

Lexical_Error::~Lexical_Error() {}

Math_Error::Math_Error(const char* who, const char* what, int errno)
  : Exception("Math_Error", who, what), rep_err(errno) {}

Math_Error::~Math_Error() {}

void Math_Error::display(ostream& out) const
{
  Exception::display(out);
  out << " (errno " << rep_err << ')';
}

Not_Found::Not_Found(const char* who, const char* what)
  : Exception("Not_Found", who, what) {}

Not_Found::~Not_Found() {}

Not_Null::Not_Null(const char* who, const char* what)
  : Exception("Not_Null", who, what) {}

Not_Null::~Not_Null() {}

Not_Root::Not_Root(const char* who, const char* what)
  : Exception("Not_Root", who, what) {}

Not_Root::~Not_Root() {}

Overflow::Overflow(const char* who, const char* what)
  : Exception("Overflow", who, what) {}
```

```cpp
Overflow::~Overflow() {}

Position_Error::Position_Error(const char* who, const char* what)
  : Exception("Position_Error", who, what) {}

Position_Error::~Position_Error() {}

Range_Error::Range_Error(const char* who, const char* what)
  : Exception("Range_Error", who, what) {}

Range_Error::~Range_Error() {}

Storage_Error::Storage_Error(const char* who, const char* what)
  : Exception("Storage_Error", who, what) {}

Storage_Error::~Storage_Error() {}

Underflow::Underflow(const char* who, const char* what)
  : Exception("Underflow", who, what) {}

Underflow::~Underflow() {}

ostream& operator<<(ostream& out, const Exception& e)
{
  e.display(out);
  return out;
}

void _catch(const Exception& e)
{
  cerr << "EXCEPTION: " << e << '\n';
  terminate();
}

static PFV term_f = 0;

PFV set_terminate(PFV f)
{
  PFV old = term_f;
  term_f = f;
  return old;
}

void terminate()
{
  if (term_f)
    term_f();
  exit(1);
}
```

Makefiles

The make facilities vary by platform. These representative files can be adapted to most make derivatives.

Macintosh MPW

The MPW version of cfront is based on Version 2.1 from AT&T/USL. It therefore does not support templates. Using the components on this platform requires a template preprocessor, tpl, available as part of the MPW version of the C++ Booch Components distributed by Rational.

```
#
#   The C++ Booch Components (Version 1.4.7)
#   (C) Copyright 1990-1992 Grady Booch.  All Rights Reserved.
#       example.make
#
# This script requires the following symbols be predefined:
# (For MPW, use the 'set' and 'export' commands)
#
# Cxx_COMPONENTS    pathname  root of directory hierarchy
# CPP           filename  program and/or options to run C preprocessor
# TPL           filename  program to translate C++ template syntax
# CC        filename  program to compile C++ programs

### Variable Definitions ###

# Directory structure:

SUPPORT    = "{Cxx_COMPONENTS}":support
BAGS       = "{Cxx_COMPONENTS}":structures:bags

OBJECT     = :object

# Program options:

INCLUDE_DIRS   = -I {BAGS} -I {SUPPORT}
CPP_SWITCHES   = -D throw=_catch -m -model far {INCLUDE_DIRS}
CC_SWITCHES    = -w1 -m -model far
LINK_SWITCHES  = -w -srt -model far -c 'MPS ' -t MPST

# Required auxiliary files:

TEMPLATE_ARGS  = str.h

TEST_FILES     = {OBJECT}:example.o     {OBJECT}:str.o
```

Source Code Listings

```
SUPPORT_FILES = ¬
    {OBJECT}:except.o   ¬
    {OBJECT}:support.o  {OBJECT}:support2.o

LIB_FILES = ¬
    "{CLibraries}"StdCLib.o ¬
    "{CLibraries}"CPlusLib.o ¬
    "{Libraries}"Stubs.o ¬
    "{Libraries}"Interface.o ¬
    "{Libraries}"ToolLibs.o ¬
    "{Libraries}"Runtime.o

### Build Rules ###

# Implicit rules:
# (order is important! -- longer sequence rules should come earlier)
#
# These rules implement the following template expansion sequence:
#    cpp      .cp  -> .tmp   (sometimes preceded by a 'cat' step)
#    tpl      .tmp -> .i
#    CC       .i   -> .o

## It might be more helpful to use the following suffixes:
##   cpp      .cp  -> .i
##   tpl      .i   -> .tpl
##   CC       .tpl -> .o
## but not all C++ compilers accept unusual suffixes.

.tmp1.cp  _    .cp
    catenate {TEMPLATE_ARGS} {DepDir}{default}.cp ¬
    > {TargDir}{default}.tmp1.cp

.tmp2.cp  _    .tmp1.cp
    {CPP} {CPP_SWITCHES} {TargDir}{default}.tmp1.cp ¬
    > {TargDir}{default}.tmp2.cp

.tmp.cp   _    .cp
    {CPP} {CPP_SWITCHES} {DepDir}{default}.cp ¬
    > {TargDir}{default}.tmp.cp

.o        _    .i
    {CC} -s {default} {CC_SWITCHES} {TargDir}{default}.i ¬
    -o {TargDir}{default}.o

.o        _    .cp
    {CC} -s {default} {CC_SWITCHES} {DepDir}{default}.cp ¬
    -o {TargDir}{default}.o

# Directory dependency rules (MPW specific):
```

```
{OBJECT}: _    {OBJECT}:
{OBJECT}: _    {SUPPORT}:
{OBJECT}: _    :
{OBJECT}: _    {BAGS}:

### Dependencies ###

# Final targets:

example  _    example.cp {TEST_FILES} {SUPPORT_FILES}
    link {LINK_SWITCHES} {TEST_FILES} {SUPPORT_FILES} {LIB_FILES} _
    -o {Targ}
    echo "{Targ}"

### Explicit Build Rules ###

# The explicit .i -> .o dependencies are needed because
# the .cp -> .o rule would short-circuit

{OBJECT}:example.i _ {OBJECT}:example.tmp.cp
    "{TPL}" {NewerDeps} > {Targ}
{OBJECT}:example.o _ {OBJECT}:example.i

{OBJECT}:support.i _    {OBJECT}:support.tmp.cp
    "{TPL}"  -X "Bag<String>" _
      -X "Bag_Active_Iterator<String>" _
      -X "Bag_Passive_Iterator<String>" _
      -X "Bounded_Bag<String, 100U>" _
      -X "Simple_Vector<String, 100U>" _
      -X "Unsigned_Vector<100U>" _
    {NewerDeps} > {Targ}
{OBJECT}:support.o  _    {OBJECT}:support.i
{OBJECT}:support2.i _    {OBJECT}:support.tmp.cp
    "{TPL}" _
      -X "Simple_Vector<unsigned, 100U>" _
    {NewerDeps} > {Targ}
{OBJECT}:support2.o _    {OBJECT}:support2.i

# Dependencies

{OBJECT}:example.tmp.cp        _    str.h
{OBJECT}:support.tmp.cp        _    str.h
{OBJECT}:support2.tmp.cp       _    str.h
```

GLOSSARY

Active agent — An **active agent** is one that embodies its own thread of control, and thus may operate autonomously.

Component: — A **component** is a set of one or more classes, where each member of the set is related to one or more of the others through a direct relationship inheritance, containment, friendship, or use.

Monolithic — A **monolithic** structure is one that is always treated as a single unit: there are no identifiable, distinct components, and thus referential integrity is guaranteed.

Polylithic — A **polylithic** structure is one in which structural sharing is permitted; for example, we may have objects that denote a sublist of a longer list, a branch of a larger tree, or individual vertices and arcs of a graph.

BIBLIOGRAPHY

[Booch 90] Booch, G., and M. Vilot, "The Design of the C++ Booch Components," *OOPSLA/ECOOP Conference*, Ottawa, Canada, October 1990.

[Booch 91] Booch, G., *Object Oriented Design with Applications*, Benjamin/Cummings, Redwood City, CA, 1990.

[Ellis 90] Ellis, M., and B. Stroustrup, *The Annotated C++ Reference Manual*, Addison-Wesley, Reading, MA, 1990.

[Lippman 89] Lippman, S., *C++ Primer*, AddisonWesley, Reading, MA, 1989.

[Lippman 90] Lippman, S., "A Tour of Cfront, Release 2.0/2.1 C++," Tutorial: *USENIX C++ Conference*, San Francisco, CA, April 1990.

[Stroustrup 91] Stroustrup, B., *The C++ Programming Language*, 2nd ed., AddisonWesley, Reading, MA, 1991.

INDEX

SYMBOLS

#include directives, 38

A

abstract base classes, 7, 8, 22, 29, 33, 37, 42-44, 153
abstract class, 8-10
abstractions
  forms, 8
    bounded, 8, 17
    guarded, 9
    sequential, 9
    synchronized, 9
    unbounded, 8, 17
  layering, 19

active agents, 9, 25-29
active iterators, 35-38
agents, active, 9, 25-29
algorithms, 2-7
aliasing, 20
analysis, domain, 18, 23
Arbitrary_Tree class, 115-122
arguments, template, 2, 13-14
assignment operators, 21-22, 29-31
Association_Node class, 23
AT&T style, 44
AT&T task library, 28

B

Bag class, 4, 46-51
    program, 37-42
bag.[C,cpp,cp] source code,
    220-226
bag.h source code, 217-219
bag_b.[C,cpp,cp] source code,
    228-231
bag_b.h source code, 226-227
Binary_Tree class, 122-127
Booch, Grady, xv
Bound class, 6
bounded forms, 8-9, 17
bounded heaps, 27
bounded monolithic structures, 27
bounded polylithic structures, 27
Bounded_Bag class, 38
Bounded_Heap class, 27, 184-188
Bounded_Map class, 28
Bounded_Queue class, 11
Bounded_Simple_List class,
    173-178

C

categories of classes
    Structures, 3-5
    Support, 3, 6
    Test, 3
    Tools, 3-6
    see also classes
Character_Utilities class, 154-157
class libraries, 2-11
classes
    abstract, 8-10
    abstract base, 7-8, 22, 29, 33,
        37, 42-44, 153
    Arbitrary_Tree, 115-122
    Association_Node, 23
    Bag, 4, 46-51

Binary_Tree, 122-127
Bound, 6
Bounded_Bag, 38
Bounded_Heap, 27, 184-188
Bounded_Map, 28
Bounded_Queue, 11
Bounded_Simple_List,
    173-178
Character_Utilities, 154-157
concrete, 8, 42, 153
container, 11-13
Controlled, 26
Counter, 195-198
Counting_Node, 23
Deque, 4, 51-56
Directed_Graph, 56-66
Double_List, 76-83
Double_Node, 23
Except, 6
Exception, 178-181
families, inheritance, 8-11
Filters, 6
Float_Utilities, 157-160
Free, 6
Graph_Node, 23
Graph_Search, 140-142
Graph_Sort, 149-151
Graphs, 4
guarded, 29-30
Heap, 6
Input_Filter, 131-133
Integer_Utilities, 160-162
Lists, 4
List_Search, 143-145
Lock, 198-202
Managed, 25
Map, 4, 89-93
Monitor, 198-202
Multiple_Read_Write_Monitor,
    32
Node, 6, 23, 188-195

INDEX

Output_Filter, 133-135
Pattern_Match, 6, 137-140
Process_Filter, 135-137
Queue, 4, 94-98
Read_Lock, 32
Read_Write_Monitor, 32
Ring, 5, 98-102
Search, 6, 147-149
Semaphore, 28, 198-202
Set, 5, 103-107
Shared, 6, 195-198
Simple_Bounded_List, 18, 27
Simple_List, 18, 27, 202-206
Simple_Vector, 18, 206-209
single base, 4
Single_List, 83-89
Sort, 6, 151-154
Stack, 5, 107-110
Storage_Manager, 24-25, 181-184
String_Utilities, 162-168
Strings, 5
Synch, 6
synchronized, 30-31
template, 11-15
Tree_Node, 23
Tree_Search, 145-147
Trees, 5
Unbound, 6
Undirected_Graph, 66-76
Utilities, 6
Variable_String, 34-35, 110-115
Vector, 6
Write_Lock, 32
components, setting up and using program, 38-42
concrete classes, 8, 42, 153
  subclasses, 8
concurrent systems, 9
constructors, 14, 21, 24-27, 40-43
  copy, 22, 29, 31, 34
container classes, 6, 11-13
containment, 11
Controlled class, 26
controlled storage management, 25
copy constructors, 22, 29-31, 34
Counter class, 195-198
Counting_Node class, 23

D

data structures, 2-7
Deque class, 51-56
Deques catgegory, 4
design rules, 6
design, object-oriented, *see* OOD
destructors, 24-25, 43
Directed_Graph class, 56-66
directives, #include, 38
domain analysis, 18, 23
Double_List class, 76-83
Double_Node class, 23

E

error notification, 11, 16
example.[C,cpp,cp] source code, 211-213
Except class, 6
except.[C,cpp,cp] source code, 244-248
Exception class, 178-181
exceptions, 15-17

F

families of classes, 5
  inheritance, 8-11
Filters class, 6
Float_Utilities class, 157-160
forest of classes, 4

forms of abstractions, 8
Free class, 6
functions
    modifier, 24
    selector, 32, 43

G

goals, class library, 2
Graph_Node class, 23
Graph_Search class, 140-142
Graph_Sort class, 149-151
graphs, 13
Graphs class, 4
guarded class, 29-30
guarded forms, abstractions, 9

H-I

Heap class, 6
heaps, bounded, 27

inheritance, families of classes, 8-11
Input_Filter class, 131-133
Integer_Utilities class, 160-162
iterators, 34-37
    active, 35-38
    passive, 35-36

L

layering abstractions, 19
libraries
    AT&T task, 28
    organization, 6-11
List_Search class, 143-145
lists, 18
Lists catgegory, 4
Lock class, 198-202

M

Macintosh MPW source code, 248-250
Managed class, 25
managed storage management, 24
managing storage, 22-28
Map class, 89-93
Maps class, 4
methods, OOD (object-oriented design), 3-6
modifier functions, 14, 24, 33
modifier member functions, 32
Monitor class, 198-202
monolithic structures, 23
    bounded, 27
multiple process synchronization, 31
Multiple_Read_Write_Monitor class, 32

N-O

Node class, 6, 23, 188-195
nodes, 23
notification of errors, 16

object-oriented design, *see* OOD
OOD (object-oriented design) method, 3-6
operators, assignment, 21-22, 29-31
optimization, 12
Output_Filter class, 133-135

P

passive iterators, 35-36
Pattern matching class, 6
Pattern_Match class, 137-140

polylithic structures, 23
  bounded, 27
preprocessor #include directives, 37-38
Process_Filter class, 135-137
processes, synchronizing, 28-34
programs,
  categories, Bag, 37-42
  components, setting up and using, 38-42

Q-R

Queue class, 4, 94-98

Read_Lock class, 32
Read_Write_Monitor class, 32
reporting errors, 11
representation, 17-22
Ring class, 5, 98-102
rules, design, 6

S

Search class, 6, 147-149
selector functions, 32, 43
semantics, time and space, 8, 17
Semaphore class, 28, 198-202
sequential forms, abstractions, 9
sequential systems, 9
Set class, 5, 103-107
Shared classes, 6, 195-198
Simple_Bounded_List class, 18, 27
Simple_List class, 18, 27, 202-206
Simple_Vector class, 18, 206-209
single base class, 4
single process synchronization, 31
Single_List class, 83-89
Sort class, 6, 151-154

source code
  bag.[C,cpp,cp], 220-226
  bag.h, 217-219
  bag_b.[C,cpp,cp], 228-231
  bag_b.h, 226-227
  example.[C,cpp,cp], 211-213
  except.[C,cpp,cp], 244-248
  Macintosh MPW, 248-250
  str.[C,cpp,cp], 214-216
  str.h, 214
  support.[cpp,cp], 216-217
  support2.[cpp,cp], 217
  svector.[C,cpp,cp], 233-240
  svector.h, 231-233
Stack class, 5, 107-110
storage management policies, 24
  controlled, 25
  unbounded forms, 22
Storage_Manager class, 24-25, 181-184
str.[C,cpp,cp] source code, 214-216
str.h source code, 214
String_Utilities class, 162-168
Strings class, 5
Structures category of classes, 3-5
  Arbitrary_Tree, 115-122
  Bag, 46-51
  Binary_Tree, 122-127
  Deque, 51-56
  Directed_Graph, 56-66
  Double_List, 76-83
  Map, 89-93
  Simple_Vector, 206-209
  Single_List, 83-89
  Queue, 94-98
  Ring, 98-102
  Set, 103-107

Stack, 107-110
Undirected_Graph, 66-76
Variable_String, 110-115
structures
    data, 2-7
    monolithic, 23
        bounded, 27
    polylithic, 23
        bounded, 27
styles, AT&T, 44
subcategories, 5
subclasses, concrete, 8
Support category of classes, 3, 6
    Bounded_Heap, 184-188
    Bounded_Simple_List, 173-178
    Counter, 195-198
    Exception, 178-181
    Lock, 198-202
    Monitor, 198-202
    Node, 188-195
    Semaphore, 198-202
    Shared, 195-198
    Simple_List, 202-206
    Storage_Manager, 181-184
support.[cpp,cp] source code, 216-217
support2.[cpp,cp] source code, 217
svector.[C,cpp,cp] source code, 233-240
svector.h source code, 231-233
Synch class, 6
synchronization process, 9, 28-34
synchronized class, 30-31
systems
    concurrent, 9
    sequential, 9
synchronized forms, abstractions, 9

T

template arguments, 2, 13-14
template class, 11-15
Test category of classes, 3
time and space semantics, 8, 17
Tools category of classes, 3-6
    Character_Utilities, 154-157
    Float_Utilities, 157-160
    Graph_Search, 140-142
    Graph_Sort, 149-151
    Input_Filter, 131-133
    Integer_Utilities, 160-162
    List_Search, 143-145
    Output_Filter, 133-135
    Pattern_Match, 137-140
    Process_Filter, 135-137
    Search, 147-149
    Sort, 151-154
    String_Utilities, 162-168
    Tree_Search, 145-147
Tree_Node class, 23
Tree_Search class, 145-147
Trees cagtegory, 5
type parameterization, 7-8

U-Z

Unbound class, 6
unbounded forms, 8-9, 17
    storage management, 22
Undirected_Graph class, 66-76
unmanaged storage management, 24
Utilities class, 6

Variable_String class, 34, 110-115
Vector class, 6
vector searching, 153
vectors, 18

Write_Lock class, 32

Take the Rational approach to object technology...

The C++ Booch Components: Reuse them again and again!

A comprehensive, well-documented class library of data structures, tools, and tests. Delivered in C++ source code complete with a 250-page class catalog, support for templates and exceptions, and no royalties.

Data structures: bags, collections, deques, graphs, lists, maps, queues, rings, sets, stacks, strings, and trees.

Tools: filters; four different pattern-matching algorithms; eight different search algorithms; ten different sort algorithms; utility classes for manipulating characters, strings, integers, and floating-point numbers

The C++ Booch Components are built in a forest structure to facilitate incorporation with other class libraries and your own code. When you use the components, you can tune your storage use to optimize the space/performance trade-off. Support for concurrency is included so that you can develop single- and multithreaded applications.

- for PC, Macintosh - $495   - for SPARC, RS/6000, HP 9000 - $695

(Server, site, and corporate licenses available.)

Rational Rose for Windows: Tool Support for the Booch Method

A powerful analysis-and-design tool that automates the development process.
- Supports class, object, state-transition, process, and module diagrams
- Provides multipage, large-model capability
- Exports diagrams and templates to word processors
- Performs consistency checking with method

- for Windows - $495   - for OS/2 - coming in spring 1993   - UNIX versions available - call for details

Booch-Certified, Object-Oriented Training and Consulting

Rational's training department offers a range of services customized to meet your needs, from one-day introductory seminars to in-depth consulting services.

Prices are subject to change without notice. All prices are in U.S. dollars.

```
To place an order call 1-800-767-3237
```

RATIONAL   3320 Scott Boulevard   Santa Clara, California, 95054-3197   012

What's On The Disk

Source code and example programs for the Bounded Bag Booch component.

Installing The Floppy Disk

Follow this procedure to copy the files on the disk to your hard drive:

1. From a DOS prompt, change to the drive that contains the installation disk. For example, if the disk is in drive B:, type **B:** and press Enter.

2. Type **INSTALL drive** (where *drive* is the drive letter of your hard drive), and press Enter. For example, if your hard drive is drive C:, type **INSTALL C:** and press Enter.

This will install all the files to a directory called \POWERPAK on your hard drive. Be sure to read the README.TXT file for more information.